Charleston, Savannah & the Coastal Islands

Charleston, Savannah & the Coastal Islands

A Great Destination

Cecily McMillan

The Countryman Press   Woodstock, Vermont

EIGHTH EDITION

To George McMillan, who introduced me to the beauty
and social complexity of the Lowcountry, and to our son, Tom,
with whom I continue to love it; and to Priscilla Johnson McMillan,
whose wisdom and support has allowed me to understand it.

Copyright © 2011, 2014 by Cecily McMillan

Charleston, Savannah & the Coastal Islands: A Great Destination, 8th edition

ISBN 978-1-58157-233-9

Interior photographs by the author unless otherwise specified
Maps by Erin Greb Cartography, © The Countryman Press
Book design by Bodenweber Design
Composition by Eugenie S. Delaney
Published by The Countryman Press, P.O. Box 748, Woodstock, VT 05091

Distributed by W. W. Norton & Company, Inc., 500 Fifth Avenue, New York, NY 10110

Printed in the United States of America

10 9 8 7 6 5 4 3 2 1

Acknowledgments

MANY LONGTIME FRIENDS in Charleston, Beaufort, and Savannah have helped improve this book, most of all Beth Scott. I am also grateful for the lovely design created by the professionals at The Countryman Press, which has made the book easier to use and enjoy.

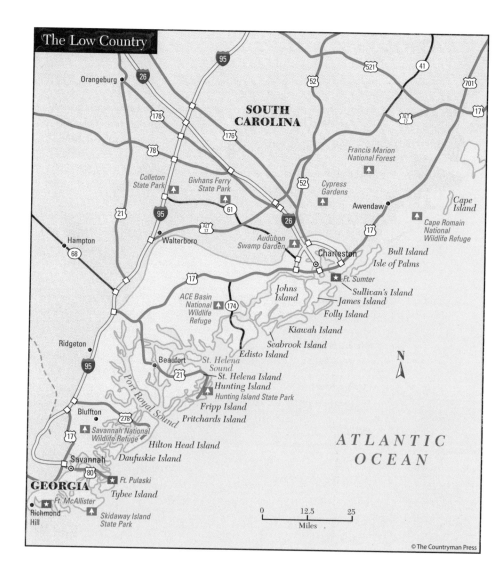

The Low Country

Orangeburg

SOUTH
CAROLINA

Francis Marion
National Forest

Colleton
State Park

Givhans Ferry
State Park

Cypress
Gardens

Awendaw

Cape
Island

Cape Romain
National
Wildlife Refuge

Hampton

Walterboro

Audubon
Swamp Garden

Charleston

Ft. Sumter

Bull Island
Isle of Palms

Johns
Island

Sullivan's Island
James Island

ACE Basin
National
Wildlife
Refuge

Folly Island

Kiawah Island

Ridgeton

Seabrook Island
Edisto Island

N

Beaufort

St. Helena
Sound

St. Helena Island
Hunting Island
Hunting Island State Park
Fripp Island
Pritchards Island

ATLANTIC
OCEAN

Bluffton

Port Royal Sound

Savannah National
Wildlife Refuge

Hilton Head Island
Daufuskie Island

Savannah

Ft. Pulaski

GEORGIA

Tybee Island

Ft. McAllister

Richmond
Hill

Skidaway Island
State Park

0   12.5   25

Miles

© The Countryman Press

Contents

Introduction

THERE ARE SOME PLACES about which we have such strong impressions that when we finally go there they seem familiar. The Lowcountry seems to have lodged itself securely in so many imaginations that I often find, when I am asked about it, that what I have to say matters less than the opportunity for someone to focus the picture they already have.

Where these clustered impressions come from—a history lesson on the Civil War, a friend, novel, or movie—seems less important than the fact that they feel fully conceived. This isn't surprising: The Lowcountry has earned our permanent attention. It is a compelling world. Like other places that have witnessed tremendous historic upheavals and whose residents have had to adjust to changed circumstances, it evokes a natural sympathy in us for its stories.

I like listening in and locating the presence of the past: on the shores of St. Helena Sound, where I catch crabs on a string or dig for clams much as Native Americans might have done; at Drayton Hall, where beds of lilies bloom, as they did in Jefferson's Monticello garden; at Penn Center, where descendants of slaves honor their heritage and the strength of their forebears in song; on the squares of Savannah, laid out more than 275 years ago and still possessing a power of geometry that untangles nature and orders urban life. The region's physical beauty is evocative. The landscape is soft and flat, edges softened by marsh grass and sand. The air, weighted by moisture, wraps it like a package. The light changes several times a day, and very dramatically from season to season.

This book is intended to both introduce you to some of the long-standing pleasures and pastimes found in the Lowcountry and point you to where you might discover ones of your own as the region's cities and towns flourish in the 21st century. Your efforts may be studious—admiring architecture, exploring sites of historic and cultural significance. Or you may be content to satisfy your senses: to walk a beach, smell the marsh, watch a pelican dive, taste fresh shrimp. Don't neglect to listen for old stories, either.

You could end up joining those who visit and return for good. The glossy residential resorts like Kiawah and Palmetto Bluff shine like jewels; Beaufort can't stay off "Best Small Town" lists as newcomers enliven its culture; and Savannah and Charleston keep reinventing themselves as art and restaurant destinations. Today, restaurants, bookstores, jazz and blues clubs, clothing shops, art galleries, and B&Bs are embedding themselves in the old Lowcountry places. They are enlarging the remnant world, just as spats fasten on oyster banks and make them grow.

Cecily McMillan
St. Helena Island, South Carolina

The Way This Book Works

THIS BOOK is divided into five chapters, four of which cover specific regions of the Lowcountry. Brief historical summaries introduce them; recommendations and reviews follow. They cover a range of options according to style and price, and will help you make decisions, whether you are staying in one area or intend to travel the region.

Some entries, most notably those in the Lodging and Dining sections of chapters, include detailed information (telephone, address, hours, etc.) organized for easy reference at the beginning of each listing. All such information has been checked for accuracy as close to the time of publication as possible, but things change, so it's best to check in advance. Wherever possible I have included websites where you may learn, among other information, if the establishment has a social media presence you can follow. The best of the sites provide creative and useful links to local blogs. For year-round tourist information and seasonal activities, see Chapter Five, *Information*.

PRICES

Prices change, too, and for that reason I've avoided listing specific prices in favor of noting their range. Lodging price codes are based on a per-room rate, double occupancy in the high-season months; they do not include room taxes or special service charges that might apply during your stay. Ask about AAA, AARP, and other discounts. Low-season rates, which generally apply in December and January, are usually about 20 percent less. In the high season many places, small and large, require a minimum two-night stay and may also have specific rules regarding adequate notice and refunds in the event of cancellation. It is assumed that payment by credit or debit card is accepted, and that is true 99 percent of the time, but I've noted the exceptions.

You might also confirm information provided about policies concerning such things as handicapped access, smoking, and how adaptable the site is for children and pets.

Restaurant prices indicate the cost of a meal including appetizer, entrée, and dessert, but not bar beverages, tax, or tip. Here again, the season of your visit may bring on special conditions: When there are crowds, most restaurants extend their hours of operation, serving meals both earlier and later. In the winter, they may shut down for a day or two or longer in the rural areas.

Price Codes

	Lodging	*Dining*
Inexpensive	Up to $80	Up to $15
Moderate	$80 to $140	$15 to $30
Expensive	$140 to $200	$30 to $50
Very expensive	Over $200	Over $50

History

"NO FAYRER OR FYTTER PLACE"

LONG BEFORE THE ENGLISH LANDED in the Lowcountry, before Jamestown and Plymouth Rock, Captain Jean Ribaut and 150 Huguenot colonists landed near Beaufort, at what is now the Marine Corps Recruit Depot on Parris Island. In a report he stated there was "no fayrer or fytter place" than the area of Port Royal Sound, one of the "goodlyest, best and frutfullest countres that ever was sene"; where egrets were so plentiful bushes "be all white covered with them"; where there were "so many sortes of fishes that ye may take them without net or angle." He wrote that in 1562.

To a modern traveler who chances upon a rookery in Hunting Island State Park or Edisto's Botany Bay Preserve, or to the youngster throwing a cast net and needing the strength of two to draw it in, little has changed. The natural resources of the Lowcountry are breathtakingly impressive. There will be schools of dolphin by your boat off Hilton Head, hundreds of loggerhead turtles' nests from the ACE Basin shoreline to Port Royal Sound and the Atlantic, and thousands of terns, which—when they rise all at once off a sandbar in St. Helena Sound—appear as a cloud of smoke on the horizon. There will be late-afternoon light so intense and golden it makes the dun bark of the grayest sycamore shimmer.

And, when Ribaut called the Lowcountry a place "where nothing lacketh," Charleston, Beaufort, and Savannah had not even been invented.

It only took about 50 years from their founding at the turn of the 17th and 18th centuries for each of these cities to develop the self-consciousness we now recognize as the spirit of place; a short time, perhaps because the raw ingredients were there all along, waiting to be shaped, tapped, and exploited. History has shown us that such loyalty, such an abiding sense of legacy and protection, can get you into trouble, and a war was fought here in part over that kind of crazy pride. And I have felt of people I know that if they ever left the city limits of Charleston or Savannah, or crossed the bridge away from St. Helena Island, they would vaporize.

LEFT: Bonaventure Cemetery, full of sculpture and history, has drawn visitors for more than 150 years. Savannah Area Convention & Visitors Bureau

A beach on the edge of the ACE Basin, where three rivers meet the ocean. Peter Loftus

Yet there's something to be said for deep connections, and it is interesting and worthwhile to explore a region and observe the ways place, heritage, custom, and culture resonate to this day, across racial lines and personal history. The activity of reinterpreting and understanding the past drives a new generation who have less need to be insular and more incentive to be curious.

Several distinct ecosystems make up the Lowcountry: swamps, estuaries, marshes, maritime and bottomland forests, dunes and interdune meadows, tidal creeks and sounds, alluvial and blackwater rivers. Perhaps the most common sight is the field of smooth cordgrass (*Spartina alterniflora*) that makes up the salt marsh and the muddy banks and flats that cut through it. Rimmed by wax myrtle, nandina, and Carolina cherry laurel on its banks, overshadowed by huge live oaks whose limbs are draped with Spanish moss (an air plant, member of the pineapple family), and dotted with resurrection fern, the salt marsh is nature's most productive nursery. The Lowcountry has more of it than anywhere on the Southeast coast.

What you see is this: filter-feeders

A Pleasing Music

A beautiful green frog inhabits the grassy, marshy shores of these large rivers. They are very numerous, and their noise exactly resembles the barking of little dogs, or the yelping of puppies: these likewise make a great clamour, but as their notes are fine, and uttered in chorus, by separate bands or communities, far and near, rising and falling with the gentle breezes, affords a pleasing kind of music.

—*From* Travels of William Bartram *(New York: Viking Penguin, 1988. First published in 1791.)*

Sand Hills

I continued through this forest nearly in a direct line towards the sea coast, five or six miles, when the land became uneven, with ridges of sand hills, mixed with sea shells, and covered by almost impenetrable thickets, consisting of Live Oaks, Sweet-bay, Myrica, Ilex . . . The dark labyrinth is succeeded by a great extent of salt plains, beyond which the boundless ocean is seen. Betwixt the dark forest and the salt plains, I crossed a rivulet of fresh water, where I sat down a while to rest myself, under the shadow of sweet Bays and Oaks; the lively breezes were perfumed by the fragrant breath of the superb Crinum, called by the inhabitants, White Lily. This admirable beauty of the sea-coast islands dwells in the humid shady groves, where the soil is made fertile and mellow by the admixture of sea shells . . . and the texture and whiteness of its flowers at once charmed me.

—*From* Travels of William Bartram *(New York: Viking Penguin, 1988. First published in 1791.)*

such as snails, crabs, oysters, shrimp, and mullet ingesting the detritus—a potent mixture of decomposed marsh grass, animal matter, algae, and fungi. Or a heron or raccoon eating its smaller prey. The fiddler crabs with their lopsided claws gather and disperse like a muddy cavalry. As the tide recedes, you will hear the marsh release oxygen and pop like 100 pricked balloons. The slightly sweet, sulfurous smell of "pluff mud" fills the air. Locals call that smell "puffy." If you venture to the edge of the marsh and get your sneakers wet, when they dry you'll see it's not mud at all, rather fine gray material that shakes off like dust.

Even the cities are overcome by nature's exuberance. Streets and gardens burst with azaleas and flowering dogwood in the spring. Honeysuckle, jessamine, wisteria, and trumpet vine tumble wildly over walls and race up tree trunks. And then there are the birds: the tiny, sassy Carolina wren that makes its nest in a flowerpot; mourning doves that coo from telephone wires; chuck-will's-widows that frantically chant at dusk; the mockingbird that mimics 200 songs; and the birds of prey that soar overhead.

The first African slave was brought to the first Charleston settlement in 1670 with English settlers from Barbados, a group that would define governance, slave codes, and the establishment of a new society. The story of the Lowcountry and the narrative that draws visitors begins with this unequal racial relationship: Every historic building or landscape you see is a part of its legacy. Slaves, freedmen and women, and their heirs have contributed in the most essential way imaginable to its politics, economic growth, folkways, art, culture, and language. The enterprise of managing slaves as individuals and as economic assets, along with the fear of uprising, especially after the Denmark Vesey rebellion in Charleston in 1822, made for a regulation of life unknown outside the South. This was true in both the cities and the country.

In the cities, black and white residents would pass each other in the street. Black people may have been politically invisible, but their presence was known. By contrast, the plantation world that generated wealth was isolated and self-sufficient, marked by seasonal activities: gathering marsh hay for fertilizer; harvesting, clearing and burning the fields; building and repairing fences and dikes; growing food crops and raising cows and hogs for slaughter; moting and ginning cotton, packing it in the cotton house, and taking it to the landing for shipment. For cotton and food crops, the tool was a hoe to chop weeds and a team of oxen to dig the furrow. Cultivating rice required more knowledge about tidal flow and the operation of rice dikes. Drayton Hall and Middleton Place outside Charleston and even modest plantation properties on the Sea Islands are now grand and silent; they were once fantastically busy. As you tour the countryside, try to imagine it dominated by open fields punctuated by orderly windbreaks of trees, rather than the scrub you see today. The Lowcountry was a vast rice and cotton factory, and the plantations were run like a business with as much acreage under cultivation as possible.

Within that world and responding to its demands arose the Gullah or Geechee culture. It reflects a West African heritage of competencies and sensitivities that survived the Middle Passage and much more. It flourished, and its legacy survives today, because slaves kept a sense of personal and community

Born into slavery, Robert Smalls was a Civil War hero and prominent Reconstruction-era congressman from Beaufort.

The Mock-Bird

This ancient sublime forest, frequently intersected with extensive avenues, vistas and green lawns, opening to extensive savannas and far distant Rice plantations, agreeably employs the imagination, and captivates the senses by scenes of magnificence and grandeur. The gay mock-bird, vocal and joyous, mounts aloft on silvered wings, rolls over and over, then gently descends, and presides in the choir of the tuneful tribes.

—*From* Travels of William Bartram *(New York: Viking Penguin, 1988. First published in 1791.)*

identity alive in unregulated places like plantation praise houses, brush arbors, and extended families, and later in churches and schools. Descendants' stories are continuing to be told and they inform significant new interpretations of historic sites.

It is not possible to overestimate the way in which the Civil War disrupted the order imposed by the plantation world and the society it held in check. When recovery was to come to the Lowcountry, it would come to the countryside last.

If the Lowcountry is seen by visitors as a place rich in references to the Civil War, both physical and cultural, perhaps it is because there was such a difference in the "before" and "after." But even before the Civil War, the Lowcountry had been undergoing a slow transformation, a political and economic drift that marginalized it from the center of national opinion. As Mary Boykin Chesnut wrote in her diary at the time of secession: "South Carolina had been rampant for years. She was the torment of herself and everyone else. Nobody could live in this state unless he were a fire-eater."

In December 1860, South Carolina seceded, led by planters from Edisto and Beaufort. The following year, Georgia followed suit. Soon, the harbor forts that watched over both cities—Fort Sumter and Fort Pulaski—were battle sites. Both of the forts can be visited today, and the story of their defense is a dramatic one.

A less well-known chapter of Civil War history, having Beaufort as its center, concerns the efforts of Northern abolitionists to live among the newly freed slaves and prepare them for full "citizenship." The enterprise followed by several months the Union invasion of Port Royal in November 1861. This "Gideon's Band" set up schools for slaves young and old in front parlors and cotton houses. The occupying Union army converted the old houses to hospitals, barracks, and offices.

Impoverished after the Civil War,

Secession is the fashion here. Young ladies sing for it; old ladies pray for it; young men are dying to fight for it; old men are ready to demonstrate it.

—*From a dispatch to the* London Times, *April 1861, sent from Charleston by English journalist William Howard Russell*

Market Hall defined the head of the Charleston city market area where every commodity, including slaves, was bought and sold.   Peter Loftus

Voluptuous Charm

Picket life was of course the place to feel the charm of the natural beauty on the Sea Islands. We had a world of profuse and tangled vegetation around us, such as would have been a dream of delight to me, but for the constant sense of responsibility and care which came between. Amid this preoccupation, Nature seemed but a mirage, and not the close and intimate associate I had before known. I pressed no flowers, collected no insects or birds' eggs, made no notes on natural objects, reversing in these respects all previous habits. Yet now, in the retrospect, there seems to have been infused into me through every pore the voluptuous charm of the season and the place; and the slightest corresponding sound or odor now calls back the memory of those delicious days.

—From Army Life in a Black Regiment *by Thomas Wentworth Higginson*
(New York: W. W. Norton, 1984. First published in 1869.)

To describe our growing up in the lowcountry of South Carolina, I would have to take you to the marsh on a spring day, flush the great blue heron from its silent occupation, scatter marsh hens as we sink to our knees in the mud, open you an oyster with a pocketknife and feed it to you from the shell and say, "There. That taste. That's the taste of my childhood." I would say, "Breathe deeply," and you would breathe and remember that smell for the rest of your life, the bold, fecund aroma of the tidal marsh, exquisite and sensual, the smell of the South in heat, a smell like new milk, semen, and spilled wine, all perfumed with seawater.

—From The Prince of Tides *by Pat Conroy (Boston: Houghton Mifflin Company, 1986)*

people simply went home. Older white residents hoarded their gentility as they might their last pennies, taking in sewing, teaching, and renting rooms to boarders. In the country, everyone concentrated on making a modest living. People were thrown back on their resources—fishing, hunting, and farming—and they made do. Only small numbers of black freedmen actually received, and were able to hang on to, land they had been promised for purchase. Often families banded together to buy land from Northern speculators, giving rise in the 20th century to extremely complicated efforts to unwind ownership of "heirs' property" in which descendants own fractional claims.

Although phosphate mining, timbering, and shipyards emerged as centers of postwar activity, the economy was slow to repair itself. An idea of just how poor conditions were, right up until World War II, can be glimpsed in the work of photographers sent by the Farm Security Administration to document it. Many of these images can be accessed online in the records of the Library of Congress.

The legacy of poverty was just as crucial in preserving the built environment of the Lowcountry as prosperity had been for bringing it to life. As early as the 1920s, Charlestonians were organizing to save their old buildings. In 1931, the city passed the nation's first Historic District zoning ordinances; some 20 years later, the Historic Savannah Foundation was founded to oppose the demolition of the Isaiah Davenport House. Ever since, these cities' Historic Districts and properties in the country nearby have been central attractions to generations of tourists, inspiring legions of architects, landscape gardeners, historians, novelists, and anthropologists.

Charleston

A CITY OF STORIES

CHARLESTON is one of the nation's oldest urban environments. It has been the site of some of the most dramatic events in American history, and scores of buildings and vistas that tell its story remain intact. Unlike many American cities, it didn't reinvent itself over time—partly because after the Civil War its leaders preferred provincial insularity to the risks of change, and partly because it was too worn down to do much but carry on in the old ways, its people too habituated to roles they inherited long after the society which had assigned them disappeared.

In the early 20th century, with the attack on Fort Sumter fresh in living memory, Charlestonians got a second chance to protect the life they knew and valued, this time with more favorable results. A group of women spearheaded the country's earliest preservation efforts, reacting strongly to demolitions and setting a vision, and it is their legacy that shapes the city today, both its structure and its spirit. The environment they and later generations saved serves as the backdrop to a vibrant urban culture of restaurants, art galleries, shops, and live performances, and to accommodations ranging from an old parlor to a luxury suite. The city is neither an "authentic reproduction" nor an outdoor museum, but a place with character and style.

The energy that enlivens the old city is most obviously on display during the annual Spoleto Festival, held for two weeks in May and June and marked by dozens of world-class productions in opera, dance, theater, chamber music, and art (see Culture). Other seasonal events, like the annual Festival of Houses & Gardens in May and June, and the Fall Tours of Homes and Gardens, sponsored by historic preservation organizations, get you behind the gates to experience for yourself the indoor and outdoor spaces nurtured by Charleston's elite for some three centuries. You can take your history in smaller doses, too, on 90-minute walking tours that focus on ghosts, plantation life, pirates, politicians, or war (Revolutionary or Civil).

LEFT: The South of Broad neighborhood has its share of historic plaques, but it never feels like a re-created environment. Peter Loftus

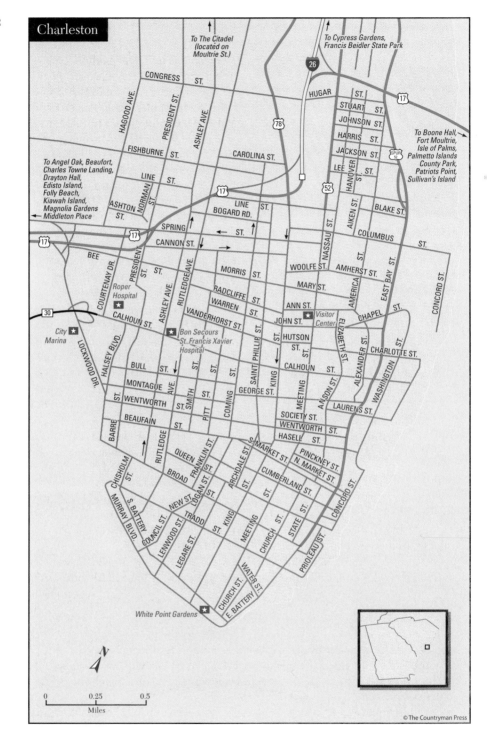

Charleston

To The Citadel (located on Moultrie St.)

To Cypress Gardens, Francis Beidler State Park

CONGRESS ST.

HUGAR

26

17

HAGOOD AVE.

PRESIDENT ST.

ASHLEY AVE.

STUART ST.

JOHNSON ST.

78

HARRIS ST.

JACKSON ST.

To Boone Hall, Fort Moultrie, Isle of Palms, Palmetto Islands County Park, Patriots Point, Sullivan's Island

SPUR 52

FISHBURNE ST.

CAROLINA ST.

To Angel Oak, Beaufort, Charles Towne Landing, Drayton Hall, Edisto Island, Folly Beach, Kiawah Island, Magnolia Gardens Middleton Place

LINE ST.

LEE ST.

HANOVER ST.

NORMAN ST.

17

LINE ST.

BLAKE ST.

ASHTON ST.

BOGARD RD.

AIKEN ST.

52

SPRING ST.

COLUMBUS ST.

17

CANNON ST.

NASSAU ST.

17

BEE

MORRIS ST.

WOOLFE ST.

AMHERST ST.

EAST BAY ST.

CONCORD ST.

COURTENAY DR.

PRESIDENT ST.

ASHLEY AVE.

RUTLEDGE AVE.

RADCLIFFE ST.

MARY ST.

AMERICA ST.

Roper Hospital

WARREN ST.

ANN ST.

Visitor Center

CHAPEL ST.

VANDERHORST ST.

JOHN ST.

30

CALHOUN ST.

City Marina

Bon Secours St. Francis Xavier Hospital

HUTSON ST.

ELIZABETH ST.

ALEXANDER ST.

CHARLOTTE ST.

WASHINGTON ST.

HALSEY BLVD.

BULL ST.

SAINT PHILLIP ST.

KING ST.

CALHOUN ST.

LOCKWOOD DR.

MONTAGUE AVE.

SMITH ST.

GEORGE ST.

MEETING ST.

ANSON ST.

LAURENS ST.

WENTWORTH ST.

COMING ST.

SOCIETY ST.

BARRE ST.

BEAUFAIN ST.

PITT ST.

WENTWORTH ST.

HASELL ST.

QUEEN ST.

FRANKLIN ST.

ARCHDALE ST.

S. MARKET ST.

PINCKNEY ST.

N. MARKET ST.

CHISHOLM ST.

RUTLEDGE ST.

BROAD ST.

LOGAN ST.

CUMBERLAND ST.

CONCORD ST.

S. BATTERY ST.

MURRAY BLVD.

NEW ST.

TRADD ST.

KING ST.

MEETING ST.

CHURCH ST.

STATE ST.

PRIOLEAU ST.

COUNCIL ST.

LENWOOD ST.

LEGARE ST.

White Point Gardens

CHURCH ST.

WATER ST.

E. BATTERY ST.

N

0   0.25   0.5
Miles

© The Countryman Press

Creative newcomers and a younger generation of locals are building on traditions and introducing transformative perspectives on what it means to be "Charleston." There is a dynamic, collaborative community of chefs, farmers, and foodies who capitalize on a long growing season and easy access to fresh produce and seafood. They are envied by their peers across the country. A new food and wine festival (www.charlestonwineandfood.com) on a March weekend shows them off (see Dining). Groups of galleries promote emerging and established artists and sponsor monthly walks and festivals (see Culture). An appreciation for design and antiques—practically coin of the realm in the city—is newly evident in stores along 15 blocks of King Street, a greatly expanded district, and in the dozens of galleries in the French Quarter a few minutes by foot to the east.

For all its urbanity, Charleston is deeply tied to its natural environment, which more than ever is accessible to visitors through kayaking and eco-tours. Beach communities are about 30 minutes away by car, from resorts like Kiawah to the south to the laid-back Sullivan's Island, Folly Beach, and Isle of Palms. On the other side of the peninsula, up the Ashley River, stand the big houses at Magnolia Plantation, Drayton Hall, and Middleton Place. After more than 250 years, the creative breezes blowing through the region are gently ruffling them, too.

While there's still a nod to the past and a story on every corner, it's far from what it was in 1941, when the classic WPA *Guide to the Palmetto State* noted that

Kayaking is a unique way to become acquainted with Charleston.   Beaufort Regional Chamber VCB
(Banker Optical Media)

The Circular Congregational Church was a favorite of the New England merchants who came to Charleston after the American Revolution.   Peter Loftus

one "may live in Charleston, a city that competes with the New Jerusalem in his dreams; or he may live in a drafty Georgian country house," but he "recalls his past glory with a pride that surpasses his ability to appreciate thoroughly the good things of the present." That cannot be said of Charleston today.

A BRIEF HISTORY

The Carolina Province, as claimed by the English, came into view during the Restoration, when Charles II gave a group of Lord's Proprietors vast tracts of land in the New World. Sir John Colleton, who had lived in Barbados, convinced his associates that a similar plantation-based society using slaves to develop the lower coast could be profitable. Several exploratory voyages ensued, and in 1670 a ship nosed into a creek upriver from Charleston under the guidance of the cacique, or chief, of the Kiawah tribe.

The earliest years of the colony have been brought to life at Charles Towne Landing, a restored living history village that conveys the precariousness of periodic hostilities and the challenges of self-sufficiency. After a decade, and augmented by new arrivals, the colonists and their slaves relocated from Albemarle Point to a site on the peninsula at the mouth of the harbor, where they laid out their city.

It was all go from there. Churches and houses whose architecture recalled the classic Barbadian design of raised basements and upstairs piazzas went up along streets like Church, Broad, Meeting, Tradd, and Queen; some of them stand today. It was a time of defense and expansion, of building walls to protect residents and opening the network of creeks and rivers to the countryside, where planters put thousands of acres under cultivation with rice, indigo, and cotton.

Rice brought the first tidal wave of wealth, producing a small, landed gentry—deeply connected by marriage and property, including their slaves—that was the richest in the colonies. By 1742, when there were 7,000 people living in Charleston, Savannah's population numbered in the hundreds. Prosperous as the planters were, many became increasingly as fed up with the taxes and political tactics of the British as their Northern neighbors, and joined the revolutionary cause, repelling an attack at Fort Moultrie on Sullivan's Island in 1776.

The years following brought Charleston's next phase, with an influx of entrepreneurs finding new markets for cotton while buying land and slaves. Although the profitable bounty on indigo was lost, the invention of a new cotton gin capable of removing seeds from cotton faster than a slave's fingers drove Lowcountry expansion. The boom, which lasted until about 1820, dramatically changed the look of the city, and the Federal style houses, with delicately carved mantels, tapered columns, and graceful proportions you see today, were built in that period.

As Charleston emerged with its social rules and rituals, its dual devotion to piety and pleasure, Africans and African Americans created their own unique culture, known as Gullah. Scholars have identified "Africanisms" that point to its roots on the West African coast—rice-growing techniques, folk tales, patterns of speech and dress, basketry and cooking, song, dance, and spirit belief, to name a few—but it was also shaped as a personal response to hardship and a way to preserve identity. A deepening respect for its contributions and its complexity as a culture has brought the Gullah experience, past and present, into focus for a much wider audience. The Charleston region, more than others on the coast, is the first, best place to understand it.

Some historians have said that Charleston's golden age was effectively over by the 1830s, battered by economic competition from cotton lands to the west and other factors. Where it had been influential, now other places held supremacy. When it came time to defend its position and attitude, it left the Union. The cost of the move was so high that it took the city nearly up until World War II to recover.

GETTING THERE

Charleston International Airport (www.chs-airport.com) is served by major airlines with direct flights to many cities. It's easily navigated; car rental is convenient with adjacent lots. To downtown, a 25-minute ride, a group shuttle costs about $12 and cab service about $27 (a third person is charged a flat rate of about $13). Charleston Aviation Authority (843-767-7010) also runs small airports on John's Island (Charleston Executive) and Mount Pleasant Regional (Faison Field) to serve private aircraft.

Greyhound (1-800-231-2222; www.greyhound.com) and Amtrak (1-800-872-7245; www.amtrak.com) make daily stops in North Charleston. The Greyhound depot (3610 Dorchester Rd.; 843-744-4247) is open daily, but with limited hours according to bus schedules. The Amtrak station at 4565 Gaynor Ave. also has limited hours, timed to arrivals and departures, usually morning and evening. Cab fare from North Charleston to downtown is about $27.

The Charleston City Marina (843-723-5098; www.charlestoncitymarina.com), 17 Lockwood Dr., is at Mile Marker 469.5 on the Atlantic Intracoastal Waterway. Transient fees start at $2/foot/night, with a minimum length of 30 feet.

Distances: Charleston is 512 miles from Washington, D.C.; from Jacksonville, 214 miles. Asheville is 265 miles to the west, Charlotte is 200 miles, and Atlanta is 286 miles.

Public transportation in Charleston is handled by CARTA (843-724-7420; www.ridecarta.com), and its DASH shuttle covers the downtown peninsula with stops at major sites. A one-day pass is $6.

Lodging

Best places to stay in Charleston, and what you'll find nearby . . .

President George Washington toured the Lowcountry in 1791, lodging with planters and in "public houses" alongside messengers, small farmers, and merchants. The modest but attentive hospitality they offered existed well into the 20th century. It was a custom, like most, that had its roots in necessity: During the years of poverty following the Civil War, taking in guests provided income for families or Confederate widows who still lived in the commodious houses.

These days, if you stay in an old home that has been transformed into a glossy bed & breakfast—and they are among the most romantic lodgings—the only Confederate widow in evidence will be a portrait on the wall. They are elegant places, with Jacuzzi tubs and fireplaces, where you are likely to be served with old silver and over-

A classic "single house" with the side-facing piazza, decorative gouge work on the door surround, and coffered soffit—the epitome of 19th-century architecture. Peter Loftus

look walled gardens dense with flower beds, fragrant olive trees, camellias, and azaleas.

Charleston also has luxury hotels; inns renovated from former commercial buildings; its share of attractive options from national name brands; rooms and suites within old houses or in their "dependencies," like kitchen houses and stables; and, on its outskirts, upscale beach resorts. A sampling follows. If you intend to spend most of your time in the city, consider the 25- to 35-minute travel time to the beach. Alternatively, if golf, tennis, boating, and being on the ocean are at the center of your trip, or especially if you're traveling with children, you could make a resort or rental home your base.

The hospitality industry is highly evolved, a point of civic pride. Even the B&B units, where a home's owner is your host, offer extras like jogger's maps, a selection of menus, tips on neighborhood sights, and, of course, history lessons. WiFi access is common but worth asking about, as are day passes to fitness facilities. Some hotels and inns have on-site babysitting services; other places have policies about children as guests. Pets are sometimes allowed; smoking is regulated; and wheelchair access, by ramps or elevators, in bathrooms or bedrooms, does vary. Not everyone offers parking, so check: Lot rates can be as high as $32 per day. Deposit/cancellation policies are strictly followed in smaller inns and B&Bs. High (expensive) season is March through June and September and October.

HOTELS AND LARGER INNS

Charleston Place (843-722-4900 or 1-888-635-2350; www.charlestonplace .com), 205 Meeting St., Charleston, SC 29401. Very expensive. Its construction some 30 years ago created a luxury microclimate with its own elegant boutiques at the central historic district intersection of Market and Meeting. It's home to Charleston Grill, one of the city's best restaurants, a full-service European spa, a rooftop pool, and grand decorating gestures, like a spectacular curved staircase and a huge chandelier, massive pots of flowers, shiny marble floors, and rooms of polished furniture. Special rate packages, which include tickets to Spoleto performances and reasonable off-season rates, are worth looking into.

Embassy Suites—Historic District (843-723-6900 or 1-800-362-2779; www.historiccharleston .embassysuites.com), 337 Meeting St., Charleston, SC 29403. Expensive–Very expensive. Located in a fine makeover of the 19th-century Citadel building where generations of Southern boys attended military school, it has a massive, theatrical feel with lit palm trees, a courtyard, and crenellated turrets, but the outdoor pool and sundeck soften the institutional edges. Suites allow for flexible arrangements for families or work, and flat screens for television or gaming. On Marion Square, near the visitor center where many tours and trolley services originate.

Francis Marion Hotel (843-722-0600 or 1-877-756-2121; www.francis marioncharleston.com), 387 King St., Charleston, SC 29403. Expensive–Very expensive. This old chestnut with 200-plus rooms from the 1920s was overhauled, redecorated, and placed on the National Register of Historic Places. There are wide stairs and hallways, wood paneling, plaster moldings covered in gold leaf, a lobby with big windows and club chairs, and high ceilings. It overlooks Marion Square (with great views of Charleston from rooms

Hidden gardens thrive in the microclimates of the city that mimic Mediterranean conditions.
Peter Loftus

on the upper floors), and from the coffee bar you can watch the goings-on in the upbeat College of Charleston neighborhood.

HarbourView Inn (843-853-8439 or 1-888-853-8439; www.harbourview charleston.com), 2 Vendue Range, Charleston, SC 29401. Very expensive. Just steps from Waterfront Park and featuring many rooms with stunning views and harbor breezes. The right mix of elegance and understatement characterizes the best of Charleston design: sea grass/rush carpeting, cream-colored walls, big windows (some with broad slatted "plantation" shutters), perhaps one framed print, and an armoire made by a local woodworking company. Many of the rooms have fireplaces, some have balconies, some have whirlpool baths. A good deal of attention is paid to detail here, even in the choice, framing, and hang-

ing of art in the hallways, and it really shows.

King Charles Inn (843-723-7451 or 1-866-546-4700; www.kingcharles inn.com), 237 Meeting St., Charleston, SC 29401. Expensive. A Best Western choice for visitors on a budget. An outdoor pool located on an elevated, screened terrace affords good privacy for an establishment in the heart of downtown. It may be modest and your neighbors may have rolled in on a motor coach tour, but the service is attentive, there's free parking, and the location is unbeatable.

The Mills House (843-577-2400 or 1-800-874-9600; www.millshouse .com), 115 Meeting St., Charleston, SC 29401. Expensive–Very expensive. Completely renovated in 2008 to better recall its 1853 origin, you can imagine what it was like when cotton planters, politicians, and brokers roamed the first floor and terraces. If you're walking the city, it's about 0.5 mile to East Bay Street, the Market area, the South of Broad neighborhood, two historic house museums, the Gibbes Museum of Art, and the French Quarter Art District. Nice pool, adjacent (for a fee) parking, and a few handicapped-accessible rooms. A Wyndham Grand Hotel.

Renaissance Charleston Hotel (843-534-0300 or 1-888-236-2427; www.renaissancecharlestonhotel.com), 68 Wentworth St., Charleston, SC 29401. Very expensive. A large hotel (162 rooms) in the Marriott chain with an outdoor heated pool and fitness center in a good location just north of Market Street and the hipper sections of upper King Street. Decor is a little more mainstream than other hotels (more colors, valances, and dust ruffles), but locals send people here—management knows its small-business neighbors and can recommend less-obvious choices for shopping and dining.

SMALLER LUXURY INNS

Ansonborough Inn (843-723-1655 or 1-800-522-2073; www.ansonborough inn.com), 21 Hasell St., Charleston, SC 29401. Expensive–Very expensive. This circa-1901 stationer's warehouse two blocks from the City Market was given new life as a boutique inn, but reminders of its past use—including huge beams, plank floors, and walls of exposed brick—remain. Forty-five suites, from small split-level loft rooms to two-room kings, generally feature a wet bar and microwave/mini-refrigerator. Terrific view across the river from rooftop patio.

Battery Carriage House Inn (843-727-3100 or 1-800-775-5575; www.batterycarriagehouse.com), 20 S. Battery, Charleston, SC 29401.

Hidden alleys connected dependencies like kitchens and carriage houses long before New Urbanism theories of neighborhood planning.   Peter Loftus

Expensive–Very expensive. South Battery opens on to White Point Gardens and the harbor promenade, the edge of the historic residential district known as "South of Broad." This is the neighborhood that comes to mind when most people think of Charleston, a place of iron gates entwined with jasmine, and houses with massive columns set on high foundations. There are 11 guest rooms whose small dimensions are alleviated by access to a narrow piazza and a lovely back garden. Continental breakfast and the newspaper arrive at your door, or you can start your day under the rose arbor.

Fulton Lane Inn (843-720-2600 or 1-800-720-2688; www.charminginns .com), 202 King St., Charleston, SC 29401. Expensive–Very expensive. Located in the heart of the downtown antique and gallery district. The 27 rooms have a refreshing, airy look: sisal, wicker, and muslin decorating accents; louvered shutters; wall coverings and paint in soft, liquid colors like celadon, pale peach, and lemon. The

feel is summer in the Lowcountry. You can go simple or deluxe, with canopied beds and fireplaces, kitchens and whirlpool baths. Part of a local consortium of inns with knowledgeable concierge service.

Governor's House Inn (843-720-2070 or 1-800-720-9812; www .governorshouse.com), 117 Broad St., Charleston, SC 29401. Expensive–Very expensive. Once home to Governor Edward Rutledge, who at 26 signed the Declaration of Independence and at 30 was a patriot under arrest. The stunning restoration of this grand home suggests he appreciated the finer things in life. The nicest rooms have 12-foot ceilings and their own veranda access, with views of Charleston's fanciest neighborhood. A kitchen house with an original 1760 fireplace has two suites. It's an excellent spot for an indulge-yourself weekend.

John Rutledge House Inn (843-723-7999 or 1-800-476-9741; www.john rutledgehouseinn.com), 116 Broad St., Charleston, SC 29401. Very expen-

Joggling boards are as common as tree houses in Charleston backyards. Peter Loftus

sive. George Washington did visit this house, which dates from 1763 and whose guest rooms, including several spacious suites, are decorated with antiques, sumptuous fabrics, and carved mantelpieces. It's a National Historic Landmark. You can stay in the main house or in two carriage houses set in a charming courtyard. Suites in the main house include an additional sitting room and fireplace; some have Jacuzzi tubs. Like the Governor's House, it's a minute's walk to get to South of Broad.

Planters Inn (843-722-2345 or 1-800-845-7082; www.plantersinn .com), 112 N. Market St., Charleston, SC 29401. Very expensive. A location at the intersection of North Market and Meeting Streets makes this larger inn within five blocks of practically every Charleston asset. It feels a bit more hip than its peers, more in the center of the action, especially because it's so convenient to take a midday breather on the verandas or in the courtyard. Member of Relais & Cha-teaux. The acclaimed Peninsula Grill, perennially on national "Best of" lists, is located here (see Dining).

Two Meeting Street Inn (843-723-7322 or 1-888-723-7322; www .twomeetingstreetinn.com), 2 Meeting St., Charleston, SC 29401. Very expen-sive. A massive Queen Anne mansion that looks like a picture on a postcard, with its wraparound porches and rock-ing chairs overlooking the Battery, oak-paneled sitting rooms, and nine guest rooms filled with Oriental rugs and period family accessories. Some have Victorian-style tubs or private balcony access. Honeymooners and celebrating couples often book a year in advance—especially for those rooms with canopied four-posters needing a special set of stairs to reach. Continen-tal breakfast and an elaborate after-

noon tea are included. Credit cards not accepted.

Wentworth Mansion (843-853-1886 or 1-888-466-1886; www.went worthmansion.com), 149 Wentworth St., Charleston, SC 29401. Very expen-sive. This Second Empire–style man-sion (built in 1886 for a cotton baron) will turn your head with its carved plasterwork ceilings, marble fireplac-es, Tiffany glass, mahogany paneling, intricately tiled floors, and a cupola, accessed by a stairway for the brave, which yields a panoramic view of the city. There are 21 rooms with king-sized beds, whirlpools, and fireplaces. A stately library is a late-night refuge. It's about a 10- to 15-minute walk to downtown. Circa 1886, in the Carriage House, is another of Charleston's best restaurants (see Dining).

BED & BREAKFAST LODGINGS IN PRIVATE HOMES AND GARDENS

A central listing service, Historic Charleston Bed and Breakfast (843-722-6606 or 1-800-743-3583; www .historiccharlestonbedandbreakfast. com) offers accommodations from single rooms to houses, which are photographed and well-described on the website. Their phone lines are open weekdays from 9–5. Credit cards can be used to pay a deposit, but the balance is usually cash or check only. They can be budget-friendly choices. The South Carolina Bed & Breakfast Association (www.southcarolinabedand breakfast.com) is a members' group with online listings and links to inns across the state on its comprehensive, well-indexed website. Reviews for many of these establishments can be found at www.bedandbreakfast.com.

1837 Bed & Breakfast (843-723-7166 or 1-877-723-1837; www.1837bb

.com), 126 Wentworth St., Charleston, SC 29401. Expensive. Nine guest rooms, porches with rockers, full breakfast. Located a few blocks north and west of Charleston Place.

Fantasia B&B (843-853-0201 or 1-800-852-4466; www.fantasiabb.com), 11 George St., Charleston, SC 29401. Expensive. Suites in dependencies or the 1813 traditional Charleston "single" house, beautifully preserved, with kitchenettes, private baths and balcony access. In the Ansonborough neighborhood, about a 10-minute walk to Broad Street.

4 Unity Alley (843-577-6660; www.unitybb.com), 4 Unity Alley, Charleston, SC 29401. Expensive. Three suites with bedroom and sitting room, and communal dining area, located in a restored brick warehouse just off East Bay Street in the French Quarter, a mix of commercial (galleries, fancy restaurants) and residential uses.

Phoebe Pember House (843-722-4186; www.phoebepemberhouse.com), 26 Society St., Charleston, SC 29401. Expensive–Very expensive. The walled meditation garden and a studio that offers yoga classes, meditation instruction, and massage send a message of healing. Rooms in the 1807 main house or in a carriage house.

Thomas Lamboll House (843-723-3212 or 1-888-874-0793; www.lambollhouse.com), 19 King St., Charleston, SC 29401. Moderate–Expensive. Open the French doors from your bedroom onto the piazza of this pre-Revolutionary house located steps from the Battery. Two rooms with private baths and fireplaces.

21 East Battery Bed & Breakfast (843-556-0500 or 1-888-721-7488; www.21eastbattery.com), 21 E. Battery, Charleston, SC 29401. Very expensive. A newly renovated carriage house and adjacent two-story former slave quarters form a private residence that can accommodate 10, tucked in the historic Edmonston–Alston House museum complex. A complimentary tour of that property is included.

27 State Street (843-722-4243; www.charleston-bb.com), 27 State St., Charleston, SC 29401. Expensive–Very expensive. Enter your private suite (with kitchenette) through the courtyard of a foursquare, circa-1800 house in the French Quarter, a block off East Bay Street and its wonderful restaurants and close to the Waterfront Park for morning jogging.

CHARLESTON ENVIRONS

The Inn at Middleton Place (843-556-0500 or 1-800-543-4774; www.theinnatmiddletonplace.com), 4290 Ashley River Rd., Charleston, SC 29414. Expensive–Very expensive. Located on a bluff adjacent to the astonishing gardens at Middleton Place (see "Historic Homes, Gardens & Religious Sites" under Culture), about 25 minutes from downtown. For serenity, long walks along the Ashley River or at Middleton Place (admission waived for guests), kayaking, and horseback riding, come here. It's handsomely modern on the outside, splendidly understated inside. There are 53 rooms in four buildings, each with working log fireplaces, custom-made furniture, soft colors, and large bathrooms. Some are handicapped accessible. Floor-to-ceiling windows with louvered shutters filter the light and air in the woodland setting. The restaurant at Middleton Place serves lunch and dinner daily.

FOLLY BEACH

Tides Folly Beach (843-588-6464; www.tidesfollybeach.com), 1 Center

St., Folly Beach, SC 29439. Expensive. A recently renovated oceanfront Holiday Inn 9 miles from Charleston. Blu, its contemporary bar and restaurant, has gotten local raves for its small plate menu and fresh seafood. Folly Beach is a down-to-earth, lively mecca for surfers and families. Handicap access and nonsmoking rooms; pets OK for a fee.

ISLE OF PALMS

The Palms Hotel (1-888-484-9004; www.thepalmshotel.us), 1126 Ocean Blvd., Isle of Palms, SC 29451. Moderate–Expensive. There are 68 rooms, some with views or partial views, in a great location with all the beach and pool amenities.

RESORTS AND RENTALS— CHARLESTON AREA SEA ISLANDS

The Sea Island resort areas are popular year-round, with golf and tennis every day and ocean swimming for all but about four months. Each resort has a well-supervised children's activity program. For longer stays of a week or more, you may want to contact some of the rental agents who specialize in private beach properties, including villas and houses located within the resorts and outside of them. Note that rental rates for some especially fancy private homes within the resorts can be as much as twice the average rates quoted below.

Rental accommodations are fully furnished, including washer and dryer, but you should check to see if you need to bring anything, if there are special features like handicap access, or if a fee for cleaning after your departure is included. Deposits are necessary and during summer months minimum stays are usually required.

Typical summer rental prices for a two-bedroom, oceanfront house generally start from $2,500 per week, but properties by a lagoon or in the woods are less expensive. November through February are low-season months. The resorts offer numerous packages covering a long weekend or week's stay to attract golfers, honeymooners, Thanksgiving get-togethers, and visitors coming for the tours of historic homes in the fall and spring.

Kiawah Island Golf Resort and The Sanctuary (843-768-2121 or 1-800-654-2924 for the golf resort; 843-768-6000 or 1-800-576-1570 for The Sanctuary; www.kiawahresort.com), One Sanctuary Beach, Kiawah Island, SC 29455. Very expensive. Kiawah is a world-class resort with a rambling inn, hundreds of villa accommodations in several sizes, and private, architect-designed homes that aren't anything like a sandy house on stilts. The beach is private and 10 miles long; 30 miles of paved bike trails wind around five golf courses and recreational areas, ultimately linking two distinct resort villages. The Sanctuary, a self-enclosed luxury hotel complex with 255 guest rooms, a luxurious spa, and two ocean-front restaurants, is the latest addition to the resort.

Seabrook Exclusives (843-768-3635 or 1-800-845-6966; www.pam harringtonexclusives.com), 4343 Betsy Kerrison Pkwy., Johns Island, SC 29455. Very expensive. Seabrook is a 2,200-acre private country club community. Visitors rent cottages, villas, or homes. Its unique asset is its equestrian center and miles of riding trails, but it also has golf and tennis, a beach and beach club, and a fitness center.

Wild Dunes Resort (843-886-6000 or 1-866-513-9841; www.wilddunes .com), 5757 Palm Blvd., Isle of Palms, SC 29451. Expensive–Very expensive.

A small resort located on the northeast end of the modest Isle of Palms, the closest of the resorts to Charleston. Sullivan's Island, an old, nonresort beach community with a smattering of restaurants and nightlife, is close by. Guests choose accommodations in the 93-room Boardwalk Inn or in villas, townhouses, and cottages.

BEACH RENTAL AGENTS

Beachwalker Rentals (843-768-1777; www.beachwalker.com), Freshfields Village, Johns Island, SC 29455.

Accommodations on Kiawah and Seabrook Islands with many family-friendly properties.

Carroll Realty (843-886-9600 or 1-800-845-7718; www.carrollrealtyinc.com), 103 Palm Blvd., Isle of Palms, SC 29451. Homes and villas by the week, month, or year on Isle of Palms, Wild Dunes, and Sullivan's Island.

Island Realty (843-886-8144 or 1-866-380-3983; www.islandrealty.com), 1304 Palm Blvd., Isle of Palms, SC 29451. Rentals and golf packages on Sullivan's Island, Isle of Palms, and the more remote Dewees Island.

Dining

Taste of the town . . . local restaurants, cafés, bars, bistros, etc.

Dining is one Lowcountry ritual that remains important, honoring family, tradition, the art of conversation, and the resourcefulness of the cook who brings African and West Indian traditions to the table. As the extraordinary Southern chef Edna Lewis said: "The birds are just the beginning. In the South you put everything you have on the table." In Charleston that means an incredible harvest of seafood, game, rice and grits, and vegetables. Over the last 20 years, the number and quality of restaurants has skyrocketed, as have creative chefs for whom Charleston is a mecca. You can hear what some of the city's most respected foodies and authors have to say: John Martin Taylor (www.hoppinjohns.com) the brothers and authors Matt and Ted Lee (www.mattleeandtedlee.com), a blog by a classically trained former food critic (www.charlestonchow.blogspot.com), and one about foodways (www.slowfoodcharleston.blogspot.com).

Many restaurants are clustered on Upper King Street and East Bay Street, or in the Market area. These choices reflect all price ranges and cuisines, with smaller or more informal places listed at the end of the section. The general price range is meant to reflect the cost of a single meal, usually dinner, featuring an appetizer, entrée, dessert, and coffee. Cocktails, beer, wine, gratuity, and tax are not included in the estimated price. Lunches are generally less expensive, and in some cases, noted as a bargain. During Spoleto, restaurants relax their hours to feed the crowds. Good picnicking spots are found at Waterfront Park at the foot of Queen Street, in the shady grove of Washington Square, or on a bench at the Battery.

Amen Street Fish and Raw Bar (843-853-8600; www.amenstreet.com), 205 E. Bay St. Open for lunch and dinner daily, with full bar until 2 AM. Moderate. One of the city's newest additions and a favorite among locals, with an extensive raw bar and fun late-night crowd that comes for a half-dozen or dozen with a glass of wine or craft beer. The emphasis is on fresh

Local farm and seafood crops and creative chefs who buy them daily have made Charleston a culinary destination.

Charleston Area Convention & Visitors Bureau

American-style cooking, unencumbered by too much sauce.

Basil (843-724-3490; www.eatatbasil.com), 460 King St. Open for lunch weekdays, dinner daily. Moderate. Gallery owners, creative types, families, and professors flock here. If there's a line (no reservations), duck into a companion restaurant that serves tapas next door. Thai standards include crispy duck and spicy noodle soups, dishes with peanuts and coconut and curries. The grill is open, with seating at the chef's counter, or at tables, booths, or a tiny bar. Lunch is a bargain. A simple and elegant standout.

Boulevard Diner (843-216-2611; www.dinewithsal.com), 409 W. Coleman Blvd., Mount Pleasant. Open Mon.–Sat. for breakfast, lunch, and dinner; brunch on Sunday. Moderate. A favorite with locals. This low key diner features fresh seafood and daily specials. Folks come for the fried green tomatoes, catfish po' boy, and tomato and pimento cheese pie.

Charleston Grill (843-577-4522; www.charlestongrill.com), 224 King St., at Charleston Place. Open daily for dinner. Expensive–Very expensive. Elegant but not stuffy, excellent service, the tables shine like little jewels against the wood paneling of a large room. Jazz seven nights a week. Chef Michelle Weaver is committed to local farmers and her menus are arranged by theme, so you can select something "Pure" like vegetables or "Lush" mélanges of roe and lobster. The desserts are like little works of art.

Circa 1886 (843-853-7828; www.circa1886.com), 149 Wentworth St. Open Mon.–Sat. for dinner. Expensive–Very expensive. Deluxe and cozy, about 50 seats off the beaten track in a renovated stable behind the Wentworth Mansion. Once common local ingredients like conch, quail, and fresh beets turn up with fruit and sweet accents and spicing inspired by the West Indies. There's a vegetarian entrée, but big servings of beef tenderloin and lamb chops, too. Notable wine list.

Fish (843-722-3474; www.fishrestaurantcharleston.com), 442 King St. Open Mon.–Sat. for lunch and dinner. Moderate–Expensive. Hidden in an 1837 single house with its side-to-the-street entryway used for outdoor dining, this is a casual restaurant with a neighborhood feel. The winter menu might feature fresh root vegetables and soups, and when shad are running in the Edisto River, sweet roe. Near the visitor center, a bargain lunch stop before or after a tour.

Fulton Five (843-853-5555; www .fultonfive.com), 5 Fulton St. Open Mon.–Sat. for dinner. Moderate– Expensive. It's said Gian Carlo Menotti chose Charleston for his Spoleto Festival USA because it had a Mediterranean feel, a serene charm as easy to appreciate and as softly worn as stucco walls. That's what it feels like here. The Northern Italian menu includes duck breast, veal, risotto dishes, and fresh seafood specials.

Gaulart & Maliclet (843-577-9797; www.fastandfrenchcharleston .com), 98 Broad St. Open Mon.–Sat. for breakfast and lunch; Tues.–Sat. for breakfast, lunch, and dinner. Inexpensive. Known as "Fast and French," it's the most popular, enduring little place in the Historic District for later dinners or a quick afternoon bite. You'll find platters of pâté, sausages, selections of cheeses, and French bread; hearty soups; fondues; excellent wine. Vegetarian options.

Hank's (843-723-3474; www.hanks seafoodrestaurant.com), 10 Hayne St. Open daily for dinner. Moderate–Expensive. A good-natured, festive throwback to family seafood houses of the 1950s, except there's no sawdust on the floor and the grilled fish entrées could come with buerre blanc. The chef's specials hit a home run.

High Cotton (843-724-3815; www.mavericksouthernkitchens.com), 199 E. Bay St. Open daily for dinner; brunch Sat. and Sun. Expensive–Very expensive. Glossy, unabashed, and high energy, a destination for visitors. Robust entrées include smoked meats and fowl, roasted pork, homemade sausages, as well as seafood standards. Jazz brunch Sunday.

Hominy Grill (843-937-0930; www.hominygrill.com), 207 Rutledge Ave. Open Mon.–Fri. for breakfast, lunch, and dinner; brunch and dinner Sat., brunch on Sun. Inexpensive–Moderate. Hominy has remained modest and graceful even after heaps of national praise have diners lining up outside for its celebrated buttermilk pie, among other delights. Off the beaten path from downtown in an old barbershop with a tin ceiling. A day that starts with butcher-paper tablecloths, thick mugs of coffee, biscuits, and bacon proceeds to a fried green tomato BLT or pimento spread sandwich, then moves on to linens, catfish, and starlight in the walled garden.

Magnolia's Uptown/Down South (843-577-7771; www.magnolias -blossom-cypress.com), 185 E. Bay

Shrimp fresh from the creek.
SC Lowcountry Tourism Commission

St. Open Mon.–Sat. for lunch; dinner nightly; brunch on Sun. Moderate–Expensive. This big and breezy place put Charleston on the map foodwise, with new twists on basic Southern foodstuffs—greens, black-eyed peas, grits, and shrimp. It's very popular, with more visitors than locals during the high season, but has kept its touch and still delivers. Sunday brunch lasts past 3 PM for late risers.

McCrady's (843-577-0025; www.mccradysrestaurant.com), 2 Unity Alley (off E. Bay St.) Open daily for dinner. Expensive–Very expensive. With its space in a beautifully redone 18th-century tavern, McCrady's is an understated treasure whose chef, Sean Brock, is a leader in the local food movement. The cooking has classic French underpinnings with art-world presentation. Cozy wine bar.

Peninsula Grill (843-723-0700; www.peninsulagrill.com), 112 N. Market St. Open daily for dinner. Expensive–Very expensive. An elegant room with velvet walls, sometimes a bit noisy, but more like a steady hum than a roar. The light is suffused with soft gold overtones, as if the color had been rubbed on the air. Jell-O would taste good here. Offering "simple" entrées like strip steak, Carolina trout, grouper, and your choice of sauces and sides. Champagne and small plates are always on the menu.

Virginia's on King (843-735-5800; www.virginiasonking.com), 412 King St. Open Mon.–Fri. for breakfast and lunch; Mon.–Sat. dinner; brunch Sat. and Sun. Moderate–Expensive. Passed-down family favorites, lovingly served. Find Frogmore Stew, fried okra, she-crab soup, and extras like mashed potatoes and fried tomatoes. Located a block north of King Street's intersection with Calhoun Street, it's a great destination after shopping.

Bakeries/Coffee Houses

Cru Café (843-534-2434; www.crucafe.com), 18 Pinckney St. A local favorite for lunch, homemade soups and wraps, wines, and seating on the porch of the 18th-century house near the Market.

Cupcake (843-853-8181; www.freshcupcakes.com), 433 King St. Located at a perfect place for a sugar fix if you're shopping in the Upper King Street Design District.

Dixie Supply Bakery & Café (843-722-5650; www.dixiecafecharleston.com) 62 State St. Open Tue.–Sun. for breakfast and lunch. This unassuming café, next to a convenience store, may be small but they turn out one of the best tomato pies in the city, served with sweet potato cornbread. Baked goods, pancakes, eggs, and bacon for breakfast. This is where the cops and lawyers eat.

Saffron (843-722-5588; www.eatatsaffron.com), 333 E. Bay St. The racks of fresh bread and the glass cases filled with daily specials like chocolate-chip scones and pastries could lead to a gourmet picnic if you don't want to eat here.

Pizza, Sandwiches, and Faster Food

Andolini's (843-722-7437; www.andolinis.com), 82 Wentworth St. College-style joint, order as you enter, eat in a high-backed booth or on the back patio.

Closed for Business (843-853-8466; www.closed4business.com), 453 King St. Inexpensive comfort food and burgers that locals think are the best in Charleston. Lunch and dinner.

Juanita Greenberg's Nacho Royale (843-723-6224; www.juanitagreenbergs.com), 439 King St. Big burritos, handmade nachos in portions made for two. You can start with a margarita at 4 PM.

Touring

Fun in the Historic District
and beyond.

Tour operators are licensed and patient with questions; they really know their stuff. Tours range from an hour to two and a half hours, longer for out-of-town sites and scheduled stops at house museums, with prices in town starting at about $15 for children and $21 for adults, then escalating quickly according to the length of the trip. Reservations recommended. Those with a nature emphasis are described more fully in the Recreation section later in this chapter.

Many tours begin at the Charleston Visitor Center (843-724-7174; www .charlestoncvb.com), 375 Meeting St., where there are maps, docents, and an audiovisual presentation. Purchase a nine-site combination ticket for substantial admission discounts (www.heritagefederation.org). Water-based tours put Charleston's history in perspective and provide an invaluable sense of place. They generally depart from the Aquarium Wharf Dock, 360 Concord St., or the Maritime Center, 10 Wharfside St.

BY BUS OR MINIVAN

The cool of a minivan or bus tour has its virtues. The audio and video are high quality, and extra-large windows offer great views. These tours also travel to sites

Many Charleston houses that are one room deep date from before the Revolution. Often an office was on the first floor.   Peter Loftus

Tours on the water can give a spectacular view of 19th-century homes lining the Charleston Battery. Charleston Area Convention & Visitors Bureau

out of the city limits, but larger vehicles are restricted in some neighborhoods with narrow streets. They are a good choice for handicapped passengers, the eager visitor who wants to cover a lot of ground in a day, and groups of six or more.

Motorized tours generally pick up and deliver passengers from major downtown hotels and the visitor center.

Charleston Tours (843-571-0049; www.charleston-tours.com).

Doin' The Charleston (843-763-1233; www.dointhecharlestontours.com).

Sites and Insight Tours by Al Miller (843-552-9995; www.sitesandinsights tours.com) Emphasizing African American history and Gullah culture.

Talk of the Towne (843-795-8199; www.talkofthetowne.com).

BY BOAT

Sandlapper Water Tours (843-849-8687; www.sandlappertours.com) History, nature, and sunset cruises aboard a 45-foot catamaran.

Schooner Pride (1-800-344-4483; www.schoonerpride.com) An 84-foot-tall ship.

Spiritline Harbor Tour (843-722-2628; www.spiritlinecruises.com).

BY BICYCLE

Discovering the nooks and crannies of the historic districts under your own steam is an intimate way to imagine the past. Rental rates start at $28 per day or $7 per hour. Shop staff has maps and ideas for longer rides. Helmets, child seats, and locks are provided at low or no cost.

Affordabike (843-789-3281; www.affordabike.com), 534 King St.

The Bicycle Shoppe (843-722-8168; www.thebicycleshoppecharleston.com), 280 Meeting St.

BY FOOT

As guiding has evolved, so have tours tailored to specific interests. With sufficient advance notice, some private guides will craft a unique tour for your group, or offer bilingual service. Walking tours generally last up to two hours and are scheduled in morning and afternoon. Ask how large the group can get—a dozen is good. Reservations are recommended, in some cases required. Prices start at about $20 per person.

Architectural Walking Tours (843-893-2327 or 1-800-931-7761; www.architecturalwalkingtoursofcharleston.com).

Bulldog Tours (843-722-8687; www.bulldogtours.com) Specializing in ghosts, graveyards, and Charleston's haunted side.

Charleston Strolls (843-722-8687; www.bulldogtours.com).

Culinary Tours of Charleston (843-722-8687; www.bulldogtours.com) Visit chefs, bakers, and food artisans on one of two walks lasting two-plus hours.

Gullah Tours (843-763-7551; www.gullahtours.com).

BY CARRIAGE

Tours generally last one hour, scheduled throughout the day and evening. Prices per person are about $20 for adults, $15 for children. These companies leave from stables in the Market area.

Old South Carriage Co. (843-723-9712; www.oldsouthcarriage.com).

Olde Towne Carriage Co. (843-722-1315; www.oldetownecarriage.com).

Palmetto Carriage Works (843-723-8145; www.carriagetour.com).

Culture

Great places to see and things to do.

ART

Gibbes Museum of Art (843-722-2706; www.gibbesmuseum.org), 135 Meeting St. Open Tues.–Sat. 10–5; Sun. 1–5; closed Mon. and holidays. The permanent collection presents Charleston from the 18th century, including Charles Fraser's exquisite miniatures of prominent citizens, and interpretations of 20th-century plantation and rural life by Alice Ravenel Huger Smith, Alfred Hutty, and Anna Heyward Taylor. Traveling exhibits every few months. Fine museum shop. Adults $9; seniors, students, military $7; children $5.

GALLERIES

The Charleston Fine Art Dealers Association (www.cfada.com) is a force for appreciation of both the work of the Charleston Renaissance artists of the 20th century and the New Renaissance artists in the Charleston of the 21st. The site is the best resource for arts-related events. An association of artists (843-805-8052; www.frenchquarterarts.com) holds quarterly walks in the French Quarter on the first Friday evening of March, May, October, and December. And two-hour gallery tours for six to eight people, led by artists, showcase the contemporary scene (843-860-3327; www.charlestonarttours.com) at a cost of $49 per person.

Anglin Smith Fine Art (843-853-0708; www.anglinsmith.com), 9 Queen St. Representing painter Betty Anglin Smith and her accomplished triplets—painters Jennifer Smith Rogers and Shannon Smith and photographer Tripp Smith—as well as the best artists on the local scene.

The Charleston Renaissance Gallery (843-723-0025; www.charleston renaissancegallery.com), 103 Church St. Located in a beautifully restored post-Revolutionary brick building, the gallery is at the forefront of renewed interest in Charleston's 20th-century art and sculpture.

Coleman Fine Art (843-853-7000; www.colemanfineart.com), 79 Church St. Members of the gallery include a number of artists working in a realistic style in oils and watercolors, as well as the paintings of portraitist and illustrator Mary Whyte. Smith Coleman III, who owns the gallery, also restores damaged works of art and makes lovely frames. The gallery is located in the former studio of Eliza-beth O'Neill Verner.

Gaye Sanders Fisher Gallery (843-958-0010; www.gayesandersfisher.com), 124 Church St. Located in an 18th-century single house, the gallery features watercolors that burst with the feeling of Lowcountry landscape and architecture.

John Carroll Doyle Art Gallery (843-577-7344; www.johncdoyle.com), 125 Church St. A Charleston native, Doyle is one of the painters in the "new" Charles-ton Renaissance, capturing people in intense moments (like blues harmonica play-ers) and teasing that intensity out of landscapes and animals.

Martin Gallery (843-723-7378; www.martingallerycharleston.com), 18 Broad St. Contemporary art and elegant craft work, including jewelry incorporating pre-cious stones and sculpted gold.

The Sylvan Gallery (843-722-2172; www.thesylvangallery.com), 171 King St. Representing more than 30 artists, the gallery features sculpture and 20th- and 21st-century representational art.

Wells Gallery (843-576-1290; www.wellsgallery.com), One Sanctuary Beach Dr., Kiawah Island. Contemporary art of nationally recognized artists. Fine art, watercolors, jewelry, and glass.

HISTORIC HOMES, GARDENS & RELIGIOUS SITES

A reasonable schedule, once you've made your difficult choices, would include visits to two or three city sites in a day and a tour of some kind. Museum Mile on Meeting Street (www.charlestonmuseummile.org) is an orienting, first-day walk. Allow a half-day for a plantation or boat tour. Visitors are welcome to enter religious sites, but are asked to observe the worship schedule and related courtesies, as few of the sites offer regular tour services. Handicapped access is sometimes limited in the old buildings, and there are usually rules regarding strollers. Many plantation properties have various scales for admission fees, depending on the tours offered.

Aiken-Rhett House (843-723-1159; www.historiccharleston.org), 48 Elizabeth St. Open Mon.–Sat. 10–5; Sun. 2–5. Built in 1817 with Greek Revival and Rococo interiors, it is preserved in a somewhat less formal way than other houses, full of atmosphere, a little worn at the edges. During the fiercest shelling of Charleston in the Civil War, it was the headquarters of Confederate General P. G. T. Beauregard. The intact work yard is a compelling example of African American urban life. Adults $10; reduced admission with combination tickets to selected historic properties.

Boone Hall Plantation (843-884-4371; www.boonehallplantation.com), 1235 Long Point Rd., Mount Pleasant. Open Mon.–Sat. 9–5; Sun. 1–4. Of particular interest are the nine mid-18th-century brick slave cabins; the Gin House, used for processing cotton; and the magnificent avenue of oaks, which runs 0.75 mile. A new living history presentation highlights Gullah culture. Adults $20, children $10.

Congregation Beth Elohim (843-723-1090; www.kkbe.org), 90 Hasell St. Open Mon.–Fri. 10–noon for tours. The country's oldest synagogue in continuous use, built in 1840 to replace an earlier building that was destroyed by fire, it is a superb example of Greek Revival architecture.

Drayton Hall (843-769-2600; www.draytonhall.org), 3380 Ashley River Rd., 9 miles northwest of Charleston. Open Mon.–Sat. 9–3:30; Sun. 11–3:30. Closed on major holidays. Built between 1738 and 1742, and set on a lovely Ashley River site, it is one of the most architecturally significant dwellings in America. The house is unfurnished, with stunning examples of plasterwork and carving. Hourly tours (written tours in English, Spanish, French, and German available), African American history tours, and self-guided walking tours available. Not to be missed even if it's raining. Adults $18, youth $8, children $6.

Edmonston-Alston House (843-722-7171; www.edmondstonalston.com), 21 E. Battery. Open Tues.–Sat. 10–4:30; Sun. and Mon. 1:30–4:30. First built in 1825 by one wealthy man, and later enlarged by another, its structure, lavish decoration, documents, family furnishings, silver, and china reveal the lifestyle some Southerners fought to protect. Adults $12, children $8; reduced admission with combination tickets to selected historic properties.

Emanuel A. M. E. Church (843-722-2561; www.emanuelamechurch.org), 110 Calhoun St. The Free African Society, composed of free blacks and slaves, was formed in 1791, and by 1818, under the leadership of Morris Brown, this independent congregation built a small church for its services. Denmark Vesey planned his slave insurrection there. The current church was built in 1891.

French Protestant (Huguenot) Church (843-722-4385; www.huguenot -church.org), 136 Church St. French Huguenots fleeing religious persecution worshipped in Charleston as early as 1687. This church, built on the site of earlier ones, dates from 1845.

Heyward-Washington House (843-722-2996; www.charlestonmuseum.org), 87 Church St. Open Mon.–Sat. 10–5; Sun. 1–5; last tour at 4:30. Built in 1772 by a rice planter and home of Thomas Heyward Jr., signer of the Declaration of Independence, it was George Washington's headquarters in 1791. Its furniture collection, including several 18th-century Charleston-made pieces and the magnificent Holmes bookcase, is unmatched, as is a formal colonial garden. Adults $10, children $5; discounted admission with combination ticket to other Charleston Museum properties.

Joseph Manigault House (843-722-2996; www.charlestonmuseum.org), 350 Meeting St. Open Mon.–Sat. 10–5; Sun. 1–5; last tour at 4:30. The outside of this structure is three stories of brick; the inside is something like shaped light.

Drayton Hall is known for its stunning architectural details. Charleston Area Convention & Visitors Bureau

Designed by native son Gabriel Manigault for his brother and completed in 1803, it exudes a beauty-loving sense of detail by an artist educated in Europe and exposed to sophisticated design ideas and decorating schemes. The furniture is of the period: English, American, and French. Adults $10, children $5; discounted admission with a combination ticket to other Charleston Museum properties.

Magnolia Plantation and Gardens (1-800-367-3517; www.magnoliaplantation .com), 3550 Ashley River Rd., 10 miles northwest of Charleston. Open daily 8–5:30; shorter hours in winter. The current building was floated here by barge in 1873, but the entire tract dates back to the time of the Barbadian planters and the Drayton family. The gardens and their design reflect three centuries of horticulture, including 250 varieties of *Azalea indica* and 900 varieties of *Camellia japonica.* Family friendly with bike and walking paths, a nature train, and boat tours. This is also the site to enter the Audubon Swamp Garden. Admission to the plantation and gardens: adults $15, children $10, with additional costs for tours of the house and rides on the nature preserve train.

Middleton Place (843-556-6020 or 1-800-782-3608; www.middletonplace .org), 4300 Ashley River Rd., 14 miles northwest of Charleston. Open daily 9–5. The formal gardens, laid out in 1741 and constructed by 100 slaves over a decade, feature terraces, camellia allées, butterfly lakes, and hillside drifts of azalea. The strong landscape design can be appreciated even when little is in bloom. Adjacent stables and a farmyard evoke the plantation era, with artisan demonstrations and tours focusing on African American life. The main house was sacked by Union

The flying staircase at the Nathaniel Russell House. Charleston Area Convention & Visitors Bureau

forces; tours of a remaining wing honor the Middletons, but the real reason to come here is what's outside. A good restaurant serves lunch and dinner. Adults $28, children $10; house tours cost an additional $15 per person.

Nathaniel Russell House (843-724-8481; www.historiccharleston.org), 51 Meeting St. Open Mon.–Sat. 10–5; Sun. 2–5. A circa 1808 brick townhouse, it represents the epitome of the Adam style in the city—its stairway appears to float, a lovely combination of function and fantasy—and it is one of the most thoroughly conceived and exquisitely executed neoclassical dwellings in the nation. $10.

Old Exchange & Provost Dungeon (843-727-2165; www.oldexchange.org), 122 E. Bay St. Open daily 9–5. Built as a British Customs House in 1771, its commanding location at the foot of Broad Street defined an end boundary for the city and a waterfront point of arrival. The British held political and military prisoners in the basement. Adults $8, children $4.

St. Michael's Episcopal Church (843-723-0603), Meeting St. at Broad St. Open daily 9–4:30. This church and its bells are still the center of many lives, as they have been since 1761. It is part of the famous "Four Corners of Law," an intersection that represents religious, civic, judicial, and federal order. There is a tranquil walled churchyard to explore.

St. Philip's Episcopal Church (843-722-7734; www.stphilipschurchsc.org), 142 Church St. Constructed in 1835–38, facing a central park, and flanked by its gravestones, St. Philip's seems out of the Old World of Europe. The building is sheathed in a mottled, tan, stucco material that reflects the gradual shifting in light over the course of a day.

MILITARY MUSEUMS & SITES

The Citadel Museum (843-953-6846; www.citadel.edu), 171 Moultrie St. The museum is open Mon.–Thurs. 12–5; the archives are open Mon.–Thurs. 9–5; closed school vacations. Located on the campus of the Military College of South Carolina, founded in 1842, it tells the history of the school and the Corps of Cadets. Dress parades take place most Fridays at 3:45 during the academic year. Free admission.

The Confederate Museum (843-723-1541), 188 Meeting St., in Market Hall. Open Tues.–Sat. 11–3:30. There's a Gullah expression that sums up this museum: When you ask someone on the telephone "Is that you?" the person may reply, in a weary tone laced with irony, "That's what's leff of me." The Daughters of the Confederacy care for its uniforms, tattered flags, documents, artifacts, and a fragrant sense of the Lost Cause. Adults $5, children $3.

Fort Lamar Heritage Preserve (803-734-3893; www.dnr.sc.gov), Fort Lamar Road, James Island (take SC 171 to Battery Island Road; left for about 8 miles to Fort Lamar Road; right for about 5 miles to small parking lot on left). Open daily dawn–dusk. The site of the Battle of Secessionville, waged in the predawn darkness of June 16, 1862, when federal troops attacked this Confederate earthwork fort. The self-guided walking tour directs you across what was an open field rimmed by marsh and woods, around the simple M-shaped field fortification, by the magazines, dry moat, earthworks, and the likely mass grave of federal wounded.

Two signers of the Declaration of Independence are buried in St. Philip's Episcopal Church's west cemetery.   Peter Loftus

Fort Moultrie (843-883-3123; www.nps.gov/fosu), 1214 Middle St., Sullivan's Island, 10 miles east of Charleston. Open daily 9–5. The base of Charleston's seacoast defense system, from its first test in the American Revolution. The palmetto-log fort that repelled the British fleet is gone, but buildings and earthworks dating from 1809 convey the sense of fragility and isolation the early patriots must have felt. A 20-minute film in the visitor center provides an excellent introduction. It is also the burial site of the Seminole warrior Osceola who, meeting under a flag of truce, was imprisoned here in 1838. Adults $3, family $5, under 15 free.

Fort Sumter National Monument (843-883-3123 or 1-800-789-3678; www .nps.gov/fosu or www.fortsumtertours.com for boat tour information). Cruises depart from a National Park Service interpretative center at 340 Concord St. by the Charleston Aquarium and Patriot's Point. Trips usually two or three times each day, year-round, but fewer in winter months to the place where the Civil War began. National Park Service rangers answer your questions, but you can explore at your own pace. The entire tour lasts just over two hours. Adults $16, seniors $14.50, children ages 6–11 $10.

H. L. Hunley Exhibit (843-743-4865 for information or 1-877-448-6539 to purchase tickets; www.hunley.org), Warren Lasch Conservation Center, 1250 Supply St., Bldg. 255, North Charleston. Open Sat. 10–5; Sun. noon–5. The *H. L. Hunley* was the forerunner of a modern submarine, most famous for its sinking of the *Housatonic* outside Charleston Harbor. Its last voyage ended in disaster; all eight men aboard died. The 40-foot submersible, powered by men pedaling a crankshaft, is undergoing restoration. $12.

Fort Moultrie was a significant presence in the Revolutionary and Civil Wars.
Charleston Area Convention & Visitors Bureau

The USS *Yorktown* berthed at Patriots Point.   Charleston Area Convention & Visitors Bureau

Patriots Point Naval and Maritime Museum (843-884-2727; www.patriots point.org), 40 Patriots Point Rd., Mount Pleasant. Open daily 9–6:30. Visit the aircraft carrier *Yorktown*, the World War II–sub *Clamagore*, and the destroyer *Laffey* and examine aircraft, guns, missiles, and quarters. The view of peninsular Charleston from the platform of the *Yorktown* is unbeatable. Snack bar and gift shop. Adults $18, children $11, seniors $15 and military with ID $15, free to uniformed soldiers.

MUSEUMS

Avery Research Center for African-American History and Culture (843-953-7609; www.avery.cofc.edu), 125 Bull St. Tours Mon.–Fri. 10:30–3:30; reading room hours are Mon.–Fri. 10–5; center is closed from 12:30–1:30. Housed in one of the first schools dedicated to educating freed slaves, the center is an archive and library of printed materials, photographs, and objects related to the heritage of the region's African Americans.

Charleston Museum (843-722-2996; www.charlestonmuseum.org), 360 Meeting St. Open Mon.–Sat. 9–5; Sun. 1–5. Founded in 1773, this is the oldest museum in America and reflects more than two centuries of the city's self-consciousness. Exhibits interpret subjects like flora and fauna, fashion, the art of silversmithing, Native American life, and plantation culture. The section on slavery is superb. Adults $10, children $5; combination tickets to museum and its historic properties available at a discount.

Charles Towne Landing 1670 (843-852-4200; www.southcarolinaparks.com or www.charlestowne.org), 1500 Old Towne Rd. (SC 171 between I-26 and US 17). Open daily 9–5. This 664-acre park is an outdoor living history museum that documents lives of the first settlers in a village, on a 17th-century replica of a typical coastal trading vessel, and in "wilderness," as found in the Animal Forest, where birds and beasts common to the area in 1670 roam in a secured habitat. A visitor center offers expanded interpretation of first contact with the Kiawah tribe and of recent, ongoing archaeological investigations. Adults $7.50, children $3.50.

Old Slave Mart Museum (843-958-6467; www.oldslavemart.org), 6 Chalmers St. Open Mon.–Sat. 9–5. This newly renovated museum has dramatically improved the portrait of the domestic slave economy that enabled Charleston's growth. One section focuses on the slave trade at large, which forcibly relocated some 1 million American-born slaves throughout the South between 1789 and 1861; and the other highlights individual stories, letters, and documents related to African Americans, slave traders, and the way the slave market complex functioned. Adults $7, children $5.

South Carolina Aquarium (843-577-3474; www.scaquarium.org), 100 Aquarium Wharf. Open Mar.–Aug., daily 9–5; Sept.–Feb., daily 9–4. Displays of the state's aquatic habitat, from the mountain streams of the Upcountry to Lowcountry marshes. More than 10,000 creatures reside here in the 330,000-gallon Ocean Tank, in living habitat exhibits, and in the hands-on water tables. Twice daily you can visit the sea turtle hospital for an additional $10 for adults and $5 for children. A super-realistic 4-D theater shows 30-minute films for $5. Adults $24.95, children (4–12) $14.95.

MUSIC

Charleston has a symphony orchestra (www.charlestonsymphony.com) and all the performances of the Spoleto Festival (www.spoletousa.org), as well as annual events like the 10-day Blues Bash (www.bluesbash.com) in February, the Moja Arts Festival (843-724-7305; www.mojafestival.com; 180 Meeting St.) in September, and Spirituals Concerts, which often take place in conjunction with spring and fall house tours.

Nightlife

After-hours attractions and activities.

For dancing and concerts, the younger crowd and college kids from out of town head to Music Farm (843-577-6969; www.musicfarm.com), 32 Ann St., but the hard-core, disco/house-beat crowds pack Club Pantheon (843-577-2582) 28 Ann St., which opens after 10 PM Fri.–Sun. Check listings at www.charlestoncitypaper.com.

There are several milder places, from cozy to cool, to have a nightcap, tapas, bar food, or coffee and dessert. There might be soft jazz, dance music, or jukebox tunes in the background. Uptown, 39 Rue de Jean (843-722-8881; www.39ruedejean.com), 39 John St., is a brasserie that is as lively and good-looking as its clients, with full and late-night menus, indoor and outdoor seating. In the

middle of the Historic District are Charleston Grill (843-577-4522; www
.charlestongrill.com), 224 King St. at Charleston Place, the classiest option with
incredible desserts and live jazz; The Blind Tiger Pub (843-577-0088; www
.blindtigercharleston.com), 36 Broad St., a favorite local's bar; and Social Wine
Bar (843-577-5665; www.socialwinebar.com), 188 E. Bay St., where the beautiful
people go.

SPOLETO

For 18 days at the end of spring, a time of budding oleander, fading azalea, and
unapologetically fragrant magnolias, Spoleto comes to Charleston and Charleston
becomes the artistic city it loves to be with first-rate international performances
and art. Founded in 1977, each season offers more than 100 scheduled events,
including premieres of opera and dance as well as dozens of chamber music,
choral, jazz, and orchestral shows. Performances take place indoors and out—in
parks, plantation gardens, amphitheaters, and auditoriums. Contact Spoleto
Festival USA (843-722-2764; box office 843-579-3100; www.spoletousa.org),
14 George St., Charleston, SC 29401.

Start planning early—the website is best. Tickets usually go on sale in January
and quickly sell out, as the festival draws visitors from around the world. You can
order by a ticket package or individual performances, which take place in several
venues. You can try your luck at the last minute for standing room, or order on the
phone, often up to the morning before the performance.

More than 600 Piccolo Spoleto performances (often free) are organized by
the city's Office of Cultural Affairs (843-724-7305; www.piccolospoleto.com), 180
Meeting St., Charleston, SC 29401.

THEATER

More than a dozen companies, theater departments, or experimental groups
make up the Charleston theater community; www.theatrecharleston.com provides
comprehensive ticketing information.

Charleston Stage (843-577-7183; www.charlestonstage.com) Productions at
Dock Street Theatre (135 Church St.) by a residential theater group that offers
classics and family-friendly shows.

Dock Street Theatre (843-577-7183), 135 Church St. This is a lovely
interpretation of a Georgian-style theater of the sort 18th-century Charlestonians
may have patronized. Rebuilt during the Depression within the old Planters Hotel
(circa 1809) as a project of the Federal Works Progress Administration, cypress
interiors, intimate box seats, and terrific acoustics make it a wonderful place to
attend performances.

Footlight Players (843-722-4487; www.footlightplayers.net), 20 Queen St.
A community theater group, founded in 1931, performs in a renovated cotton
warehouse in the French Quarter.

Sottile Theater (843-953-0833; www.sottile.cofc.edu), 44 George St.
Featuring lectures, recitals, dance, and plays—college and noncollege productions.

Theatre 99 (843-853-6687; www.theatre99.com), 280 Meeting St.
Improvisation in a high-energy, informal setting. Cocktails available.

Recreation

Active pursuits in and around Charleston.

BASEBALL

Charleston RiverDogs, a Class-A Minor League Affiliate of the New York Yankees, plays April through August at Joe Riley Jr. Park (843-577-3647 for tickets; www.riverdogs.com), 360 Fishburne St. Tickets are $8–19.

BEACH ACCESS

The beaches are flat and wide, without rocks, overlooked by dunes or maritime forest, sometimes punctuated by fishing piers. The surf ranges from placid to roiling (the Washout at Folly Beach is considered a top surfing spot). Lifeguards are not on duty at every beach access point, and swimming may be extremely hazardous: It is not wise to swim in unmonitored areas. Walking on the dunes, picking the sea oats, and driving on the beach are forbidden. Some places offer changing areas, restrooms, showers, and parking. Others are mere paths in the sand. Check with individual beach parks about rules concerning dogs.

Sullivan's Island and Isle of Palms are located north of the city on US 17 and SC 703. The beach at Sullivan's is marked by walkways. You may park along the side of streets unless otherwise posted. County parks (www.ccprc.com) are open daylight hours in the summer and limited hours in the off-season. They include Isle of Palms County Park (843-886-3863), 1st through 14th Avenues and Palm Boulevard, with $7 parking, restrooms, and changing facilities. Located to the south, off US 17 on SC 171, Folly Beach County Park (843-795-4386), 1100 W. Ashley Ave., offers 4,000 feet of oceanfront access, lifeguards, changing rooms, showers, $8 standard vehicle parking, $20 RV/camper parking, and a 1,045-foot fishing pier. You may rent beach chairs and umbrellas. A bit farther south, off US 17 at the gate to Kiawah Island, is Beachwalker Park (843-768-2395), Beachwalker Dr., Kiawah Island, a much smaller destination.

SHORE REFUGES

Cape Romain National Wildlife Refuge (843-928-3264; www.fws.gov/cape romain), 5801 US 17 North, Awendaw. Covers 22 miles of coast consisting of numerous landscapes and habitats: Bull Island, a 5,000-acre barrier island; Cape Island, a favorite spot for loggerhead turtles to nest; Garris Landing, the site of ferry services and an observation pier just right for birders; and Raccoon Key Island, a popular spot for shelling.

Coastal Expeditions (843-884-7684 for ferry information; www.coastal expeditions.com) offers exclusive ferry service to Bull Island, weather permitting. Ticket prices are $40 for adults and $20 for children under 12. From March through November, the ferry makes two round-trips daily every Tuesday, Thursday, Friday, and Saturday. From December through February there's one trip only, on Saturday. Reservations are not required, but tickets must be paid for by cash or check. No credit cards. You can take a fat-tired bike on the ferry.

Another refuge is Capers Island—a classic, undisturbed barrier island managed by the South Carolina Department of Natural Resources (843-953-9001; www.dnr.sc.gov/mlands). You can get there in a sea kayak from Coastal

Expeditions (843-884-7684; www.coastalexpeditions.com), 514-B Mill St., Mount Pleasant; or on a 40-foot boat with Barrier Island Eco-Tours (843-886-5000; www .nature-tours.com), 50 41st Ave., Isle of Palms. A 3½-hour tour led by a naturalist and marine biologist costs $38 for adults, $28 for children. They offer many other tours and fishing expeditions, too.

BIRD-WATCHING

The barrier islands mentioned above provide the least-disturbed habitats for birds and wildlife, but if you can't make it there, other places are accessible. Because of its location on the North American flyway and its diverse natural environment, the Lowcountry attracts scores of wading, shore-, and songbirds, some of them as unusual as the roseate spoonbill and parasitic jaeger. Woodcocks flock in plowed fields, owls hover in roadside forests, and hawks soar over open grassland. Local Audubon groups have reported more than 200 types of birds. Sites recommended by local birders include:

Bears Bluff (843-559-2315; www.fws.gov/warmsprings/bearsbluff), southeast of Charleston on Wadmalaw Island. This 31-acre fish hatchery offers sensational viewing of common and endangered species in a lovely rural setting that's also good for picnics. You can download a self-guided tour brochure from their website.

Bear Island (843-844-8957; www.dnr.sc.gov/managed/wild), south of Charleston off US 17 at Green Pond. Operated by the South Carolina Department of Natural Resources, Bear Island is an extensive habitat characterized by old rice fields, meandering creeks and rivers, marshes, and all sorts of woodlands. Open daylight hours in designated areas from Feb. 9–Oct. 31, Mon.–Sat.

I'on Swamp (www.sctrails.net), 15 miles north of Mount Pleasant off US 17 on US Forest Service Road 228. Spring brings warblers—possibly even the shy Bachman's—and also resident upland birds, including red-cockaded woodpeckers, who make their home here.

Mount Pleasant, the area leading to the old Pitt Street Bridge. Sightings of marbled godwits, oystercatchers, grebes, and mergansers have been reported here. Activity is best at half tide, especially in fall and winter. A spotting scope is useful.

Sewee Visitor and Environmental Education Center (843-928-3368; www .fws.gov/seeweecenter), 5821 US 17 North, Awendaw. Exhibits featuring forest to sea ecosystems and an orientation film on Cape Romain National Wildlife Refuge.

Sullivan's Island, around the beach behind Fort Moultrie. Here, in fall and winter, you might see peeps or an occasional purple sandpiper.

US 17 by the Ashepoo and Combahee River crossings. Anhinga, rails, and gallinules nest in the remnant rice fields.

BOATING

Canoeing and Kayaking

The Edisto River, thought to be the nation's longest free-flowing blackwater stream, offers calm waters and great bird and wildlife observation, like great blue herons wading by the oak-lined riverbank or hummingbirds feeding at wildflowers. The trail follows an ancient waterway used by Native Americans and early settlers.

Just over the Ravenel Bridge from Charleston, the Memorial Park in Mount Pleasant is a favorite place to fish, watch outdoor movies, and enjoy an incredible view.
Charleston Area Convention & Visitors Bureau

Colleton State Park (843-538-8206; www.southcarolinaparks.com), US 15, Canadys, 12 miles north of Walterboro, and Givhan's Ferry State Park (843-873-0692; www.southcarolinaparks.com), SC 61, 16 miles west of Summerville, are along the route. The Walterboro-Colleton Chamber of Commerce (843-549-9595; www .colletoncounty.org), 403 E. Washington St., Walterboro, SC 29488, can assist you with paddling in the ACE Basin (Ashepoo, Combahee, and South Edisto Rivers).

Nearer Charleston, boats are available for rent at James Island County Park (843-795-4386; www.ccprc.com), 871 Riverland Dr. and Palmetto Islands County Park (843-884-0832), 444 Needlerush Pkwy., Mount Pleasant.

The following companies offer kayak rentals, tours, and instruction. The price for rentals of kayaks, safety equipment, and basic instruction is about $35–80 per day; $45 per half-day. Tours, depending on their length, cost between $58 and $88.

Coastal Expeditions (843-884-7684; www.coastalexpeditions.com).

Nature Adventures Outfitters (1-800-673-0679; www.kayakcharlestonsc.com).

Jet Skiing

Jet Skis (aka personal watercraft and WaveRunners) let you navigate the shallow creeks at a fast, noisy clip. You can rent them by the hour ($99–135) at Tidal Wave Watersports (843-886-8456; www.tidalwavewatersports.com), Isle of Palms.

Sailing

A sailor unfamiliar with Lowcountry coastal waters will encounter dramatic tides and strong currents. If you're interested in renting a sailboat, either for a day's excursion or a sunset cruise, reserve early. It's also wise to check local conditions and discuss your plans with the rental outfitter before you go. (Some boats come with their own skippers, if you get nervous.)

Sailboats in a range of sizes are available for hire or tours from the following:

Aqua Safaris (843-886-8133; www.palmettobreeze.com), P.O. Box 309, Isle of Palms, SC 29451.

OSA Sailing (843-971-0700; www.osasailing.com), 24 Patriots Point Rd., Mount Pleasant, SC 29464. Half-day sails in Charleston Harbor.

Public boat landings with unmonitored parking and ramps are listed by Charleston County Parks (843-795-4386; www.ccprc.com); South Carolina Marine Resources Division (843-762-5000), P.O. Box 12559, Charleston, SC 29412; and Lowcountry Resort Islands and Tourism Commission (843-717-3090 or 1-800-528-6870; www.southcarolinalowcountry.com), 1 Lowcountry Ln., Yemassee, SC 29945.

CAMPING

Buck Hall, Francis Marion National Forest (1-877-444-6777 for reservations; www.forestcamping.com), Wambaw Ranger District, P.O. Box 106, McClellanville, SC 29458. Nineteen sites; hiking trails, boat ramp, fishing.

James Island County Park (843-795-4386; www.ccprc.com), 871 Riverland Dr., Charleston, SC 29412. Has 124 RV sites, 10 three-bedroom cottages on the marsh, primitive camping area, shuttle service to downtown Charleston, paved trails, fishing and crabbing docks, playgrounds, and picnic shelters.

Lake Aire RV Park and Campground (843-571-1271; www.lakeairerv .com), 4375 SC 162, Hollywood, SC 29449. A hundred sites, including full hook-ups, primitive sites, and camper sites. Seven-acre fishing lake, swimming pool, paddleboat and canoe rentals, showers, laundry, recreation area, bike and foot trails.

Oak Plantation Campground (843-766-5936; www.oakplantationcamp ground.com), 3540 Savannah Hwy., Charleston, SC 29455. Full hook-ups with 30- and 50-amp service; 200 RV sites, propane, laundry, groceries, bathrooms.

Wood Brothers Campground (843-844-2208), 8446 Ace Basin Pkwy., Green Pond, SC 29446. Located 37 miles south of Charleston. Wooded and open sites for RVs, campers, and tents; grocery, propane, showers, fishing pond.

FAMILY FUN

Blackbeard's Cove Family Fun Park (843-971-1223; www.blackbeardscove. net), 3255 SC 17 North, Mount Pleasant. Laser tag, go-carts, climbing wall, golf, and arcade games.

James Island County Park and Palmetto Islands County Park (www .ccprc.com) offer a variety of water park and climbing wall activities, biking, and fishing.

FISHING

Opportunities and endless and year-round: fly-fishing in the inland flats, fishing from a pier, fishing with bait from small (15 to 26 feet) and large (up to 54 feet) craft, fishing off an artificial reef, surf casting from the beach, trolling in the Gulf Stream. Charter fees include equipment, instruction, fuel (sometimes extra), bait, licenses, and food or drink if applicable. For small craft, the price is generally based on two people, $50 for each additional person (size of party limited by size of boat). Large craft may include one or two groups fishing together. Prices for charter boat rentals are from $400 for one to three passengers for a four-hour excursion, inshore, to $1,400 for one to three anglers for a long day of Gulf

Shrimp boats at rest.

Stream adventure. If you head out on your own, the cost for an unguided power-boat starts around $90 per hour (capacity is from four to eight people), rental gear extra. You need to purchase a saltwater fishing license if you fish from a boat; a license is not necessary for shore-based fishing or recreational harvest of crab and shrimp.

Avid Angling Private Fishing Charters (843-566-3433; www.avidangling .com), 10 Wharfside St. Inshore, nearshore, fly-fishing and fly-casting lessons, surf fishing, cobia and tarpon trips for all levels of anglers and ages. They also offer crabbing and shark teeth hunting for the younger set.

Bohicket Boat (843-768-1280; www.bohicket.com), Bohicket Marina, 1880 Andell Bluff Blvd., Johns Island. Large selection of boats from 14 to 55 feet for inshore bass and trout fishing, jetty fishing, and offshore fishing for shark, mackerel, tuna, and marlin. Full- and half-day trips, on your own or with a guide.

Headshaker Charters (843-810-0495; www.headshakercharters.com), Mount Pleasant. Captain Legare Leland grew up fishing here and arranges trips in Charleston Harbor and nearby estuaries to troll for redfish, trout, flounder, and other species.

FITNESS, WELLNESS, AND SPAS

Your hotel concierge or host may recommend a personal trainer or offer a day rate for a gym. Resorts and large hotels have their own facilities or spas. Fees vary widely according to service.

Charleston Power Yoga (834-513-3400; www.charlestonpoweryoga.com), 557 King St. Baptiste Affiliate hot power yoga. Check website for downloadable waiver and class schedules.

Earthling Day Spa & Pilates Studio (843-722-4737; www.earthlingdayspa .com), 245 E. Bay St.

Sophia Institute (843-720-8528; www.thesophiainstitute.org), 26 Society St. Drop-in yoga and a full program of lectures and day retreats focused on spiritual healing and wellness.

Spa Adagio (843-577-2444; www.spaadagio.com), 387 King St. Full-service day spa located in the Francis Marion Hotel.

GOLF

The first golf course in America was built in Charleston, and courses take advantage of its ocean vistas and forest boundaries. Charleston Area Golf Guide (1-800-774-4444; www.charlestongolfguide.com) is a central information and reservation service for tee times, accommodations, and discount airfares.

Fees vary according to six seasonal categories. Lowest rates are usually December through February and after 4 PM. Carts are required at peak playing times on many courses. For resort play, golf privileges are sometimes extended to nonresort guests; check with your concierge or call the resort directly. Reservations are often made three months in advance at the resorts. Club rentals and instruction are available at all courses, and you can usually reserve tee times online. Weekday rates generally assume play Monday through Thursday only.

Public and Semiprivate Courses

Charleston Municipal Course (843-795-6517; www.charleston-sc.gov), 2110 Maybank Hwy. Par 72, 6,432 yards. Greens fees during the week start at $15 if you walk, $30 with cart rental; on weekends, $17 if you walk, $32 with cart rental.

Charleston National (843-884-4653; www.charlestonnationalgolf.com), 1360 National Dr., Mount Pleasant. Par 72 on 5,086- to 7,064-yard courses. Fees range from $50–$99.

Coosaw Creek Country Club (843-767-9000; www.coosawcreek.com), 4110 Club Course Dr. Par 71 on 5,064-yard forward course to 6,619-yard champion course. Fees: $35–69 (weekdays) and $35–65 (weekends). An Arthur Hills design.

Dunes West (843-856-9000; www.duneswestgolfclub.com), 3535 Wando Plantation Way, Mount Pleasant. Par 72 on 5,208-yard forward course to 6,859-yard champion course. Fees in six seasonal categories range from $38–80 (weekdays) to $38–96 (weekends).

The Links at Stono Ferry (843-763-1817; www.stonoferrygolf.com), 4812 Stono Links Dr., Hollywood. Par 72. Range: 4,912-yard forward course to 6,756-yard championship course. Fees: $50–88, with some seasonal variation.

Patriots Point Links (843-881-0042; www.patriotspointlinks.com), 1 Patriots Point Rd., Mount Pleasant. Par 72. Range: 5,562-yard forward course to 6,955-yard championship course with panoramic views of the harbor and Fort Sumter. Fees: $40–65 (weekdays) and $55–85 (weekends).

Shadowmoss Plantation Golf Club (843-556-8251 or 1-800-338-4971; www.shadowmossgolf.com), SC 61. Par 72. Range: 5,169-yard forward course to 6,701-yard championship course. Fees: $36–$49 (weekdays) and $39–$55 (weekends).

Courses at Charleston Area Resorts

Kiawah Island (1-800-576-1570; www.kiawahresort.com), One Sanctuary Beach Dr., Kiawah. Five championship courses have been carved out of Kiawah's gorgeous Sea Island landscape by the game's top designers: Pete Dye, Jack Nicklaus, Gary Player, Tom Fazio, and Clyde Johnston. The Ocean Course (par 72; range: 5,327-yard forward course to 7,356 championship course) hosted the 1991 Ryder Cup and was cited by *Golf Digest* as the toughest resort course in the country. Osprey Point (par 72; range: 5,023-yard forward course to 6,932-yard championship course) is consistently ranked in the country's top 75 courses, with a landscape that includes four lakes, a maritime forest, and creeks. Cougar Point (par 72; range: 4,776-yard forward course to 6,875-yard championship course) and Turtle Point (par 72; range: 5,210-yard forward course to 7,062-yard championship course) make good use of Kiawah's unique geography—bracketed by the Atlantic and the river. Oak Point (par 72; range: 4,954-yard forward course to 6,701-yard championship course) is part of the resort but located on nearby Haulover Creek.

Seabrook Island (843-768-2500 or 1-866-650-7918; www.discoverseabrook .com), 130 Gardener's Circle, Seabrook Island, offers two courses: Crooked Oaks (par 72; range: 5,250-yard forward course to 6,832-yard championship course, designed by Robert Trent Jones Sr.) and Ocean Winds (par 72; range: 5,524-yard forward course to 6,805-yard championship course, a Willard Byrd design). They won the resort a silver medal commendation from *Golf* magazine. Both of these courses are certified members of the Audubon Cooperative Sanctuary Program for Golf.

Wild Dunes (843-886-2164; www.wilddunes.com), Isle of Palms, boasts two courses designed by Tom Fazio. The Links (par 72; range: 4,907-yard forward course to 6,709-yard championship course) offers oceanfront golf at its best. The Harbor (par 70; range: 4,689-yard forward course to 6,359-yard championship course) features challenging holes that are, in some cases, an island apart.

HORSEBACK RIDING

If you want to take a trail ride during your visit, call one of the following stables to make advance arrangements. They may take you from a cypress swamp to the edge of a rice field. Prices start at about $50 per hour.

Middleton Place Equestrian Center (843-556-8137; www.middletonplace .org), 4290 Ashley River Rd., Charleston.

Mullet Hall Equestrian Center (843-768-5867; www.ccprc.com), 2662 Mullet Hall Rd., John's Island.

HUNTING

The Lowcountry has the longest deer season in the country and is considered the best spot on the East Coast to bag marsh hens, but you can also find wild turkey, dove, quail, and duck. There are six Game Management Areas; hunters at work within them are required to have a variety of licenses and permits, abide by strict size and bag limits, obtain landowners' permission before hunting on private lands, and observe safe and ethical hunting practices in the field. Contact the Wildlife and Marine Resources Department (803-734-3886; www.dnr.sc.gov). Outdoor recreation stores that specialize in hunting also provide tips, information, and licenses.

Some of the most popular public hunting grounds in the Charleston area are located in the Francis Marion National Forest (843-336-3248), 2421 Witherbee

Rd., Cordsville, Webb Wildlife Management Area (803-625-3569; www.dnr.sc
.gov), SC 1, Garnett, Palachucola Wildlife Management Area (803-625-3569;
www.dnr.sc.gov), Garnett, and Bear Island (843-844-8957), Green Pond. For
hunting licenses call 1-866-714-3611. Limited hunting is also permitted in the
ACE Basin (www.fws.gov/acebasin).

The Southeastern Wildlife Exposition (www.sewe.com), which takes place
every February in Charleston, is the region's most comprehensive gathering of
fishermen, hunters, outfitters, and artists who specialize in subjects of interest to
sportsmen. Display sites scattered throughout the Charleston area feature Lowcountry and Western collectibles, crafts, decoys, antiques, and posters. In addition,
there are presentations and demonstrations.

NATURE PRESERVES

If you are interested in the ecology of the Lowcountry, the life cycle of the marsh,
the effects of tidal flow on vegetation, and the interdependence of plant and animal life, these sites will give you a feel for the rhythms beneath the surface.

Ernest F. Hollings ACE Basin National Wildlife Refuge (843-889-3084;
www.acebasin.fws.gov), access off US 17; take SC 174 through Adams Run and

An ancient cypress garden in the swamp.   Charleston Area Convention & Visitors Bureau

follow signs to headquarters. A consortium was formed to preserve some 350,000 acres of diverse habitat, including several islands, creating one of the largest estuarine sanctuaries on the East Coast. ACE takes its name from the area it embraces: the lands and waters amid the Ashepoo, Combahee, and Edisto Rivers on both sides of St. Helena Sound, a fishery so rich and pristine it accounts for nearly 10 percent of the state's shellfish harvest. Open year-round, daylight to dusk; you may park and walk in. Extensive trail maps online.

Audubon Swamp Garden (843-571-1266 or 1-800-367-3517; www.magnolia plantation.com/swamp_garden.html), 3550 Ashley River Rd. Sixty acres of blackwater cypress and tupelo swamp, with trails and footbridges through virgin pine forests, wildflowers, and exotic plants: This is a place that impressed John J. Audubon 150 years ago. Self-guided tour. Basic admission $13.

Caw Caw Interpretive Center (843-889-8898; www.ccprc.com), 5200 Savannah Hwy., Ravenel, 20 miles south of Charleston. Elevated boardwalks overlook the wetlands and rice fields that originally marked this plantation. There are 6 miles of trails and exhibits that highlight the contributions of the African Americans who worked here long ago. A good stop if you're heading down the coast to Edisto, Beaufort, or Savannah. Closed Monday and Tuesday. Admission $1.

Cypress Gardens (843-553-0515; www.cypressgardens.info), 3030 Cypress Gardens Rd., Moncks Corner; I-26 west to exit 209-A, then SC 52 west. Take a guided tour through an old rice plantation reserve, now a protected natural swamp garden that blooms year-round. Open daily 9–5. Adults $10, seniors $9, children $5, under 5 free.

Francis Beidler Forest in Four Holes Swamp (843-462-2150; www.beidler forest.audubon.org), 336 Sanctuary Rd., Harleyville. An 11,000-acre sanctuary contains the largest remaining virgin stand of bald cypress and tupelo gum trees in the world. There's a self-guided 1.75-mile boardwalk that is handicapped accessible. Open Tues.–Sun. 9–5. Adults $8, children $4, under 6 free.

TENNIS

The City of Charleston manages 74 public courts in several locations, and only two facilities charge a nominal fee for use: the Charleston Tennis Center (843-769-8258), 19 Farmfield Ave., west of Charleston, has 15 outdoor hard courts, lit for night play; and the Maybank Tennis Center (843-406-8814), 1800 Houghton Dr., James Island, has 11 courts, including three clay. Visitors should call ahead to check availability, or may reserve by paying in advance. The professional women's tournament Family Circle Cup (1-800-677-2293; www.familycircletenniscenter. com) is played in a spectacular stadium at Daniel Island. There are 13 clay courts and four hard, all lit and open to the public except for tournament week in April. Call 843-849-5300 for court times. Hourly rates are $10–15.

Some resorts also offer playing time for nonresort guests on a space-available basis. Fees vary depending on season and time of day. Reservations are required. Inquire about tennis packages.

Kiawah Island (1-800-576-1570; www.kiawahresort.com). Hourly rates $34–44.

Wild Dunes (843-886-2113; www.wilddunes.com), Isle of Palms. Hourly rate $25.

The surfing hub is at Folly Beach, with shops noted below. They provide lessons, gear, repairs, and tips. Check surf conditions online at www.mckevlins.com for McKevlin's surf report, and surf in well-known areas. Many resorts have sailboards and other equipment to rent, or provide instruction first on land, then in sheltered creeks or on a quiet stretch of beach.

McKevlin's Surf Shop (843-588-2247; www.mckevlins.com), 8 Center St., Folly Beach.

Ocean Surf Shop (843-588-9175; www.oceansurfshop.com), 31 Center St., Folly Beach.

Shopping
Shops and markets
that will pique your interest.

A local shopping scene, informed and supported by residents, still thrives in Charleston. The main sections are King Street from Broad Street to Line Street; Queen Street and Church Street (for art, especially); and around the old city market (North and South Market Streets east of Meeting Street). The Market area tends to attract tourists; the most notable items for sale in and around the handsome brick-and-lattice sheds are the sweetgrass baskets, hand-woven by African American women. Nonetheless it's festive. At Charleston Place, the complex at the head of the Market, national chain stores have set anchor.

ANTIQUES

While taste, or a good eye, is hard to define, it seems clear that the very experience of living in Charleston has produced antique dealers who have absorbed its lessons of enduring beauty. They seem to know what fits—whether it's a pair of simple sterling candlesticks or a stunning chest-on-chest. Here are some specialists. King Street is the traditional center of the city's antique stores (www.king streetantiquedistrict.com), but warehouse-type enterprises a bit farther afield are fun to poke in, too.

Carolina Antique Maps and Prints (843-722-4773; www.carolinaantique prints.com), 91 Church St. Deep inventory and a knowledgeable staff; early botanicals, 19th-century maps, woodblocks, and hand-colored pieces.

George C. Birlant & Co. (843-722-3842; www.birlant.com), 191 King St. In business for more than 80 years, selling brass, silver, crystal, and small and large English antiques, which they import directly. Big old-fashioned picture windows open onto the street, and there's lots of room to walk around inside. Reproductions of Charleston's own cypress-and-iron "Battery Bench" available.

Moore House Antiques (843-722-8065; www.moorehouseantiques.com), 143 King St. Fine 18th- and 19th-century American pieces where styles from England show through, as in Sheraton side tables and Chinese export porcelain.

Terrace Oaks Antique Mall (843-795-9689; www.terraceoaksantiques .com), 2037 Maybank Hwy./SC 700. A short drive from Charleston, this well-known establishment houses 20 dealers who sell an amazing assortment of rugs, glassware, silver, large pieces, and accessories.

The Silver Vault (843-722-0631; www.silvervaultcharleston.com), 195 King St. Historic silver objects and tableware from America, England, and the Continent, as well as decorative art and antique jewelry.

BOOKS

Barnes & Noble (843-556-6561), 1812 Sam Rittenberg Blvd.; (843-216-9756), 1716 Towne Centre Way, Mount Pleasant.

Blue Bicycle Books (843-722-2666; www.bluebicyclebooks.com), 420 King St. A committed independent bookstore that supports local writers and whose staff is knowledgeable about what's come in—used, rare, and of regional interest. You could also pick up great advice about what to see and do in the city.

Charleston is a destination for collectors of fine antiques from the South, Europe, and Asia. Charleston Area Convention & Visitors Bureau

Historic Charleston Foundation Museum Shop and Bookstore (843-723-1623; www.historiccharleston.org), 108 Meeting St. If you want to know more about Lowcountry history and the decorative arts, preservation efforts, architecture, and related topics, stop in. Many volumes about historic properties here and elsewhere, as well as an excellent children's section.

Preservation Society of Charleston (843-722-4630; www.preservationsociety .org), 147 King St. The society's headquarters has an unhurried, Old World feeling, a very special place with many books on Charleston history, art, architecture, and culture, as well as small food and gift items.

CLOTHING

Menswear in Charleston is still a funny combination of casual hunting/outdoorsy preppy, along with sharp bow ties, fedoras, and stylish eyeglasses. Women, however, have more to choose from in stylish cuts that wouldn't look out of place in New York City.

Ben Silver (843-577-4556; www.bensilver.com), 149 King St. This shop is the epitome of the classic Charleston look for men and women, with lots of English hunting overtones.

Berlin's (843-722-1665; www.berlinsclothing.com), 114 King St. Men's and women's clothes in traditional styles and top-quality brands. Since 1883.

Bits of Lace (843-577-0999; www.bitsoflace.com), 302 King St. Fine lingerie and other little fancy things for women.

Bob Ellis Shoes (843-722-2515; www.bobellisshoes.com), 332 King St. Vast selection of fine footwear for men and women and a sales staff that keeps bringing out the boxes.

Butterfly (843-577-8404; www.butterflyconsignments.com), 482 King St. Gently worn designer and couture fashion for women.

Christian Michi (843-723-0575; www.christianmichi.com), 220 King St. High fashion for women from top European and American designers. It's as if a small section of SoHo left Manhattan for life in the provinces. Tableware and linens, too.

Kids on King (843-720-8647; www.kidsonking.com), 195½ King St. The old smocked dresses and seersucker suits of yesteryear are mixed in with European styles for kids of all ages and sizes.

M. Dumas & Sons (843-723-8603), 294 King St. Even the wallpaper here is riding to hounds. Since 1918, the go-to store for outdoor wear.

RTW (843-577-9748; www.rtwcharleston.com), 186 King St. A boutique for women who delight in gorgeous fabrics, sweaters that tumble with color, one-of-a-kind shirts, hats, scarves, and accessories, and for those who like to dress with a sense of individuality and esprit. A rare find in any city.

Worthwhile (843-723-4418; www.shopworthwhile.com), 268 King St. This wonderful, crazy store defies easy categorization: It's ironic (it could be a 5&10 for yuppies, with lots of small beautiful objects for the house) but sweet (flax and linen clothes for women, goofy baby hats, cotton sweaters, and leggings).

CRAFTS

The Lowcountry's coiled Sweetgrass Baskets are beautiful and functional works of art with a long history in the African American community, made for plantation tasks of winnowing, storage, and carting. The basket weavers are out every day along Broad Street at its intersections with Meeting and King Streets, in the Market. Prices vary for items as small as keepsake decorations or as large as fanner baskets and hampers. You're welcome to watch the process, which incorporates strips of palmetto frond and pine straw with the pale grass. Other weavers sell their work at roadside stands on the Sweetgrass Basket Makers' Highway, a part of US 17 north in Mount Pleasant. A new pavilion dedicated to their work and providing workspace can be found in Mount Pleasant's Memorial Waterfront Park, and an annual festival takes place there (www.sweetgrassfestival.org).

Charleston Crafts (843-723-2938; www.charlestoncrafts.org), 161 Church St. Crafts and exhibits by members of this local co-op who are considered superior in their fields, be they weavers, sculptors, or photographers.

Cone 10 Studios (843-853-3345; www.cone10studios.com), 1080-B Morrison Dr. A working gallery for potters, sculptors, papermakers, and other local artists.

FARMS AND FARMERS' MARKETS

Several outdoor markets convene between April and December, selling everything from bull grapes and greens to tomato pie and pepper jelly. Visit the Charleston Farmers' Market (843-724-7305; www.charlestonfarmersmarket.com) at Marion Square (Calhoun Street at King Street) on Saturdays (8–2) for a thriving festival of juried crafts, music, and prepared food, like crepes. Others near Charleston are

Vendors set up in the old market sheds that date from the 19th century. Peter Loftus

Stono Farm Market (843-559-9999; www.stonofarmmarket.com), 842 Main Rd., John's Island, and Rosebank Farms (843-768-0508; www.rosebankfarms.com), 4475 Betsy Kerrison Pkwy., John's Island. They are working farms and collaborate with others—fishermen, bakers, cooks, and gardeners—to provide an abundance of fresh foods.

The Charleston Tea Plantation (843-559-0383; www.charlestonteaplantation .com), 6617 Maybank Hwy., Wadmalaw Island, is unique in the nation. A 30-minute trolley tour ($10; discount for families) and a free factory tour explain the growing and processing of the leaves. Open daily. Take US 17 to SC 171. Turn east toward Folly Beach, and soon after turn south on SC 700, Maybank Highway. The plantation is located at nearly the end of this road. The Lowcountry Loop Trolley (843-654-5199; www.lowcountrylooptrolley.com) runs the Island Sip & See tour on Tuesday and Thursday, departing from the visitor center. Visits the tea plantation, Irvin-House Vineyards, and Firefly Distillery. Adults $46, children $12.

GIFTS

Alpha Dog Omega Cat (843-723-1579; www.alphadogomegacat.com), 40 Archdale St. Some creative and often hilarious things for pets and the owners who indulge them.

Dixie Dunbar Studio (843-722-0006; www.dixiedunbarstudio.com), 192 King St. Original handmade jewelry featuring traditional gems or freshwater pearls mixed with fabric and chains.

Dulles Designs (843-805-7166; www.dullesdesigns.com), 89 Church St. A little gem located in an old Cabbage Row building, an inspiration for *Porgy* by Du Bose Heyward. Specializing in stationery, guest books, wedding accessories, and modern, elegant keepsakes.

Gallery Chuma (843-722-1702; www.gallerychuma.com), 188 Meeting St. #N1. A large gallery with unique gifts representing work by African Americans in many media, including original paintings, prints, wearable art, and crafts.

Indigo (843-723-2983; www.indigohome.com), 4 Vendue Range. Fred Moore's steel and wire sculptures stand out amid a fanciful selection of patterned tablecloths and painted mats, handmade frames, ceramics, and even painted metal bicycle bells. A spirited, joyful store.

GOURMET SHOPS AND ONLINE PURVEYORS

Bull Street Gourmet (843-722-6464; www.bullstreetgourmetandmarket.com), 120 King St. Gourmet sandwiches, wines, homemade bread, and picnic baskets.

Charleston Cooks! (843-722-1212; www.charlestoncooks.com), 194 E. Bay St. A professional test kitchen and store as well as a gourmet classroom offering "Taste of the Lowcountry," which teaches the techniques of Lowcountry cuisine. $25 for a 90-minute demonstration, plus sampling and wine.

Hominy Grill (www.hominygrill.com). See listing in Dining, but order "Recipes From Hominy Grill" ($12.95).

Matt and Ted Lee (www.boiledpeanuts.com). A catalog of dozens of Southern staples like okra pickle, sorghum, Carolina gold rice, and more from the local brothers and prize-winning cookbook authors.

Olde Colony Bakery (842-216-3232; www.oldecolonybakery.com), 1391-B Stuart Engals Blvd., Mount Pleasant. The source for benne wafers and other regional Southern treats since 1919.

HOME FURNISHINGS/KITCHENWARE

Julia Santen (843-534-0758; www.juliasantengallery.com), 188 King St. A fabulous collection of original vintage posters that make a room pop out of its dreariness.

Le Creuset (843-723-4191), 241 King St. Famous French enameled cookware at factory prices. (The factory and another store are located at Yemassee, exit 38 off I-95 if you're heading south.)

The Old Charleston Joggling Board Company (843-723-4331; www.old charlestonjogglingboard.com), 650 King St. This long, springy board (10 feet or 16 feet) that rests on rocking trestles is common in many Charleston gardens.

South of Market (843-723-1114; www.southofmarket.biz), 173 King St. A collection of original and reproduction or remade pieces that are French Country and Belgian in style: iron tables and garden accessories, oversized striped canvas pillows, sturdy bistro plates, and glass chandeliers.

The Bicycle Shoppe (843-722-8168; www.thebicycleshoppecharleston.com), 280 Meeting St. Rent or buy bikes, or shop among cases full of bike hardware and gadgets.

The Charleston Angler (843-571-3899; www.thecharlestonangler.com), 654 St. Andrews Blvd. High-end outdoor clothing, light tackle, and supplies for fly-fishing, shrimping, and crabbing.

Half-Moon Outfitters (843-853-0990; www.halfmoonoutfitters.com), 280 King St. The most durable and fashionable outdoor wear (like Patagonia) is here, plus coats, tents, packs, camping supplies, and the best advice on local outdoor adventuring to be found in the city.

If Time Is Short

What to do on a quick visit.

For a long weekend, consider at least one historic house visit, shopping north of Broad Street or ambling through the residential neighborhood south of Broad Street, a visit to the beach, if only for a drink on a restaurant's porch, and getting out in the country to one of the Ashley River plantations. Visit a bookstore for local histories. For sightseeing from the water, take an evening cruise under sail or power. The adventurous should take a kayak tour.

Governor's House Inn (843-720-2070; www.governorshouse.com), 117 Broad St., is located in the Historic District, and waking up there makes you feel as if you're a native. It's an especially good choice for two couples who might want to stay in the carriage house. My favorite large hotel is the Harbour View Inn (843-853-8439; www.harbourviewcharleston.com), 2 Vendue Range, located on the river and adjacent to the Waterfront Park, a wonderful place for a morning run or a late-night stroll. These inns will be booked months in advance during the annual Spoleto Festival (843-722-2764; www.spoletousa.org), a series of music, dance, theater, and art that occurs in late spring.

The most evocative house museums and military sites are the Heyward-Washington House (843-722-2996; www.charlestonmuseum.com), 87 Church St., built in 1772 and representing the height of colonial living; the Nathaniel Russell House (843-724-8481; www.historiccharleston.org), 51 Meeting St., completed in 1808 with its gardens and free-flying spiral staircase; and the Joseph Manigault House (843-722-2996; www.charlestonmuseum.com), 350 Meeting St., designed in 1803 by a native son and a marvelous example of adapting European taste for the Lowcountry elite. Slightly farther away on SC 61 are two nationally recognized historic sites: Middleton Place (843-556-6020; www.middletonplace.org), where the oldest landscaped gardens in America were laid out in 1741; and Drayton Hall (843-729-2600; www.draytonhall.org), an 18th-century Georgian home which is a magnificent, unfurnished example of the Palladian style. Military history buffs should visit Fort Sumter National Monument (1-800-789-3678; www.fortsumter tours.com), where the Civil War began.

Popular shops among locals are along King Street from Broad Street north. Walking along Queen Street (boutiques and art galleries) will take you to the French Quarter Art District, and so will Church Street (art galleries and antiques

Middleton Place on the Ashley River. Charleston Area Convention & Visitors Bureau

stores). Gaulart & Maliclet (843-577-9797), 98 Broad St., is a place for a quick bite, Hominy Grill (843-937-0930; www.hominygrill.com), 207 Rutledge Ave., is great for breakfast or lunch. Basil (843-724-3490), 460 King St., serves Thai cuisine to a hip local crowd. Or try the award-winning Peninsula Grill (843-723-0700; www.peninsulagrill.com), 112 N. Market St., or McCrady's (843-577-0025; www.mccradysrestaurant.com), 2 Unity Alley, which has one of the loveliest, quietest bars in town. Wind up at Charleston Grill (843-577-4522; www.charlestongrill.com), 224 King St.

2

Savannah

AN OLD CITY, A MODERN CITY

IT'S NO SECRET that the preservation of the Lowcountry's great places occurred less as a result of enlightened social policy than from post–Civil War impoverishment. Decades of stalled expectations treated Savannah as they did Charleston, and the cities do share similar assets, including vibrant, architecturally intact, downtown historic districts; a heritage that reflects the diverse contributions of generations of residents; and a culture enriched by unique African American musical, religious, culinary, and artistic contributions.

To His Excellency President Lincoln, Washington, D.C.: I beg to present you as a Christmas-gift the city of Savannah, with one hundred and fifty heavy guns and plenty of ammunition, also about twenty-five thousand bales of cotton.

—W. T. Sherman, Major-General, writing from Savannah, Dec. 22, 1864

Yet Savannah is a more complex and interesting *modern* city than Charleston. It's edgier and funkier, enlivened by art students, film festivals, and hip restaurants that would not be out of place in San Francisco. There's a more detached air about it. Behind every bold statement about its history or beauty lurks sarcasm. During the cotton boom, Savannah madly envied New York City for its commercial muscle; 170 years later, the two cities share a liking for gesture and attitude.

This trait was evident during the Civil War. Legend has it that General W. T. Sherman spared Savannah because the city was beautiful, the women were gracious, and the parties were just what he needed at the end of his blazing "March to the Sea" campaign. He took up residence, was fêted, and, in a remarkable telegraph of 1864, offered the unmolested city to President Lincoln as a Christmas gift.

LEFT: Homeowners in Savannah link their landscape to their historic architecture in a subtropical climate, meaning that palms, olive trees, myrtle, and fig are common plantings, even since 1841, when this house was built. Peter Loftus

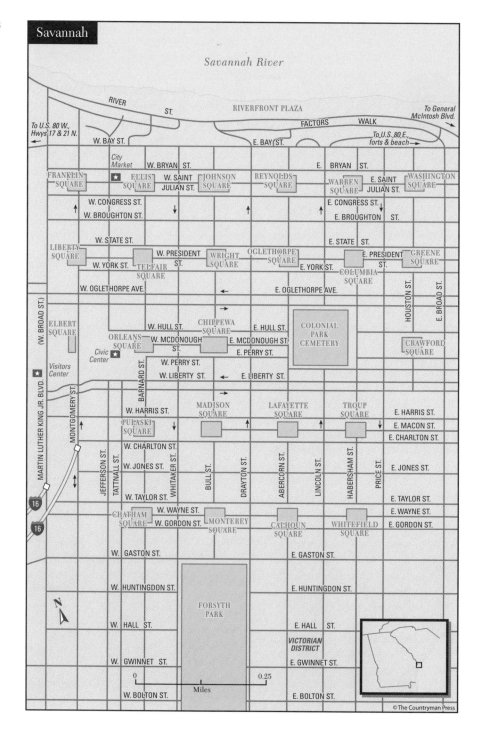

Savannah

Savannah River

RIVER ST.
RIVERFRONT PLAZA
To U.S. 80 W., Hwys 17 & 21 N.
W. BAY ST.
FACTORS WALK
E. BAY ST.
To General McIntosh Blvd.
To U.S. 80 E., forts & beach

City Market
W. BRYAN ST.
E. BRYAN ST.

FRANKLIN SQUARE
ELLIS SQUARE
W. SAINT JULIAN ST.
JOHNSON SQUARE
REYNOLDS SQUARE
WARREN SQUARE
E. SAINT JULIAN ST.
WASHINGTON SQUARE

W. CONGRESS ST.
E. CONGRESS ST.
W. BROUGHTON ST.
E. BROUGHTON ST.

W. STATE ST.
E. STATE ST.

LIBERTY SQUARE
W. PRESIDENT ST.
WRIGHT SQUARE
OGLETHORPE SQUARE
E. PRESIDENT ST.
GREENE SQUARE
W. YORK ST.
TELFAIR SQUARE
E. YORK ST.
COLUMBIA SQUARE

W. OGLETHORPE AVE.
E. OGLETHORPE AVE.
HOUSTON ST.
E. BROAD ST.

ELBERT SQUARE
W. HULL ST.
CHIPPEWA SQUARE
E. HULL ST.
COLONIAL PARK CEMETERY

ORLEANS SQUARE
W. MCDONOUGH ST.
E. MCDONOUGH ST.
CRAWFORD SQUARE

Civic Center
E. PERRY ST.
BARNARD ST.
W. PERRY ST.

Visitors Center
W. LIBERTY ST.
E. LIBERTY ST.

MARTIN LUTHER KING JR. BLVD.
(W. BROAD ST.)
MONTGOMERY ST.

W. HARRIS ST.
MADISON SQUARE
LAFAYETTE SQUARE
TROUP SQUARE
E. HARRIS ST.

PULASKI SQUARE
E. MACON ST.
E. CHARLTON ST.

16
W. CHARLTON ST.
JEFFERSON ST.
TATTNALL ST.
WHITAKER ST.
BULL ST.
DRAYTON ST.
ABERCORN ST.
LINCOLN ST.
HABERSHAM ST.
PRICE ST.
E. JONES ST.
16
W. JONES ST.

W. TAYLOR ST.
E. TAYLOR ST.

CHATHAM SQUARE
W. WAYNE ST.
E. WAYNE ST.
W. GORDON ST.
MONTEREY SQUARE
CALHOUN SQUARE
WHITEFIELD SQUARE
E. GORDON ST.

W. GASTON ST.
E. GASTON ST.

N

W. HUNTINGDON ST.
E. HUNTINGDON ST.

FORSYTH PARK

W. HALL ST.
E. HALL ST.

VICTORIAN DISTRICT

W. GWINNET ST.
E. GWINNET ST.

0   0.25
Miles

W. BOLTON ST.
E. BOLTON ST.

© The Countryman Press

Well, Savannah is still beautiful . . . and still partying. (This quality, and the world it describes, is revealed with great skill in the best book on Savannah's downtown culture, John Berendt's 1994 best-seller, *Midnight in the Garden of Good and Evil*.) The blend of reverence and hilarity, of high-mindedness and getting by, gives the city its character. When the local minor league baseball team renamed itself the Sand Gnats (the top choice in a citywide poll), it chose for its slogan "Bite Me." The city literally shuts down every St. Patrick's Day to accommodate 24 hours of revelry. There's less standing on ceremony here than in Charleston, for Charleston is an iconic Southern place, a city with such a significant, unique presence in American history that it must meet all sorts of expectations. The feeling in Savannah is more along the lines of the Baptist lyric "brighten the corner where you are."

Savannah is defined by 21 handsome squares that function as vest-pocket parks. They are embowered and rimmed with native flowering species, and are linked by one-way cross streets along their sides, which, in turn, feed a few broad parkways divided by banks of trees and shrubs. It is the nation's largest registered Urban Historic District and a National Historic Civil Engineering Landmark, containing some 1,200 notable buildings. It includes blocks of magnificent town houses, many 19th-century places of worship, and several examples of Regency architecture popularized in this country by an Englishman, William Jay. The best

Savannah's squares, a result of enlightened urban planning, allow for shortcuts and places of rest in a congested city, as well as superb views of houses on every side. Peter Loftus

Savannah, located 16 miles upriver from the Atlantic Ocean, is a thriving, modern port.
Peter Loftus

way to see them and to feel the roots of American urbanism is on foot or on a carriage or trolley tour.

The restoration and adaptive reuse of private and institutional buildings continues. The Savannah College of Art and Design (www.scad.edu) has redone more than 40 sites and sponsors nine art galleries. Its students are ubiquitous and bring with them a sense that imaginative things are happening: An old filling station on a main artery is an upscale market that sells arugula. Even the staid Telfair Museum has accommodated a makeover by architect Moshe Safdie, who convinced city leaders and preservationists that a modern addition would not detract from the beauty or scale of the Regency-style Telfair mansion, nor the views from nearby squares.

Savannah has developed in several distinctive sections. City Market is a touristy pedestrian streetscape with shops, galleries, and restaurants. Many carriage tours originate here, and visitors will be drinking sweet tea in one of the outdoor cafés before or after their ride. On River Street, 19th-century brick warehouses are filled with bars, restaurants, gift shops, and the hubbub that attracts people to other American cities that have revived real estate into festival-style marketplaces. From here, ferries zip across the Savannah River to Hutchinson Island, the International Trade & Convention Center, and Westin Savannah Harbor Resort. By night and on weekends, jugglers and street musicians entertain the crowds. Broughton Street is once again a central downtown artery where national retailers and new restaurants exist side by side. Residents in the Victorian District are tackling renovations in their neighborhood of large, fancifully designed houses and gingerbread bungalows. Entrepreneurs in smaller areas, like Wright Square and blocks of Whitaker Street, have joined together to make their address a destination for design or home and garden shops.

A BRIEF HISTORY

Savannah began as an idea in the mind of several enlightened Englishmen who came to be known as the Trustees. They petitioned for a grant in the colonies where land would be held communally and liquor, slavery, and speculation forbidden. Settlers would be selected from "impoverished classes" and under the Trustees' direction would develop exports like wine and silk and defend the region, and Charleston, from Spanish encroachment. The group of 114 who arrived in 1733 was led by General James Oglethorpe, and such was his sense of mission that when his ship *Anne* eased into Charleston Harbor to meet the royal governor, the passengers were required to remain aboard and fish for their supper, so as not to have their heads turned by the newly prosperous city. Continuing south, the *Anne* stopped at tiny Beaufort. Here passengers were allowed to fraternize with residents, whose standard of living probably appeared to be more in line with what they envisioned.

Oglethorpe chose a settlement site where "the river forms a half-moon, along the south side of which the banks are about 40 feet high, and on the top a flat, which they call a bluff." He was assisted by Colonel William Bull, an engineer with surveying experience, and guided by Tomochichi, a friendly Yamacraw chief. It was a port sufficiently deep for ships drawing up to 12 feet to navigate within 10 yards of the shore.

Oglethorpe and Bull immediately started planning the city in the wilderness. The basic form consisted of blocks of five symmetrical 60-by-90-foot lots encompassing 24 squares. Space was designated for public buildings and market areas, as well as for secure retreats for settlers living outside the city limits. Tomochichi supported the colonists' work, was instrumental in winning the trust of area tribes, and backed Oglethorpe in sporadic skirmishes with the Spanish. The existence of a trading post nearby—run by John Musgrove of South Carolina and his wife, Mary, who was part Creek Indian—also smoothed the way.

The prices for cotton negotiated at the Cotton Exchange determined Savannah's prosperity.
Peter Loftus

It was up to the settlers to clear and build, hunt and farm, and establish the Trustees' Garden. This they did, on the grants of 50 acres received by heads of families (5 acres in the city, 45 outside it for farming). By 1741, buoyed by gifts of livestock, horses, and rice from South Carolina neighbors, and growing with Irish, Scottish, Swiss, German, Italian, and Jewish settlers, the original settlement was poised for change. There were 142 homes, a courthouse, jail, storehouse, market building, and a 10-acre fenced public garden. By 1742, the liquor ban was repealed; in 1749, the ban on slavery was lifted. In 1750, the Trustees relinquished their hold on the land.

Released from Oglethorpe's idealism, the colonists proceeded to develop plantations like their neighbors to the north, and Savannah began to flourish as a colonial seat and trading port serving the Georgia backcountry and the coastal islands. In 1776, four South Carolinians and three Georgians signed the Declaration of Independence. They were indeed on the same page: The Lowcountry had pulled together, united by shared commercial and social goals, regular trade and communication, and a culture deeply affected by slavery.

GETTING THERE

Savannah/Hilton Head International Airport (912-964-0514; www.savannah airport.com) is the gateway, with some 40 stops each day from East Coast and Midwestern cities. Rental cars from all major agencies are available at the airport, as are courtesy shuttles if you are staying at a big hotel. If you are staying elsewhere, ask the proprietor for advice or select a cab service at the airport. Expect to pay $28–30 to Savannah. Greyhound (1-800-231-2222; www.greyhound.com) serves Savannah regularly with departures and arrivals from around the country at its downtown depot. Amtrak (1-800-872-7245; www.amtrak.com) offers regular daily service, but the station, located between the airport and the Historic District, is a $12 cab ride away from downtown Savannah. By car, I-95 is just 10 miles from the Historic District, with an exit at I-16 that goes directly into town. Savannah is 252 miles from Atlanta, 105 miles from Charleston, 195 miles from Charlotte, 140 miles from Jacksonville, and 467 miles from Knoxville.

Lodging

Best places to stay in Savannah, and what you'll find nearby . . .

Savannah and its Sea Island neighbor, Tybee Island, offer accommodations from upscale inns to funky beach houses and condos. The caveats of Chapter One, *Charleston,* hold true: Reservations are recommended, especially in the "high season" of spring, when a two-night minimum stay is common;

cancellation policies and room deposits are standard; and smoking takes place outside if it is allowed at all. Access for the handicapped can be problematic outside the large hotels. Carriage houses with ground-floor access are often a good bet. Ask about these and other restrictions, including whether or not children and pets are welcome. WiFi is largely in place, but if you're on a working vacation and need access, check ahead at the smaller inns. The Savannah Area Convention & Visitors Bureau (912-644-6400; www.visit

savannah.com) provides information and links, as does www.bedandbreakfastsofsavannah.com.

HOTELS AND LARGER INNS

Andaz Hotel (912-233-2116; www.savannah.andaz.hyatt.com), 14 Barnard St., Savannah, GA 31401. Expensive–Very expensive. A chic boutique hot spot with 151 rooms, including 68 suites. Heated pool, fire pit, and in-house restaurant featuring an extensive wine list. All of the rooms and suites feature luxury bedding. Located across the street from the newly restored Ellis Square.

Bohemian Hotel Savannah Riverfront (912-721-3800 or 1-888-213-4024; www.bohemiansavannah.com), 102 W. Bay St., Savannah, GA 31401. Very expensive. The newest hotel in a prime location on Savannah's riverfront offers 75 rooms, including 12 suites. British "military campaign" furniture with wood, brass, and leather elements evokes the 18th century. Its rooftop bar, Rocks on the Roof, overlooks the Savannah River and is the go-to place for the city's professional beau monde.

Hampton Inn Savannah Historic District (912-231-9700 or 1-800-576-4945; www.hotelsavannah.com), 201 E. Bay St., Savannah, GA 31412. Expensive. Heart-pine flooring, Savannah gray bricks, a rooftop pool, and an atmosphere that is both cozy and simple take the chain-hotel feeling off this renovated brick low-rise. Located

Savannah's mansions have become luxurious inns.   Savannah Area Convention & Visitors Bureau

across Bay Street from the riverfront, it's convenient and welcoming to families.

Hilton Savannah DeSoto (912-232-9000 or 1-877-280-0751; www.desotohilton.com), 15 E. Liberty St., Savannah, GA 31412. Moderate–Very expensive. A wonderful location in the heart of the Historic District, just a short walk to the riverfront. Some of the 246 rooms have private balconies, most have great views of Savannah's splendid squares. Pool and health club. At the high end of comfort and friendliness for a big, downtown hotel.

Hyatt Regency Savannah (912-238-1234; www.savannahhyatt.com), 2 W. Bay St., Savannah, GA 31412. Expensive–Very expensive. A 351-room hotel, with the trademark Hyatt atrium lobby and glass elevators, towers over the riverfront with an unparalleled view of the ship, ferry, and tugboat traffic. There's an indoor pool and shopping arcade, and you're steps away from busy River Street.

The Marshall House (912-644-7896 or 1-800-589-6304; www.marshall house.com), 123 E. Broughton St., Savannah, GA 31401. Expensive–Very expensive. A classic example of decline and rebirth on Broughton Street, where an old gem (circa 1850) is back with panache. The streetscape is bustling again with theaters, upscale restaurants, and shopping, a definite plus, but it can be noisy to stay here. Its bar draws an older, cool, local crowd. There are 68 rooms, some suites among them with separate sleeping areas. Modernized with all the amenities and putting out a high-gloss sheen.

Westin Savannah Harbor Golf Resort & Spa (912-201-2000 or 1-888-627-8457; www.westinsavannah.com), One Resort Dr., Savannah, GA 31421. Expensive–Very expensive. A full-service luxury resort complex located on Hutchinson Island, 90 seconds by water taxi across the Savannah River from the Historic District or a brief car trip over the Talmadge Bridge. From here the views of Savannah and the river traffic are stunning. It's a huge place (16 stories, 403 guest rooms) that was intended to impress with it size and modern art, and it does, although it's more likely you'll stay here as part of a high-end convention. There's an elaborate spa, fitness center, four tennis courts, a par-72 golf course, clubhouse, marina, two pools, bar, pool bar and grill, and restaurant.

SMALLER LUXURY INNS

Ballastone Inn (912-236-1484 or 1-800-822-4553; www.ballastone.com), 14 E. Oglethorpe Ave., Savannah, GA 31401. Very expensive. At Christmas, this looks like a scene out of Dickens—holly, magnolia leaves, native mistletoe, and garlands of smilax carry its grand front parlor back in time to 1838, when this townhouse was built and English taste influenced the city. The decor echoes this high-style period in rich colors (like chocolate-toned walls), drapes, and furnishings, but is updated for comfort. There are 16 rooms, including three deluxe suites—many of them with Jacuzzis and fireplaces—and a courtyard you may not want to leave. A handsome full-service bar on the first floor is a wonderful amenity, one of the coziest nooks in the city. A full Southern breakfast, afternoon tea, and hors d'oeuvres are included. No children under 14.

East Bay Inn (912-238-1225 or 1-800-500-1225; www.eastbayinn.com), 225 E. Bay St., Savannah, GA 31401. Expensive–Very expensive. Originally a circa-1853 cotton warehouse, there are now 28 guest rooms, each furnished

Savannah town houses on every square blend beautifully into the landscape. Peter Loftus

with queen-sized four-poster beds, reproduction antiques, and coffeemakers. Daily complimentary continental breakfast and wine and hors d'oeuvres reception. A modestly appointed place, it sits at a great location across the street from the busy retail and nightlife tourist hub of River Street. Pets and children are welcome. Large tour groups often book here.

Eliza Thompson House (912-236-3620 or 1-800-348-9378; www.eliza thompsonhouse.com), 5 W. Jones St., Savannah, GA 31401. Expensive–Very expensive. This 25-room inn gives off a sense of family warmth amid beautiful old objects. It was one of Savannah's first luxury inns, and while it may have been outclassed in luxury, it maintains its sense of hospitality. Its spacious courtyard and fountain, and its location

on a brick-paved street embowered by oaks and lined with iron-balconied townhouses, still fulfill the expectations of visitors who come in search of the cities of the "Old South." Many extras like breakfast in the courtyard, evening wine, coffee, and desserts.

Forsyth Park Inn (912-233-6800 or 1-866-670-6800; www.forsyth parkinn.com), 102 W. Hall St., Savannah, GA 31401. Expensive–Very expensive. A modest, quiet place with 11 rooms, including a courtyard cottage that can accommodate up to four, this inn might best be used for a romantic weekend getaway for a busy couple. The main house, a Victorian-era mansion with inlaid hardwood floors, is furnished with period antiques, reproductions, and four-poster beds.

The Gastonian (912-232-2869 or 1-800-322-6603; www.gastonian .com), 220 E. Gaston St., Savannah, GA 31401. Very expensive. This Regency/Italianate residence complex dating from 1868 has lost little of its imposing feel. Period-appropriate decor and muted colors take visitors back to the post–Civil War era when "the Old South" was becoming "the New South." Each of the 17 guest rooms and suites has a gas fireplace; many have four-poster beds and some have Jacuzzi tubs or Japanese soak tubs. The side garden has been restored to its fragrant, secret self. Local people often reserve months in advance for special occasions. Full Southern breakfast. No guests under 21 unless renting whole house.

Hamilton-Turner Inn (912-233-1833 or 1-888-448-8849; www.hamilton -turnerinn.com), 330 Abercorn St., Savannah, GA 31401. Very expensive. Home of the eccentric "Mandy" in John Berendt's book, *Midnight in the Garden of Good and Evil*, this 10,000-square-foot house is a must-see for fans of the book. Even on its own, it's an amazing place, built in the Second Empire style in 1873 and furnished with Empire, Eastlake, and Renaissance Revival antiques. The four-story house and carriage house contain 17 rooms and suites, many with private balconies, whirlpools, and fireplaces. Full breakfast and predinner treats are served in a grand dining room.

The Kehoe House (912-232-1020 or 1-800-820-1020; www.kehoehouse .com), 123 Habersham St., Savannah, GA 31401. Very expensive. This restored Victorian mansion has had several lives; this is its grandest. There

are 13 guest rooms (many with private balconies) and several opulent public rooms adorned with huge urns of fresh flowers in the main building, as well as three additional rooms in the townhouse across the courtyard. Everything here is scaled to fin de siècle oversize: the ceiling moldings, the valances, the draperies, the armoires, the library tables, even the banisters and paneling. Confirm age restrictions for guests in advance.

Mansion on Forsyth Park (912-238-5158 or 1-888-213-3671; www .mansiononforsythpark.com), 700 Drayton St., Savannah, GA 31401. Very expensive. After the initial tourist rush

Azaleas in Savannah's Forsyth Park. Savannah Area Convention & Visitors Bureau

in the mid-'80s that put Savannah on the map, the industry matured, and some of the quainter B&Bs faded. Chocolates on the pillows were not enough. The mansion may be over the top even for Savannah—a tricked-out car among the classics. It's not about a touch here, a touch there, a nice oil painting or a fondly told Civil War story/myth. This is serious deluxe, with 126 rooms, a massive gallery with hundreds of paintings and sculptures, a spa, a cooking school, and an excellent 150-seat restaurant (700 Drayton) composed of six dining rooms. Showmanship and glamour: It's rocking Savannah's world.

SMALLER ACCOMMODATIONS AND OFFBEAT LODGINGS

These are alternatives to the full-blown, fancy places. Rates are moderate–expensive. They can be a budget choice, or an option for extended families or friends traveling together.

Bed & Breakfast Inn (912-238-0518 or 1-888-238-0518; www.savannah bnb.com), 117 W. Gordon St. A mid-1850s townhouse at Chatham Square, closer to Forsyth Park than the river, but in an old neighborhood. This inn has been around for years and has many fans.

Joan's on Jones Bed and Breakfast (912-234-3863 or 1-888-989-9806; joansonjones.com), 17 W. Jones St. Good location on one of Savannah's prettiest streets. Two suites; children and some pets welcome.

Park Avenue Manor (912-233-0352; www.parkavenuemanor.com), 109 W. Park Ave. Four rooms with private baths in an owner-occupied, 1897-built bed & breakfast on the southwest corner of Forsyth Park, the leading edge of the Victorian District. On the froufrou side of decor, but much loved by many repeat visitors for 10 years. No pets; children older than 16 only.

Thunderbird Inn (912-232-2661 or 1-866-324-2661; thethunderbirdinn .com), 611 W. Oglethorpe Ave. Renovated to retro. If you're a hipster from Williamsburg (N.Y.) or SoMa (San Francisco), this is for you.

RESORTS AND RENTALS— TYBEE ISLAND

Savannah's beach is Tybee Island, the opposite of a gated resort. You have your neighbors over for a beer before lunch. While there are some new luxury homes, it's mostly raised houses with latticed skirts hiding the pilings and a deck out back. The beach is broad and public, with a pier and plenty of access points. There are shops for beachwear and boogie boards, two excellent restaurants, some fine B&Bs, oceanfront hotels, and a campground and RV park. It's also the best place to get on the water in a kayak (see Recreation). Condo complexes and inexpensive motels are typical lodgings, but some other options are listed here.

Contact the Tybee Visitor Center (912-786-5444; www.visittybee.com) for more ideas.

Beachview Bed & Breakfast (912-786-5500; www.beachviewbb tybee.com), 1701 Butler Ave., Tybee Island, GA 31328. Very expensive. Eight rooms in a circa-1910 house at the beach, one block from the water, 30 minutes from downtown Savannah. They also offer The Love Shack, a one-bedroom cottage on property which sums up the casual/funky attitude of Tybee.

Dunes Inn and Suites (912-786-4591; www.dunesinn.com), 1409 Butler Ave., Tybee Island, GA 31328. Moderate–Expensive. An upscale

Tybee Island's broad beach and friendly, nonresort atmosphere sum up the simple life.
Savannah Area Convention & Visitors Bureau

version of a chain hotel. Some of the 54 rooms have kitchenettes, some have king-sized beds and Jacuzzis. It's simple, clean, close to the beach, and has a swimming pool.

17th Street Inn (912-786-0607 or 1-888-909-0607; www.tybeeinn.com), 12 17th St., Tybee Island, GA 31328. Moderate–Expensive. Eight rooms with private entrances and full kitchens, along with a deck for all guests and plenty of room for families. Clean, friendly, funky, less than one block from the beach. Kids accommodated with beds at modest additional cost.

Tybee Island Inn (912-786-9255 or 1-866-892-4667; www.tybeeisland inn.com), 24 Van Horn Ave., Tybee Island, GA 31328. Expensive–Very expensive. Once part of the Fort Screven infirmary, this seven-room inn

is located one block from the beach on the quieter north end of the island (closer to Savannah) amid live oaks, palmettos, and many places to walk or jog.

RENTAL AGENTS AT TYBEE ISLAND

Oceanfront Cottage Rentals (912-786-0054 or 1-800-786-5889; www.ocean frontcottage.com), 717 First St., Tybee Island, GA 31328. Listing more than 30 homes on the ocean or with an ocean view. Many welcome pets, and usually provide boogie boards, bikes, and beach chairs. Some with pools and hot tubs.

Tybee Island Rentals (912-786-4034 or 1-800-476-0807; www.tybee islandrentals.com), P.O. Box 627, Tybee

Island, GA 31328. Some 65 properties are available for rent by the week or month; two-night minimum stay.

Tybee Vacation Rentals (912-786-5853 or 1-877-214-7353; www.tybee vacationrentals.com), P.O. Box 402, Tybee Island, GA 31328. Listing 254 houses, cottages, villas, and houses with pools. Pet-friendly properties. Online reservations.

Dining

Taste of the town . . . local restaurants, cafés, bars, bistros, etc.

The art and pleasure of dining stayed home-based in Savannah well into the 20th century. There were few places to dine out and few reasons to do so. You could conduct your business in a restaurant, but not your social life. Savannah's many restaurants show how that has changed. Today, the city is filled with plain and fancy places to eat. The local population, including thousands of students, is eager to dine out. While there may be fewer no-frills lunch counters and cafeterias, there are plenty of informal cafés, coffee bars, and bistros to take their place. The general price range is meant to reflect the cost of a single meal, usually dinner, featuring an appetizer, entrée, dessert, and coffee. Cocktails, beer, wine, gratuity, and tax are not included in the estimated price. Reservations are a good idea.

Delicatessens, sweet shops, and bakeries are listed below larger restaurants; gourmet and health-food stores are listed under "Gourmet Food" in the Shopping section of this chapter.

Belford's Savannah Seafood and Steaks (912-233-2626; www.belfords savannah.com), 315 W. St. Julian St. Open daily for lunch and dinner. Moderate–Expensive. Belford's opens on both sides to City Market and has patio seating, features which make it very attractive for lunch. There's a small corner bar where you can eat in a pinch, but you'd want to be in the main dining area, one side an exposed brick wall, lots of glass windows, seating around an open grill. Steaks and seafood are the best choices, and every waiter and the carriage tour operator outside will remind you that the crab-cakes have received an award. They also do a great job of Lowcountry staples like greens, shrimp with smoked bacon, and crab stew.

Casbah (912-234-6168; www .casbahrestaurant.com), 20 E. Brough-ton St. Open daily for dinner. Moderate. A decor that calls to mind Arabian folk tales and a menu that takes North African herbs and staples like tabouli, mint, almonds, saffron, and lamb and chicken to new heights. There's even belly dancing. Perhaps unlikely in old historic Savannah, but it has found its niche. Families are welcome: It's exotic and festive.

Cha Bella (912-790-7888; www .cha-bella.com), 102 E. Broad St. Open daily for dinner. Moderate–Expensive. Organic, organic, organic. Locally produced food from sustainable farms. Very creative menu that changes every day, according to what's growing and at the fish market. Whiffs of southern Spain and Provence. Sounds too good to be true, but this exuberant, modern, restaurant has uniquely hit the tone for 21st-century Savannah with its loftlike space in a former industrial building, and its nod to the art scene, with live music some nights.

Circa 1875 (912-443-1875; www .circa1875.com), 48 Whitaker St. Open

Outdoor dining is possible nearly year-round at Savannah's City Market.
Savannah Area Convention & Visitors Bureau

daily except Sun., for dinner or just for drinks and appetizers at the bar. Moderate–Expensive. Excellent French bistro cuisine and extensive wine list with many wines by the glass. Or have a perfect martini. The pub and adjacent dining room are handsome and high-ceilinged, but the white-tablecloth feel is as cozy and welcoming as a known-only-to-locals country inn in the Loire Valley. Grilled meats and poultry, the full array of local vegetables and seafood, and wonderful desserts—which many patrons take at the bar after a performance or gallery walk.

Clary's Café (912-233-0402; www .claryscafe.com), 404 Abercorn St. Open daily for breakfast and lunch. Inexpensive. A bacon-and-egg sandwich on wheat and coffee is a typical order at Clary's, a downtown eatery

where your cup stays filled and breakfast waffles can set you up for the day. At lunch, the Greek salad is big enough to share, or if you're hungry you might try the chicken potpie, which includes salad and a roll. Top it off with a root beer float. *Midnight in the Garden of Good and Evil* fame sent the crowds here, but the diet-busting food makes it worth the trip.

Crystal Beer Parlor (912-349-1000; www.crystalbeerparlor.com), 301 W. Jones St. Open daily for lunch and dinner. Inexpensive–Moderate. Located at the end of one of Savannah's prettiest residential streets on the edge of the Historic District, the Crystal is a bar with leather booths and frosted mugs that has been recently refreshed. It's been written up many times, but tends to be forgotten when it shouldn't be. Shrimp salad, fried oysters, burgers, and crab stew are popular.

Elizabeth on 37th (912-236-5547; www.elizabethon37th.net), 105 E. 37th St. Open daily for dinner. Very expensive. Reservations required. The creation of Elizabeth Terry, chef, author, and James Beard Award winner, this restaurant was one of the first in Savannah to bring seasonal products, signature flavorings, and a sense of creative possibility to mundane Southern staples like grits, grouper, and greens. It was upscale and ahead of the trend. Elizabeth is gone, but diners can still count on elaborate meals in the sumptuous setting of an old mansion. You'll need to drive or take a cab from downtown. Relax and enjoy the formality and the huge wine list, and forget about the price. Favorites include pepper crusted beef tenderloin, local fish, and seasonal offerings such as local oysters on the half shell.

The Lady & Sons (912-233-2600; www.ladyandsons.com), 102 W. Congress St. Open daily for lunch and dinner. Closed for dinner on Sun. Moderate. Owner Paula Deen has been through reputational struggles but the food is the same that made her name on the Food Network and in cookbooks. The crowded lunch buffet offers the full range of Southern specialties, including fried tomatoes, catfish, ribs, and shrimp grits, so be prepared to walk it off. Dinner seating is on a first-come, first-served basis, but they will accept reservations up to a year in advance.

Mrs. Wilkes' Dining Room (912-232-5997; www.mrswilkes.com), 107 W. Jones St. Open Mon.–Fri. for lunch. Inexpensive. The line starts to form well before 11 AM. This is homemade cooking served as it would be at home: the diners seated around large tables with heaping platters of fried chicken, baskets of biscuits, and bowls of slaw, vegetables, red rice, and black-eyed peas or green beans placed before them. If you've ever been grateful for the kindness of strangers, the one who gives you the last chicken leg could be your friend for life. No credit cards accepted.

The Olde Pink House (912-232-4286; www.plantersinn.com), 23 Abercorn St. Open daily for lunch and dinner. Expensive. Located in an elegant 18th-century mansion designated a National Landmark, where the Declaration of Independence was read in Savannah for the first time. There's a quiet dining room upstairs and a livelier tavern downstairs, with fireplaces roaring in winter, piano music, a welcoming bar, and a full dinner menu. This is one of the most popular places downtown to have a cocktail or relax after dinner—that is, if the diners release their tables. The seafood is recommended (a recent appetizer was sautéed shrimp with country ham and grits cake), but the entrées include fish, pork, steak, and lamb, many with a glazed sauce.

Olympia Café (912-233-3131; www.olympiacafe.net), 5 E. River St. Open daily for lunch and dinner. Inexpensive–Moderate. River Street is not subtle, with bars, gift shops, and crowds, but it's fun, and this is a reliable, inexpensive restaurant supported by Savannah's population of Greek descent, proud of its deep roots and civic contributions. There are Mediterranean appetizers like tzadziki and dolmadakia, and gyros and kabobs, as well as traditional Greek dishes like lemon chicken and moussaka. If you hear servers and diners shouting "Opa," it means another order of flaming cheese appetizers was a hit.

Papillote (912-232-1883; www .papillote-savannah.com), 218 W.

Broughton St. Open Wed.–Fri. 10:30–7; Sat. and Sun. 9:30–5. Moderate. This chic French bistro features shrimp and prosciutto salad, soup du jour, crab and mango tartine, cheese plates, and daily specials like a salmon burger with tomato fennel salad and béarnaise sauce on challah roll with duck fat pan-fried potatoes. You can also buy fresh-baked breads and sweets, teas and coffees, herbs and specialty vinegars in their shop. In fact, everything on the menu can be "brown-bagged" to go (except the ice cream!). Grab a picnic lunch and enjoy it in one of Savannah's beautiful squares.

Rancho Alegre (912-292-1656; www.ranchoalegrecuban.com), 402 Martin Luther King Jr. Blvd. Open daily for lunch and dinner, until 10:30 PM Fri. and Sat., when there is live jazz played at a comfortable level. The menu is Cuban, down-home style, and features 27 entrees and combinations, which include yucca, plantains, and of course rice and beans and mojo sauce. There are long tables to seat multigenerational families, for which this restaurant is a joyous favorite.

Sapphire Grill (912-443-9962; www.sapphiregrill.com), 110 W. Congress St. Open daily for dinner. Expensive–Very Expensive. A sophisticated, stylish City Market restaurant on three floors serving a first-rate dinner and open late for nightcaps. The bar can get crowded and create a lot of traffic, and the restaurant tends to be noisy. Nonetheless, it's a special place. There's always an excellent choice of beef or duck, several pan-seared or grilled fish dishes. The menu changes seasonally. All dishes emphasize heirloom, organic, and local produce along with the freshest fish and meat. For many it's the best Savannah restaurant.

Vinnie Van Gogo's (912-233-6394; www.vinnievangogo.com), 317 W. Bryan St. Open Mon.–Thurs. 4–11:30; Fri.–Sat. noon–midnight; Sun. noon–11:30. Inexpensive. Calzones and thin-crust pizza by the slice or pie (14- or 18-inch) made from dough prepared on the premises at night, then rolled and tossed while you watch from the counter. These cooks are having fun. Toppings include healthy vegetables. A large selection of imported beers and a concoction called spodeeodee (cheap red wine, 7-Up, and a splash of orange soda), which sells by the glass or pitcher as fast as they can mix it up. You're surrounded by art students, so get a sense of a population that has enlivened the old city. Credit cards not accepted. Delivery by bicycle courier to downtown area.

SAVANNAH AREA

The Breakfast Club (912-786-5984; www.thebreakfastclubtybee.com), 1500 Butler Ave., Tybee Island. Open daily 7–1 for breakfast and lunch. Inexpensive. Here is the kicked-back life of Tybee among locals sitting at booths and tables set close together. You might run into the shrimpers coming in or the early anglers and birders just setting out. If you want to get a jump on the day, or take a quiet walk on a deserted morning beach, this is a great place to start. There will be a line on weekends or by midmorning.

Crab Shack at Chimney Creek (912-786-9857 or 1-866-789-2722; www.thecrabshack.com), 40 Estill Hammock Rd. (second right past Lazaretto Creek Bridge), Tybee Island. Open daily for lunch and dinner, until 10 PM during the week and 11 PM on weekends. Moderate. No reservations. Long wait times are possible, but there are three full bars and 600 seats inside and out and you can visit the gator lagoon (with 78 baby gators you can

Breakfast on the porch in Savannah. Savannah Area Convention & Visitors Bureau

feed), the gift shack, and an aviary with rescued exotic birds. Offering local shellfish—steamed, boiled, or raw—BBQ pork, ribs, and grilled chicken. The Crab Shack is pet friendly.

Gerald's Pig and Shrimp (912-786-4227; www.tybeebbq.com), US 80 at McKenzie St., Tybee Island. Open for lunch and dinner, daily during the summer until 10 PM and operating Thurs.–Sun. in the off-season, with earlier closing times. Moderate. Dining is under an open-air shed next to the main drag on Tybee, and it's the height of informal, but the surf-and-turf baskets, pulled pork sandwiches, fried oysters, and peel-your-own shrimp draw the most discriminating locals.

Sundae Café (912-786-7694; www.sundaecafe.com), 304 First St., Tybee Island. Open Mon.–Sat. for lunch and dinner. Expensive. Don't let the strip mall exterior fool you—this is a small gem. The owners have transformed a former ice cream parlor into a destination for those in the know. Their menu is inspired Southern, focusing on steaks and seafood. The crispy scored flounder, filet mignon, and shrimp and grits inspire a loyal following. Call ahead for reservations.

Tybee Island Social Club (912-472-4044; www.tybeeislandsocialclub.com), 1311 Butler Ave., Tybee Island. Open daily for lunch and dinner. Moderate. Such an upbeat place, where everyone has freshened up after a day at the beach and donned sundresses and shorts. You select from a tapas menu with recommended beer and wine pairings, maybe three per customer, and everyone shares. Intimate tables inside and out; eat at the bar if you can't grab a table. Freshest ingredients and attentive service, votives flickering, much laughter but not noisy: Tybee neighbors and newcomers enjoying themselves.

FOOD PURVEYORS

Some of the places listed below should not be overlooked for lunch or brunch, and they are a welcome sight at midafternoon, after a day of touring.

Bakeries/Coffeehouses

Back in the Day Bakery (912-495-9292; www.backinthedaybakery.com), 2403 Bull St. Open Tues.–Sat. 8–5. Located in the up-and-coming hipster neighborhood of Starland, where there are new galleries and artists' lofts, the bakery has astonishing sweets as well as salads and sandwiches.

Forsyth Park Café (912-233-7848), Bull St. and E. Park St. Built in 1915 for Georgia National Guard training, this recently renovated fort is now open daily, serving breakfast, lunch, and early, light dinners from 7 AM–6 PM in the winter and 7–dusk in spring, summer, and fall. There is a visitor center and information kiosk on-site.

Foxy Loxy (912-401-0543; www.foxyloxycafe.com), 1919 Bull St. Besides extra-strong coffee, you can sample Tex-Mex, visit the print gallery, or listen to local musicians in informal jam sessions.

Gallery Espresso (912-233-5348; www.galleryespresso.com), 234 Bull St. Coffees, cakes, outdoor tables, and indoor art exhibits. Longtime favorite of artsy locals.

The Sentient Bean (912-232-4447; www.sentientbean.com), 13 E. Park Ave. The coffee here is terrific, along with menu items such as granola and yogurt, breakfast burritos, salad, baked goods, and homemade soups. Check the website for events and performances—they offer live music, film night, and photography exhibits.

Soho South Café (912-233-1633; www.sohosouthcafe.com), 12 W. Liberty St. Lunch starts at 11 Mon.–Sat.; Sunday brunch 11–4. Inside a hip art gallery with good things to see and good people-watching. To-go menu, too.

Starland Café (912-443-9355; www.starlanddining.com), 11 E. 41st St. Lunch is served in this converted house Mon.–Sat.,11–3. They have a loyal following, many of whom come for the Greek asparagus sandwich or the Thai tomato soup with goat cheese, salads, and many vegetarian options.

Wright Square Café (912-238-1150; www.wrightsquarecafe.com), 21 W. York St. Open Mon.–Fri. 7:30–5:30; Sat. 9:00–5:30. The wraps at lunch are terrific (the menu also includes panini and salads) and the setting is very European, with indoor and sidewalk dining, racks of fine chocolates and coffees, comfortable chairs, and a serious attention to architectural detail, from floor to ceiling. On a square with several shops for antiques, books, upscale clothing, and home furnishings.

Candy and Ice Cream

Byrd Cookie Co. (912-355-1716 or 1-800-291-2973; www.byrdcookie company.com). They have a new location at 213 W. St. Julian St. selling treats or you can tour the factory and buy products at 6700 Waters Ave. A local institution since 1924. Delicious cookies and gourmet desserts.

Leopold's Ice Cream (912-234-4442; www.leopoldsicecream.com), 212 E. Broughton St. Leopold's made lasting memories for Savannahians between 1919 and 1970. In 2004, the son of the original owners re-opened the ice cream parlor, bringing with him the original family recipes. Expect a wait, but this place is worth it—Leopold's has your old favorites plus choices like tutti-frutti, rum bisque, or seasonal homemade specials like pumpkin spice—plus sandwiches, salads, and soups.

Lulu's Chocolate Bar (912-480-4564; www.luluschocolatebar.net), 42 Martin Luther King Jr. Blvd. Open Mon.–Thurs. 5 PM–11:30 PM; Fri.–Sat. 2 PM–2 AM; Sun. 2 PM–11:30 PM. You could go for the happy hour, champagne cocktails, or the specialty martinis, but they're nothing compared to the incredible desserts which downtown partygoers savor on their last stop of the evening. Also a very worthy stop after a Saturday of sightseeing.

Savannah's Candy Kitchen (912-233-8411; www.savannahcandy.com), 225 E. River St. The largest candy store in the South, where you can see the candies made and have some sent home.

Delis and Faster Food

Betty Bombers (912-272-9326), 1108 Bull St., inside the American Legion Post 135. Tues.–Wed. 11 AM–midnight; Thurs.–Sat. 11 AM–2 AM. Burgers, tacos, wings, chili, fries, and assorted sandwiches. You can get your drinks at the Legion just down the hall, where the regulars seem to enjoy this tiny, funky establishment in their midst.

Brighter Day (912-236-4703; www.brighterdayfoods.com), 1102 Bull St. A health-food store featuring a full line of breads, organic produce, natural foods, juices, and supplements as well as fresh sandwiches to go or to eat in.

Goosefeathers Café and Bakery (912-233-4683; www.goosefeathers cafe.com), 39 Barnard St. An upscale art deco–style bakery created in the shell of a downtown storefront. Opens weekdays at 7 AM. The breads and desserts are homemade; omelets are light and fresh. Light lunches include soups and sandwiches.

Touring

Fun in the Historic District and beyond.

You might as well decide whether you want to concentrate on ghosts, the Civil War, "The Book," gardens, or old houses; and whether you want to go on foot, by carriage, trolley, air-conditioned bus or van; or by daylight or moonlight.

Most tours last one to two hours. Reservations are strongly suggested. You can also pick up a CD and map at the visitor center (301 Martin Luther King Jr. Blvd.) and walk or drive at your own pace. SavHGuide for the iPhone is available at the app store and with it you can map your own tours and read about the historic sites along the way.

Some motorized tours allow you to step off and catch up with them at a later stop. Tours that are more specifically nature-oriented, or may require equipment such as a kayak or canoe, are more fully described in the Recreation section below. Prices range from $12 to $25 for adults, from $5 to $12 for children.

BY MOTOR

Freedom Trail Tour (912-232-7477) Focuses on African American history.

Hearse Ghost Ride (912-695-1578; www.hearseghosttours.com) Yes, it's true, nine passengers ride at night in a converted hearse.

Savannah Heritage Tours (912-224-8365; www.savannahheritagetour.com).

Tours by BJ (912-233-2335; www.toursbybj.com).

A guided carriage ride lets you soak up the city's ambience, history, and architecture at a 19th-century pace. Peter Loftus

BY CARRIAGE

Carriage Tours of Savannah (912-236-6756; www.carriagetoursofsavannah.com).

Historic Savannah Carriage Tours (912-443-9333 or 1-888-837-1011; www .savannahcarriage.com).

Plantation Carriage (912-201-0001; www.plantationcarriagecompany.com).

BY TROLLEY

Oglethorpe Trolley Tours (912-233-8380; www.oglethorpetours.com).

Old Savannah Tours (912-234-8128 or 1-800-517-9007; www.oldsavannah tours.com).

Old Town Trolley Tours (912-233-0083; www.trolleytours.com).

BY FOOT

Architectural Tours of Savannah (912-604-6354; www.architecturalsavannah .com).

Ghost Talk, Ghost Walk (912-233-3896; www.ghosttalkghostwalk.com).

Savannah Haunted History Tours and Haunted Pub Crawl Tour (912-604-3007; www.ghostsavannah.com).

Savannah Walks (912-238-9255; www.savannahwalks.com).

See Savannah Walking Tours (912-441-9277; www.seesavannah.com).

BY BIKE

Savannah Bike Tours (912-704-4043; www.savannahbiketours.com).

BY BOAT

Bull River Marina Dolphin Watch (912-897-7300; www.bullrivermarina.com).
Dolphin Magic Tours (912-897-4990 or 1-800-721-1240; www.dolphin
-magic.com).
Riverboat Cruises (912-232-6404 or 1-800-786-6404; www.savannahriver
boat.com).
Sea Kayak Georgia (912-786-8732; www.seakayakgeorgia.com).

Culture
Great places to see
and things to do.

ARCHITECTURE

Savannah's architectural inventory includes Federal-period mansions and town houses; buildings designed by William Jay, the Regency-period archi-tect who delighted in fancy scrollwork and a freehand imposition of Greek motifs; grand antebellum homes; and a whole district of Victorian homes made of wood and masonry. Whatever their specific style, the older buildings downtown share a formal and restrained design that makes a cohesive whole. Their colors come from a muted palette of grays, greens, and tans, and the end result is that they resonate with the geometry of Savannah's squares.

A good place to start is the Savannah Visitor Center (912-644-6400; www.visitsavannah.com), 301 Martin Luther King Jr. Blvd., where you can join a tour or get an overview of the city's history. Open daily.

Local people appreciate your interest and are generally welcoming, but since all but a few of the historic homes are privately owned, remember that while pho-tographing is fine, entering gardens or climbing front stairs is not. For such closer looks, visit the house museums, where well-briefed and accommodating docents can answer your questions. Annual tours of private homes and gardens are spon-sored by local preservation organizations or churches. They usually take place in March, last all day, and range in price from $20 to $45. For information, contact the Savannah Tour of Homes and Gardens (912-234-8054; www.savannahtourof homes.org) or The Garden Club of Savannah (912-447-3879; www.gcofsavnogs tour.org) about its Annual NOGS Tour (that is, gardens "North of Gwinnett Street").

FILM

(See also "Theater" entries below—several local venues offer both live and film events.)
Carmike Cinemas 10 (912-353-8683), 511 Stephenson Ave.
Spotlight Theatres (912-352-3533), 1100 Eisenhower Dr.
Trademark Cinema (912-355-5000), 1915 Victory Dr.

The Savannah Film Festival (www.savannahfilmfestival.com) hosted in the fall by the Savannah College of Art and Design (SCAD) at the Trustees Theatre draws independent filmmakers from around the world.

GALLERIES

The Savannah College of Art and Design (www.scad.edu) greatly raised the profile of the city as an arts center. Frequently changing exhibitions of work are on display in college buildings throughout the city. In addition, graduates settle in and many have started arts-related businesses in film and digital media production, framing, and restoration; their work stretches the boundaries of two-dimensional representation. The increasing number of artists who teach at SCAD and wish to exhibit has led to probably a doubling of available gallery space in the last decade, including innovative "pop-up" shows in shared spaces or alternative venues, like hotel lobbies and warehouses. A glance at *Connect Savannah* (www.connectsavannah.com), a free weekly, will turn up undiscovered or short-run shows—as will www.savannahoffthebeatenpath.com.

Beach Institute (912-234-8000), 502 E. Harris St. Established in 1865 by the American Missionary Association to educate the newly freed slaves of Savannah, the Beach is now an African American cultural center that features arts and crafts exhibits. Of unique interest is the collection of hand-carved wooden sculptures, including likenesses of presidents, by acclaimed folk artist and Savannah barber Ulysses Davis. Call ahead for hours. Adults $7, students and seniors $5, children under 12 years $2.

Chroma Gallery (912-232-2787), 31 Barnard St. Contemporary art, glass, and sculpture, with new artists represented frequently. See website for schedule.

Desotorow (912-376-9953; www.desotorow.org), 2427 De Soto Ave. A nonprofit gallery and performance venue for local artists, many of whom have been affiliated with SCAD.

Ellis Gallery (912-234-3537 or 1-800-752-4865; www.rayellis.com), 205 W. Congress St. Paintings, watercolors, bronzes, books, and prints of golf and traditional maritime scenes by Ray Ellis, perhaps the best known of Lowcountry artists.

Folklorico (912-232-9300), 440 Bull St. Folk art and crafts from around the world, interestingly curated and secured through fair trade practices.

John Tucker Fine Arts (912-231-8161), 5 W. Charlton St. This handsome gallery on Madison Square features several yearly shows of established artists whose work usually reflects Southern themes.

Kobo Gallery (912-201-0304; www.kobogallery.com), 33 Barnard St. An artists' cooperative with shows by members and invited guests displaying a range of work from the very best artists working in Savannah.

Pei Ling Chan Garden for the Arts (www.scad.edu), 322 Martin Luther King Jr. Blvd. at W. Harris St. This walled garden, with individual sections reflecting African American, English, French, and Asian cultures, is the backdrop for sculpture exhibits. There is also a small amphitheater used during theatrical productions. A nice place in the thick of downtown to have a quiet moment.

shopSCAD (912-525-5180; www.shopscad.com), 340 Bull St. A gallery of SCAD featuring work by students, faculty, and occasional guests each month. It has expanded into a terrific shop.

Savannah's First African Baptist Church.   Savannah Area Convention & Visitors Bureau

HISTORIC HOMES, GARDENS & RELIGIOUS SITES

A distinguishing quality of longtime Lowcountry residents is that they are, to paraphrase the Rolling Stones, "practiced in the art of perception"; that is, they know how to see and how to honor what they see. In Savannah, this means that historic sites—be they mansions, gardens, forts, or houses of worship—are cared for in a personal way. A site is valued not just because it is important and beautiful (though they all are), but because it has given meaning to the community. Structures that could be classified as monuments are familiar touchstones. Such an attitude puts flesh on the bones of historic preservation talk. And it's not just buildings that are treated well: Savannah's squares and cemeteries are testimonials to public beauty as well.

Andrew Low House (912-233-6854; www.andrewlowhouse.com), 329 Abercorn St. Open Mon.–Sat. 10–4; Sun. noon–4; closed major holidays and first two weeks of January. A city house in the high style, although adapted to Savannah's summer heat by means of jalousied rear porches. By 1849, when it was built, Savannah was in its prime: This is how the wealthy cotton merchants lived, and there is a large collection of furniture to tell their story. It was from this house that Juliette Gordon Low founded the Girl Scouts and where she died in 1927. Adults $8, students $6.

First African Baptist Church (912-233-6597; www.theoldestblackchurch.org), 23 Montgomery St. Tours Tues.–Sat. at 11 and 2. Built in 1788 and believed to be the oldest continually active church for black worshippers in North America, it was built by slaves for slaves. Many original pews remain intact. It was the birthplace of the Civil Rights Movement in Savannah and a refuge on the Underground Railroad. Adults $7, students $6.

Georgia State Railroad Museum (912-651-6823; www.chsgeorgia.org), 655 Louisville Rd. Open daily 9–5. This National Historic Landmark is a collection of structures first built in 1838 and used as a railroad manufacturing and repair facility. Today you can see the roundhouse and turntable, a 125-foot brick smokestack, antique steam engines, diesel locomotives, and rolling stock. Adults $10, students $6.

Green-Meldrim House (912-233-3845), 14 W. Macon St. Open Tues., Thurs., and Fri. 10–4; Sat. 10–1 (last tour of the day starts 30 minutes before closing). Used as headquarters by General W. T. Sherman during his 1864 Christmas occupation of Savannah, this Gothic Revival mansion on Madison Square was the city's most expensive house when it was built in 1850. The exterior ironwork and porches are the best example of the style in the city. Adults $7, students $3.

Isaiah Davenport House (912-236-8097; www.davenporthousemuseum.org), 324 E. State St. Open Mon.–Sat. 10–4; Sun. 1–4. The proposed demolition of

One of Savannah's famous squares. Peter Loftus

this landmark—built circa 1820 by a master builder from Rhode Island for his family—to salvage the brick and make way for a parking lot galvanized Savannah preservationists. That was in 1954, and the effort marked the birth of the Historic Savannah Foundation. Today it's a museum adorned with furnishings and decorative arts of the Federal period. There's a lovely garden out back and an excellent museum shop. Adults $8, children $5.

Juliette Gordon Low National Birthplace (912-233-4501; www.juliettegordon lowbirthplace.org), 10 E. Oglethorpe Ave. Open Mon.–Sat. 10–4; Sun. 11–4. Check website as hours change seasonally. A Regency town house decorated in postbellum period style, this building commemorates the childhood of the founder of the Girl Scouts, who was born here in 1860. There's a gift shop with special things for Scouts. Adults $8, children $7.

King-Tisdell Cottage (912-234-8000), 514 E. Huntingdon St. Call for hours. This charming, original Victorian cottage (circa 1896) houses a museum of the black history and culture of Savannah and the Sea Islands. Adults $7, students and seniors $5, children under 12 years $2.

Laurel Grove—South Cemetery (912-651-6772), at the western end of 37th St. Open daily; tours by appointment. The South Cemetery of Laurel Grove was dedicated in 1852 for the burial of "free persons of color" and slaves. Many of the city's most famous African Americans are buried here. Adults $5, children $3.50.

Mercer Williams House (912-236-6352; www.mercerhouse.com), 429 Bull St. at Monterey Square. Open Mon.–Sat. 10:30–3:40; Sun. noon–4. Construction on this Italianate mansion began in 1860 and was completed in 1868. While it was built for the great-grandfather of Savannah's favorite son, Johnny Mercer, no member of the Mercer family ever lived here, and the house is most famous for its association with the late Jim Williams. Mr. Williams finished his two-year restoration of the house in 1971, and many pieces of his private collection are on display in the house, including 18th- and 19th-century portraits. The Carriage House Shop, which sells items depicting the Mercer House, is located across the square. Adults $12.50.

Owens-Thomas House (912-790-8800; www.telfair.org), 124 Abercorn St. Open Mon. noon–5; Tues.–Sat. 10–5; Sun. 1–5. Last tour at 4:30. Designed in 1816 by Englishman William Jay and considered the best example of an urban villa in his Regency style, this house contains a collection of European and American decorative arts and has a formal garden. The Carriage House is the site of one of the few discovered slave quarters in the Historic District, and its collections offer insight into the lives of urban African American slaves. Adults $15, children (6–18) $5.

Ralph Mark Gilbert Civil Rights Museum (912-777-6099), 460 Martin Luther King Jr. Blvd. Tues.–Sat. 9–5. Dr. Gilbert, who died in 1956, was a leader in early efforts to gain educational, social, and political equality for African Americans in Savannah. This museum features state-of-the-art interactive exhibits focusing on the history of the Civil Rights Movement in Savannah. You can arrange a guided tour by calling the museum in advance. Adults $8, seniors $6, students $4.

Second African Baptist Church (912-233-6163; www.secondafrican.org), 123 Houston St. Call ahead to arrange visit. The church, established in 1802, was the site of two historic occurrences: General W. T. Sherman's reading of the Emancipation Proclamation to the newly freed slaves and, nearly a century later, Dr.

Martin Luther King Jr.'s presentation of his "I Have a Dream" sermon prior to its delivery in Washington, D.C.

Temple Mickve Israel (912-233-1547; www.mickveisrael.org), 20 E. Gordon St. Call ahead to arrange visit. The Gothic-style synagogue was built in the 1870s, more than 100 years after the congregation was established. The museum and library house the oldest Torah in America, as well as letters, books, and historical documents.

Wormsloe Historic Site (912-353-3023; www.gastateparks.org), 7601 Skidaway Rd., Isle of Hope. Open Tues.–Sun. 9–5. The tabby ruins, an avenue of oaks, and artifacts excavated from the site are all that remain of the colonial plantation built by Noble Jones, a physician and carpenter who came with the first settlers on the ship Anne and established the Georgia colony. An audio-video presentation and interpreters of colonial life make the period vivid for visitors. Adults $10, children 6–17 $4.50, children under 6 $2.

MILITARY MUSEUMS & SITES

The island forts and lighthouses, in particular, recall both the sense of isolation felt by soldiers stationed there and the effort they made to create a community.

Fort Jackson (912-232-3945; www.chsgeorgia.org), 1 Fort Jackson Rd., 3 miles from downtown. Open daily 9–5. The oldest standing fort in Georgia, first established in 1809 on an earlier fortification, it was central to the Confederate network of river batteries during the Civil War. A self-guided tour leads you to military exhibits in the fort's casemates. Special military history programs enliven the fort several times each year. Adults $7; children $4; military, seniors, and veterans $5.50.

Fort McAllister Historic Park (912-727-2339; www.gastateparks.org), 3894 Fort McAllister Rd., Richmond Hill (24 miles south of Savannah on I-95). Open daily 8–5. The fall of Fort McAllister, on the Ogeechee River, signaled the end of Sherman's "March to the Sea." By that time it had outlasted other forts due to its earthen walls, which, unlike the popular masonry equivalent, could be swiftly repaired after a bombardment. There are self-guided tours, rangers on hand, and a good, small museum. Picnicking in the park is popular, but bring insect repellent. Biking trails and canoe/kayak rentals available. Adults $6.50, children $3.75. There is a $5 parking fee to use the park but no parking fee if you're only touring the fort.

Fort Pulaski National Monument (912-786-5787; www.nps.gov/fopu), Cockspur Island, US 80 east, about 30 minutes from Savannah. Open daily 9–5 until 6:00 in summer months. A young officer named Robert E. Lee had his first military assignment here, soon after the fort was built. It's a masterpiece of engineering, a huge and heavy brick building, surrounded by a moat, sitting on an unstable marsh. And yet during the Civil War, cannons blasted holes in the masonry of such forts and they became obsolete. Interpretive programs explain life at the fort during the Civil War, and you are free to roam its ramparts. An excellent selection of books is available at the gift shop. Adults $5, ages 15 and younger free.

Mighty Eighth Air Force Heritage Museum (912-748-8888; www.mighty eighth.org), 175 Bourne Ave., Pooler, GA (take I-95 exit 102 to US 80 east, then go left on Bourne Ave.). Open daily 9–5. Dedicated to the men and women who served in the "Mighty Eighth" (formed in Savannah in 1942) during World War II.

Washed up or discarded oyster shells were the key ingredient in "tabby," which when burned (into lime) and mixed with sand resulted in a building material used for foundation walls for many of the earliest Lowcountry structures. Peter Loftus

Exhibits also track later engagements, such as Operation Desert Storm, supplemented by photos and film presentations. Adults $10, children (6–12) $6, under 6 free. Discounts for seniors and military.

Tybee Island Museum and Lighthouse/Fort Screven (912-786-5801; www.tybeelighthouse.org), 30 Meddin Dr., Tybee Island, 18 miles east of Savannah. Open daily except Tues. 9–5:30; ticket sales stop at 4:30. Located within Fort Screven, which was acquired by the federal government in 1808 and used as a post through World War II, the museum and lighthouse offer visitors a glimpse of life at a beach outpost. The museum has an assortment of objects, Native American and Civil War weaponry, as well as memorabilia and illustrated newspaper accounts of the Civil War. A lighthouse has marked this site since 1736. Today you can climb this 19th-century version (more than 150 feet tall) for a wonderful view of the river. Adults $8, children $6.

MUSEUMS

Oatland Island Education Center (912-395-1212; www.oatlandisland.org), 711 Sandtown Rd. Open daily 10–4. Children will love walking the nearly 2 miles of wooded trails in this 175-acre preserve, where they can watch for animals and experience the salt marsh, forest, and wetland habitat of the Lowcountry. Sheep, goats, ponies, and swans may cross your path while bald eagles and hawks soar overhead. There is a farmyard, too. Adults $5, children $3.

Savannah History Museum (912-651-6825; www.chsgeorgia.org), 303 Martin Luther King Jr. Blvd. Open Mon.–Fri. 8:30–5; Sat.–Sun. 9–5. Audio and video presentations, displays, and objects relating to Savannah's history are housed in the old Central of Georgia railway depot train sheds in the visitor center complex. The black soldier exhibit highlights the 1st South Carolina Volunteers and the 178,895 black men who fought in the Civil War. Adults $4.25, children (6–12) $3.75.

SCAD Museum of Art (912-525-7191; www.scadmoa.org), 601 Turner Blvd. Open Tue., Wed., Fri. 10–5; Thurs. 10–8. A contemporary art focus is designed to engage art students with the work of modern practitioners, both known and obscure, and to invite viewers to share in the vision of art-making through lectures and panel discussions.

Ships of the Sea Museum (912-232-1511; www.shipsofthesea.org), 41 Martin Luther King Jr. Blvd. Open Tues.–Sun. 10–5. Ship models, a magnificent dollhouse-style construction of a huge 19th-century ship, and ships-in-bottles tell the exciting story of maritime adventure, war, commerce, and exploration in the world's oceans from the time of the Vikings forward. Located in the William Scarbrough House, a Regency jewel with a lovely garden. Adults $8.50, students and seniors $6.50.

Telfair Museum of Art/Jepson Center for the Arts (912-790-8800; www .telfair.org), 121 Barnard St. Open Sun. 1–5; Mon. 12–5; Tues.–Sat. 10–5. Savannah's premier museum, housed in a Regency-style mansion, hosts a permanent collection of American and European Impressionist paintings, drawings, prints, and sculpture. The new building displays 20th- and 21st-century art and hosts traveling exhibitions. A single admission fee allows access to three sites: Telfair Museum, Jepson Center, and the Owens-Thomas House. There's also an interactive space for kids, the ArtZeum, and a café. Single site admission: adults $12, students $5. For $20, an adult may visit three sites.

University of Georgia Marine Extension Service Aquarium (912-598-3474; www.marex.uga.edu/aquarium/SEA1.html), 30 Ocean Science Circle, Skidaway Island, 14 miles from downtown. Open Mon.–Fri. 9–4; Sat. 10–5. This is a working research lab and facility, but visitors are welcome to visit the aquarium and exhibits, which depict the underwater marine and plant life of coastal Georgia. Fossils of shark teeth and whale skulls are prominently displayed. A self-guided visit takes about an hour. Ages 13–54, $6. Afterward, you can picnic. From here it's a short hop to Skidaway Island State Park (912-598-2300; see "Camping" in the Recreation section below), where you can walk through a maritime forest, bird-watch, and observe the life of the marsh. $5.

MUSIC

Savannah Music Festival (912-234-3378; www.savannahmusicfestival.org) A terrific jazz, blues, classical, and world music festival that takes place for about two weeks in March and April at churches, halls, clubs, and auditoriums around the city. A mini-Spoleto that draws music aficionados from all over.

Savannah Stopover (www.savannahstopover.com) A new three-day festival designed for bands heading to SXSW in Austin every March, it brings buoyancy and big energy to the city through more than 80 performances.

Nightlife

After-hours attractions and activities.

Club One (912-232-0200; www.club one-online.com), 1 Jefferson St. If you're looking for Lady Chablis, who sang and carried on in the book *Midnight in the Garden of Good and Evil,* this is the spot, but check the website for Lady Chablis's specific performance schedule. Other performers and female impersonators appear nightly. Dancing on two floors.

Jazz'd (912-236-7777; www.jazzdsavannah.com), 52 Barnard St. Located downstairs at the corner of Barnard and West Broughton Street. No cover. Live music Tues.–Sun. nights starting at 9.

The Jinx (912-236-2281), 127 W. Congress St. Crazy punk and lots of hipsters. But some conventioneers find their way in, too.

Planters Tavern (912-232-4286), 23 Abercorn St. Downstairs at the Olde Pink House, Planters is a much-loved local bar with a pianist and chanteuse rolling through the songs we love when we're feeling sentimental.

Rocks on the Roof (912-721-3800; www.bohemianhotelsavannah.com), 102 W. Bay St. A rooftop bar overlooking the Savannah River and River Street. Tapas menu, creative wine and beer list. An upscale local scene.

THEATER

Lucas Theatre for the Arts (912-525-5050; www.lucastheatre.com), 32 Abercorn St. An old movie palace features films, musical performances, and theatricals. One of the venues for the Savannah Film Festival (along with SCAD's Trustees Theatre; see below), an annual, week-long event presenting professional and student filmmakers—the best in independent filmmaking (filmfest.scad.edu).

The Historic Savannah Theatre (912-233-7764; www.savannahtheatre.com), 222 Bull St. Seasonal productions of contemporary drama, musicals, and comedy.

SCAD's Trustees Theater (912-525-5051; www.trusteestheater.com), 216 E. Broughton St. A former art deco movie house transformed by the Savannah College of Art and Design into a glittering 1,105-seat performance art hall featuring movies, plays, and dramatic readings.

Recreation

Active pursuits in and around Savannah.

BASEBALL

The area's professional farm team is the Savannah Sand Gnats (912-351-9150; www.sandgnats.com), Grayson Stadium, 1401 E. Victory Dr. When at home, they play games weeknights at 7 and Sundays at 3. Admission is $8–10 for adults.

BEACH ACCESS

The only beach accessible by car on Georgia's northern coast, Tybee Island, lies 18 miles east of Savannah on US 80. Strictly enforced "No Dogs Allowed on Beach" policy. Check out www.visittybee.com for beach rules and regulations before you go.

Ossabaw Island (912-233-5104; www.ossabawisland.org) is a barrier island 20 miles south of Savannah that's run by a nonprofit foundation. There are two primitive campsites with a 30-person maximum and a 6-person minimum, as well as a two-night minimum. There is also The Clubhouse, a restored 1880s hunting lodge that can accommodate 20 people maximum, 6 people minimum with a two-night stay. Transportation and fresh drinking water are available.

Wassaw Island (912-652-4415; www.fws.gov/wassaw), located east of Savannah and Skidaway Island, can be reached by private or charter boat. It is managed by the U.S. Fish and Wildlife Service. Within its 10,000 acres are more than 20 miles of inland island trails and a 7-mile beach to explore.

BIRD-WATCHING

The best spots for birding around Savannah are part of the Savannah National Wildlife Refuge System, a complex of seven coastal parks that provide habitat on the beach and dunes as well as in abandoned rice fields, swamps, creeks, and estuarine systems. Explore Tybee Island North Beach by parking at the Tybee Island Museum (see listing under "Military Museums & Sites" in the Culture section of

By the banks of the river. Peter Loftus

Gliding in the region's hundreds of miles of estuaries and creeks puts you at eye level with an amazing number of birds. Savannah Area Convention & Visitors Bureau

this chapter). Skidaway Island State Park (912-598-2300; www.gastateparks.org), 52 Diamond Causeway, Savannah, is separated from the Atlantic by salt marsh to the east and by Wassaw Island to the south. This unique geography attracts a wide variety of songbirds as well as large ospreys and bald eagles. To get there, take exit 164 off I-16 west of Savannah and head south. It will become Diamond Causeway. Harris Neck National Wildlife Refuge (843-784-2468; www.fws.gov/harrisneck), an old World War II Army airfield, supports a large colony of wood storks and dozens of nesting wading birds. Take US 17 south to Harris Neck Road, then travel 6.5 miles to the refuge entrance. There is an interpretive kiosk near the entrance gate, providing a brief description of the refuge. Drive along the 4-mile Laurel Hill Wildlife Road for a good introduction to the area, which includes freshwater marsh, river-bottom hardwood swamp, and tidal rivers and creeks. Wilderness Southeast (912-236-8115; www.wilderness-southeast.org) offers all kinds of weekend birding trips near Savannah and farther afield.

BOATING

Canoeing and Kayaking
If you are traveling with your own boat, access points along the Savannah River and boat landings at Isle of Hope and Skidaway Island allow you to launch into tidal creeks throughout the Savannah National Wildlife Refuge complex. For outing ideas, instruction, guided tours, maps, and expedition opportunities, Sea Kayak Georgia (912-786-8732 or 1-888-529-2542; www.seakayakgeorgia.com) and Savannah Canoe and Kayak (912-341-9502; www.savannahcanoeandkayak.com)

are the experts. No experience necessary for many excursions. Trips that last three hours leave Tybee Island daily in the morning and afternoon, and longer camping expeditions are also offered. Lessons and specialized skills workshops start at $95 per person with a minimum of two participants and last three to four hours. A three-hour guided trip costs $60 per person. Daily sit-on kayak rentals cost $50 for a single, $60 for a tandem; a variety of decked models range from $60 to $130. Full-day and overnight canoe trips on the Altamaha River, including shuttle service, can be arranged.

East Coast Paddleboarding (912-484-3200; www.eastcoastpaddleboarding .com).

North Island Surf & Kayak (912-786-4000; www.northislandkayak.com), 1 C Old Highway 80, Tybee Island.

Wilderness Southeast (912-236-8115; www.wilderness-southeast.org).

Sailing

For sailors unfamiliar with Lowcountry waters and tides, renting a sailboat or having a lesson is a good way to get acquainted with local conditions. Prices vary according to length of sail lesson or charter and type of sail.

CompassSailing (912-441-3265; www.compasssailing.com), Bull River Marina. Private sails for up to six people on a 38-foot Morgan 384 cost $400 for a four-hour cruise.

Savannah Sailing Center (912-352-9996; www.savannahsailingcenter.org), at Lake Mayer Community Park, Montgomery Crossroad and Sallie Mood Dr. Offers lessons in the calm setting of the 35-acre lake, which may be easier for a beginner to negotiate. Call for rates.

BOWLING

AMF Bowling Lanes (912-925-0320), 115 Tibet Ave. Open until 2 AM Fri. and Sat.

CAMPING

River's End Campground and RV Park (912-786-5518 or 1-800-786-1016; www.riversendcampground.com), 5 Fort Ave., Tybee Island. A hundred sites, full hook-ups, tent sites, and cabin rentals. WiFi available.

Skidaway Island State Park (912-598-2300; www.gastateparks.org), 52 Diamond Causeway. A 533-acre park with 87 tent, trailer, and RV sites and three camper cabins; laundry, bathhouse, nature trail, and interpretative walks and programs.

DIVING

Serious divers explore Gray's Reef National Marine Sanctuary (www.graysreef .noaa.gov), 11,000 acres of live bottom fishery, and they get there via a fishing charter or tour.

Diving Locker and Ski Chalet (912-927-6603; www.divinglockerskichalet .com), 74 W. Montgomery Crossroads.

Island Miniature Golf (912-898-3833; www.islandminigolf.com), 7890 US 80, Whitemarsh Island. On the way to the beaches and boat landings, it includes bumper go-carts, an arcade, and batting cages.

FISHING

Inshore, there are fish in shallow water and narrow creeks when the tide is right; offshore, there are bigger game fish in the Gulf Stream. Some guides specialize in the art of saltwater fly-fishing.

A good place to plan a fishing trip is at a marina, although some sporting goods stores may have recommendations (see the Shopping section below). Noncommercial saltwater fishing does not require a license; nonresident fresh-water fishing does. Contact the Wildlife Resources Division (1-800-366-2661; www.georgiawildlife.com/fishing) for information on licenses and regulations, or talk to your guide. Licenses are available at most sporting goods stores and bait shops.

A listing of some of the many charter boat services available follows. Most boats are fully outfitted with supplies and bait, but check in advance, especially if you have questions about bringing your favorite rod—an option for fly-fishing—or if the length of the trip requires food. Always bring sunscreen, a hat, and a windbreaker. The cost does not include gratuity for the mate(s). The 2013 prices for half-day trips (generally one to three passengers for inshore fishing, four to six for offshore fishing) started at $350. A 12-hour trip can cost $1,400 and a 14-hour trip to the Gulf Stream costs about $2,400.

Bull River Marina (912-897-7300; www.bullrivermarina.com), 8005 US 80 East. Located halfway to Tybee.

Coastal River Charters (912-441-9930; www.coastalrivercharters.com) Inshore fishing and sight-seeing tours of barrier islands and secluded creeks.

Lazaretto Creek Marina (912-786-5848 or 1-800-242-0166; www.tybee dolphins.com), 1 Old Hwy. 80, Tybee Island. A full-service marina offering inshore and offshore trips for six people.

Miss Judy Charters (912-897-4921; www.missjudycharters.com), 124 Palmetto Dr. Deep-sea fishing and trolling, Gulf Stream trips, and inshore fishing with Captain Judy Helmey.

Reelemn (912-897-4990; www.reelemn.com) Up to 10 anglers fish the artificial reefs or head to the Gulf Stream.

Savannah Light Tackle Fishing Co. (912-398-8134; www.fishsav.com), at Bull River Marina, 8005 US 80 East. Inshore and fly-fishing a specialty.

Sundial Nature and Fishing Tours (912-786-9470; www.sundialcharters .com), 142 Pelican Dr., Tybee Island. Inshore fishing, crabbing, and net casting. Ask about the naturalist-led outings to Little Tybee and Wassaw Islands and overnight camping possibilities.

Tybee Island Charters (912-786-4801; www.fishtybee.com), 1 US 80 East, Tybee Island. Fish inshore from a 21-foot Carolina skiff, in deeper waters aboard a 30-foot Delta Sport, sleep aboard a 49-foot trawler, or take a nature cruise.

Coastal YMCA (www.ymcaofcoastalgeorgia.org). Three locations: 912-354-6223, 6400 Habersham St.; 912-897-1192, 66 Johnny Mercer Blvd.; and 912-786-9622, 204 Fifth St., Tybee Island. These facilities honor YMCA memberships from other parts of the country.

Spa Bleu (912-236-1490; www.spableu-sav.com), 101 Bull St. Open Mon.–Thurs. 10–6; Fri.–Sat. 10–7. Massage, skin care, manicures, and pedicures.

Savannah Yoga (912-232-2994; www.savannahyoga.com), 1319 Bull St. Offering all levels of yoga, at about $15 for walk-ins.

GOLF

The most varied opportunities for golf exist on Hilton Head and Bluffton, about 45 minutes away depending on where you go (see Chapter Four, *Hilton Head*), but here are some local options.

Bacon Park Golf Course (912-354-2625; www.baconparkgolf.com), Shorty Cooper Dr. Par 72; 27 holes across three layouts; 6,700 yards. Putting green and lighted driving range. Fees for 18 holes: $29–34 plus $13–15 cart fees.

Henderson Golf Course (912-920-4653; www.hendersongolfclub.com), 1 Al Henderson Dr. Par 71; 18 holes; 6,700 yards. Five sets of tees. Putting green and lighted driving range. Fees: $39–48, cart included.

The Wilmington Island Club (912-897-1612), 501 Wilmington Island Rd. Par 72; 18 holes; 6,876 yards. Driving range and putting green. Fees: $69, cart included.

Southbridge Golf Club (912-651-5455; www.southbridgegolfclub.com), 415 Southbridge Blvd. Par 72; 18 holes designed by Rees Jones; 6,990 yards. Driving range, putting green, and a full staff of teaching pros on-site. Fees: $40–60, cart included.

HORSEBACK RIDING

If you can spend 50 minutes in the car, the best places to ride would be on or near Hilton Head Island or St. Helena Island, where you might arrange for a beach or country ride. Expect to pay $75 per person for 90 minutes.

Norwood Stables (912-356-1387; www.norwoodstables.com), 2304 Norwood Ave.

HUNTING

As in other regions of the Lowcountry, land quarry in the Savannah area includes a variety of waterfowl, turkey, and various sizes of game. Familiarize yourself with specific hunting seasons, license requirements, and bag limits by visiting an outdoor recreation store (see the Shopping section below) or by contacting the Game and Fish Division of the Georgia Department of Natural Resources (706-557-3597; www.georgiawildlife.com).

Popular public hunting grounds in the greater Savannah area are located in the Webb Wildlife Management Area and Palachucola Management Area

Country roads of sand still mark many areas of the rural Lowcountry. Peter Loftus

(803-625-3569; www.dnr.sc.gov), at Turtle Island and Victoria Bluff in Jasper and Beaufort Counties, and in the Savannah National Wildlife Refuge (843-784-2468; www.fws.gov/savannah).

NATURE PRESERVES

Some of the most accessible and user-friendly preserves in the Lowcountry are located within 30 minutes of Savannah. They include:

Coastal Georgia Botanical Gardens at the Historic Bamboo Farm (912-921-5460; www.coastalgeorgiabg.org), Canebrake Rd. off US 17. Open Mon.–Fri. 8–5; Sat. 10–5; Sun. noon–5. A 46-acre educational and research center that started more than 100 years ago when a local bamboo fancier was given three Japanese giant timber bamboo plants and cultivated them on her property. Today there are more than 100 types of plants, flowers, and trees growing here, and more than 70 species of bamboo. Free.

Harris Neck National Wildlife Refuge (843-784-2468; www.fws.gov/harris neck/), I-95 exit 67 to US 17 south, then travel approximately 1 mile to Harris Neck Rd.; the refuge entrance is 6.5 miles on the left. Signs direct you to the driving and biking trails, which wind through this 2,700-acre area of freshwater impoundments, salt marsh, forest, and field.

Pinckney Island National Wildlife Refuge (843-784-2468; www.fws.gov /pinckneyisland/), US 278 at the foot of the Hilton Head bridge, approximately 35 minutes from Savannah. A 4,053-acre complex of small islands and hammocks set in the marsh with 14 miles of trails. A good place to spend an hour walking and birding.

The Savannah Ogeechee Canal (912-748-8068; www.savannahogeechee canalsociety.org), 681 Fort Argyle Rd., Savannah. Open Mon. and Fri. 10–4; Sat. 9–5; Sun. 1–5. Located on a barge canal dating from 1831 and threading through rice fields and swamps, this new linear park has 6 miles of footpaths and a small museum. Adults $2, children $1.

Savannah National Wildlife Refuge (843-784-2468; www.fws.gov/savannah/), I-95 exit 5 to US 17 south; 6 miles south of Hardeeville on SC 170. The refuge consists of 25,608 acres spread across land once used for growing rice. The visitor center is located on US 17 (6 miles north of Savannah and 7 miles south of Hardeeville), and is open Mon.–Sat. 9–4:30. Get a map at the visitor center and drive along the 5-mile Laurel Hill Wildlife road for a good introduction to an area that includes freshwater marsh, river-bottom hardwood swamp, and tidal rivers and creeks. Hiking trails (39 miles in all) are well marked, many of them following the path of the old rice dikes.

Victoria Bluff Heritage Preserve (803-734-3886; www.dnr.sc.gov), Sawmill Creek Rd., off US 278, 3 miles from the Hilton Head bridge. Open dawn to dusk daily. This beautiful parcel of 1,000 acres on the Colleton River was long eyed for residential or industrial development, but local residents secured its protection as a passive recreation area.

TENNIS

Seven city parks in and around Savannah have a total of 47 courts, and nearly all are lighted for night play. The custom at public parks is first-come, first-served. The locations are: Bacon Park (6262 Skidaway Rd.); Daffin Park (1001 E. Victory Dr.); Forsyth Park (Gaston and Drayton Sts.); Lake Mayer Park (Montgomery Crossroad and Sallie Mood Dr.); Stell Park (Bush Rd.); Tybee Memorial Park (Butler Ave.); and Wilmington Island Community Park (Lang St. and Walthour Rd.).

Shopping

Shops and markets that will pique your interest.

There's not much you can't buy in Savannah, from collard greens to a gilded armoire, old books to edgy art. Concentrate on Whitaker Street, Broughton Street, Abercorn Street, Wright Square, and Ellis Square. River Street is the most generic and geared toward tourists. Parking downtown can be difficult and meters are checked regularly. Make use of municipal parking garages at City Market and Bryan Street at Abercorn. Discount parking passes are sold at the visitor center, the Bryan Street garage, and at several hotels and inns.

Shopping on River Street. Savannah Area Convention & Visitors Bureau

ANTIQUES

There are antiques of every period and style in the city—or a dealer will find you what you want. Whether you live in a sleek, minimalist apartment or a farmhouse, you're likely to find a piece that works. As one man said in the paper a few years back: "We love old things. It makes life easier because you don't have to like the new ones." Popular sales are held regularly by Bull Street Auctions (912-443-9353; www.bullstreetauctions.com), 2819 Bull St.

Alex Raskin Antiques (912-232-8205; www.alexraskinantiques.com), 441 Bull St. If the setting in the Noble-Hardee mansion on Monterey Square isn't enough to get your attention, then the inventory will. Among the big, older antique vendors, it's a little more laid-back in that the furniture, rugs, paintings, and light fixtures simply overflow the space.

Arthur Smith Antiques (912-236-9701; www.arthursmithantiques.com), 402 Bull St. Four floors of rooms filled with antique tables, rugs, armoires, beds, and side pieces. It helps to know what you want.

Attic Antiques (912-236-4879), 224 W. Bay St. Next door to the antiques mall at Cobblestone Lane. Come here for browsing fun or if you collect very specific small items: fountain pens, buttons, advertising materials, etc.

Cobblestone Lane Antiques (912-447-0504), 230 W. Bay St. A 10,000-square-foot restored warehouse facing the Savannah River that hosts 20 dealers and is chockablock with relics and more.

In late February, jonquils, narcissi, and camellias are plentiful. Peter Loftus

J. D. Weed & Company (912-234-8540; www.jdweedco.com), 102 Victory Dr. W. An area native who knows just what American antiques furnished the old houses, from tea caddies and document boxes to dining tables and sideboards.

Limehouse Plantation (912-232-7212), 120 E. Jones St. European and 20th-century American furnishings with a good selection of iron and garden ornaments and accessories. Sometimes you find nice old fabric.

Pinch of the Past (912-232-5563; www.pinchofthepast.com), 2603 Whitaker St. at 43rd St. Architectural fragments and vintage house parts, including antique ironwork, door frames, columns, mantels, lighting fixtures, and hardware.

Simply Silver (912-238-3652), 236 Bull St. Most interesting is an ever-changing inventory of flatware to fill in the pieces you've lost, as well as small gift items: baby cups, fruit knives, mirrors, and frames.

V. & J. Duncan (912-232-0338; www.vjduncan.com), 12 E. Taylor St. You could browse through the files and piles of prints, maps, old advertising art, and illustrations here for hours. A comprehensive, well-organized collection of fine antique material.

BOOKS

Book Lady (912-233-3628; www.thebookladybookstore.com), 6 E. Liberty St. Used and antique volumes at this longtime city business.

E. Shaver Booksellers (912-234-7257; www.eshaverbooks.com), 326 Bull St. Downtown and great for browsing. If some topic of Lowcountry history has captured your interest, the owners will track it down, new or used. Rooms of new and rare books, history, fiction, a children's section, and excellent art books.

Ex Libris (912-525-7550; www.scad.edu), 228 Martin Luther King Jr. Blvd. This three-story bookstore provides course books and supplies for students at the Savannah College of Art and Design, and is also full of treasures for the avid reader. Also, art supplies and a nice café.

CLOTHING

There is preppy and retro fashion in Savannah, but it's still the South, after all, and there are plenty of small-scale boutiques with modern sensibility. Men's styles tend toward the casual and outdoorsy.

Gaucho (912-232-7414), 251 Bull St. and 18 E. Broughton St. Jewelry, leather, flowing scarves, and both rustic and romantic clothes for women, including lines from Eileen Fisher and many new, smart designers.

Globe Shoe Company (912-232-8161), 17 E. Broughton St. A longtime local favorite of Savannah's shoe aficionados.

Kathi Rich (912-236-7424), 2515 Abercorn St. Very hip women's clothes by young designers.

Terra Cotta (912-236-6150), 34 Barnard St. Elegant, soft cottons for the bed and bath; also, simply cut, stylish casual wear, including some vintage.

CRAFTS/GALLERIES

If you'd like to see local artists at work, drop by the City Market Art Center (www.savannahcitymarket.com), a downtown art colony located upstairs (there's elevator access) at 308 and 309 W. St. Julian St.

Atelier Galerie (912-233-3140; www.agsavannah.com), 150 Abercorn St. Handcrafted jewelry by local, regional, and international artisans.

Friedman's Fine Art (912-234-1322; www.friedmansfineart.com), 28 W. State St. A collection of the region's best representational artists is on exhibit, including young, emerging, and collectible talents. Fine-art framing and a large selection of antique botanical and maritime prints for sale.

Gallery 209 (912-236-4583; www.gallery209.com), 209 E. River St. Thirty of the region's finest artists and craftsmen show here. Their works include batik, fiber, glass, pottery, wood, paintings, and sculpture displayed in a 19th-century cotton warehouse.

Village Craftsmen (912-236-7280; www.villagecraftsmen.com), 223 W. River St. Original arts and crafts are still being created by members of this 25-year-old co-op gallery, including jewelry, books, quilts, and decorative painting.

GIFTS

Cottage Shop (912-233-3820; www.cottageshopgifts.com), 2422 Abercorn St. Linens for bed and table, stationery, lamps, and crystal. The shop recently celebrated its 60th birthday: At a time of malls and chains, it may be a throwback, but it's a very gracious one.

Davenport House Museum Shop (912-236-8097; www.davenporthousemuseum.org), 324 E. State St. Gifts with a Savannah angle in the first house restored by the Historic Savannah Foundation.

Levy Jewelers (912-233-1163; www.levyjewelers.com), 2 E. Broughton St. Family owned and operated since 1900, this store carries high-end pieces, affordable starter jewelry, designer watches, and some estate jewelry. They also have a nice gift collection.

Owens-Thomas House Museum Shop (912-790-8800; www.telfair.org), 124 Abercorn St. A superior gift shop in a recently renovated ground-floor space with a great selection of art and architecture books, travel books, small clothing items, and prints.

Paris Market & Brocante (912-232-1500; www.theparismarket.com), 36 W. Broughton St. Here is boutique shopping—linens, stationery, vintage posters, odd antique mirrors, and garden decorations—in one of the best Savannah commercial restorations. Worth it just to browse, even if all you buy is French milled soap.

GOURMET SHOPS

Parker's Market (912-233-1000; www.parkersav.com), 222 Drayton St. Face the challenge: How to take a 1930s filling station and point it in the direction of highest and best use (cool gourmet supermarket), not gasoline convenience store (but the company has those, too). Win-win. Open 24 hours, with wines and microbrews, fresh herbs and flowers, cookies and pastries baked daily, and a variety of picnic meals and take-out. The corporate website is kind of hilarious, explaining this unlikely concept.

The Paula Deen Store (912-232-1579; www.pauladeen.com), 108 W. Congress St. A storefront devoted to the culture and culinary empire of the Deens, including signed books and gift baskets that can be sent from Savannah.

HOME FURNISHINGS/KITCHENWARE

Two sections of the city have emerged as centers of home furnishing/decoration. One is the Downtown Design District, located on Whitaker Street between Charlton and Gordon Streets, and the other is the Starland Design District, just south of downtown between 37th and 41st Streets, from Whitaker to Habersham. The furnishings can be sleek and modern, hand-painted, antique, or really rustic.

Arcanum (912-236-6000; www.arcanummarket.us), 422 Whitaker St. The designers here have a way of mixing the old with the contemporary.

Kitchens on the Square (912-236-0100; www.kitchensonthesquare.com), 38 Barnard St. Quality cookware, tableware, and crazy kitchen gadgets.

One Fish Two Fish (912-447-4600; www.onefishstore.com), 401 Whitaker St. Painted chairs, benches, floor cloths, and little household accents mixed with antiques and elegant objects.

24E Design Company (912-233-2274; www.24estyle.com), 24 E. Broughton St. Modern, distressed, recreated, and whimsical (and in all combinations) furniture fills two floors in an old brick building. A changing group of smaller pieces by local and regional artists is also on sale.

Most of the following stores not only have athletic equipment and accessories for sale, but they rent equipment, too. Call ahead to reserve. For bikes, you are in a hill-free land: Ask about rails-to-trails pathways to Tybee and the forts.

Bicycle Link (912-233-9401; www.bicyclelinksav.com), 210 W. Victory Dr.

Fleet Feet Sports (912-355-3527; www.fleetfeetsavannah.com), 3405 Waters Ave.

Half Moon Outfitters (912-201-9393; www.halfmoonoutfitters.com), 15 E. Broughton St.

If Time Is Short
What to do on a quick visit.

The Gastonian (912-232-2869 or 1-800-322-6603; www.gastonian.com), 220 E. Gaston St., is a sumptuous luxury inn, and The Thunderbird Inn (912-232-2661; www.thunderbirdinn.com), 611 W. Oglethorpe, is the retro-hip alternative. My favorite historic sites are the Owens-Thomas House (912-233-9743; www.telfair.org), 124 Abercorn St., a Regency-style urban villa designed by William Jay in 1816, and Fort Pulaski (912-786-5787; www.nps.gov/fopu) on US 80, a masonry fort that is a great place for a picnic or a bicycling destination. Drop in on any gallery associated with the Savannah College of Art and Design or the Kobo Gallery. The Beach Institute (912-234-8000), 502 E. Harris St., has a permanent display of folk-art sculpture that celebrates the talent of Ulysses Davis and other African American artists. I could and do walk for hours in the Historic District, dropping in on antique stores on Bull Street, Abercorn Street, and Whitaker Street. For fine dining or a late night drink with a friend, I choose Circa 1875; at a moderate price and a great atmosphere, especially if the jazz group is on, Rancho Alegre; for a late-day pick-me-up, Vinnie Van Gogo's or any café; and Gerald's Pig and Shrimp on Tybee.

3

Beaufort, Edisto & Bluffton

SEA ISLAND GEMS

THE FIELDS, CREEKS, sandy roads, and spreading marshes of the rural Low-country, the place where its history began, have once again become a center of attention. Along the coast from Charleston to Savannah, there is an increasing awareness of what the culture of the countryside, expressed in a lifetime of habits and rituals, has meant to the two great cities that bookend the region and present themselves like magnificent finished products. It is most clearly seen in the areas around Beaufort—Lady's Island, St. Helena Island, and Port Royal—on Edisto Island, and in the old village of Bluffton.

It took years for them to recover from the Civil War, the boll weevil, and a broken agricultural economy, but recover they have as places where vistas and fields are valued as much as brickwork, porches, and Palladian windows. Although Beaufort, in particular, is a destination itself, driving or bicycling across Edisto Island or St. Helena Island—through the landscape of small homes and churches, across narrow creeks, by "rabbit-box" stores, farm and fish stands, and packing houses—puts the cities and the wealth that produced them in context.

BEAUFORT

Beaufort has been a small town for a long time. Spanish and French explorers came to the area 100 years before the Pilgrims landed at Plymouth Rock; English and Scottish settlers followed. The city of Beaufort is itself on Port Royal Island, one of more than 65 islands that make up Beaufort County. Other islands accessible by car include St. Helena, Lady's, Fripp, Hilton Head, Cat, Harbor, Hunting, Coosaw, Dataw, Parris, Cane, Bray's, Lemon, and Pinckney.

Formally founded in 1711, Beaufort was a frontier settlement and trading center, attacked at times by Yemassee Indians, beset with illness, and populated by the scrupulous and unscrupulous. Resources were plentiful: Beaufort's outlying lands sustained dense forests, which gave up shipbuilding timber and naval stores; vast tracts of land suitable for raising cattle and crops like corn, potatoes, indigo,

LEFT: The docks on Daufuskie Island.   SC Lowcountry Tourism Commission

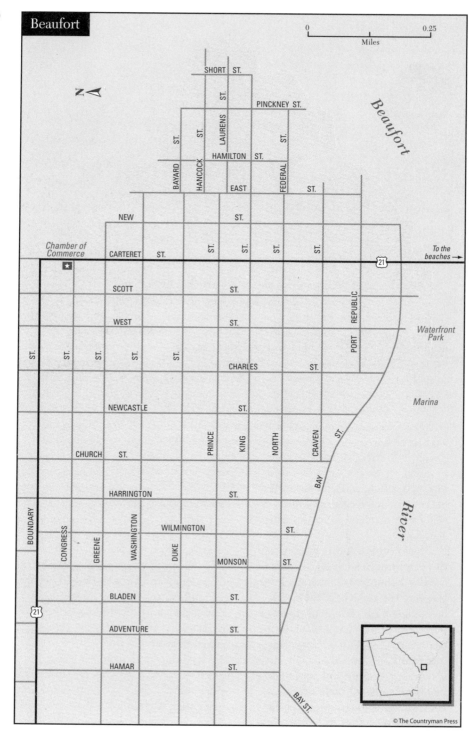

Beaufort

0   0.25
Miles

SHORT ST.

PINCKNEY ST.

LAURENS ST.

HAMILTON ST.

BAYARD ST.

HANCOCK ST.

FEDERAL ST.

EAST ST.

NEW ST.

Chamber of Commerce

CARTERET ST.

SCOTT ST.

WEST ST.

CHARLES ST.

NEWCASTLE ST.

PRINCE

KING

NORTH

CRAVEN

CHURCH ST.

HARRINGTON ST.

BOUNDARY

CONGRESS

GREENE

WASHINGTON

WILMINGTON ST.

DUKE

MONSON ST.

BLADEN ST.

ADVENTURE ST.

HAMAR ST.

ST.

REPUBLIC

PORT

BAY ST.

Beaufort

River

Waterfront Park

Marina

To the beaches →

© The Countryman Press

The Green in Beaufort's Point neighborhood, rimmed by antebellum homes, is protected as open space. Peter Loftus

rice, and cotton; and rich marshes to feed fowl and game. The maze of waterways provided fish and shellfish in abundance.

Beaufort was bustling even before the American Revolution, although the first boom came immediately after the war. The stability of the newly independent country, the increase in population (both slave and free), the southward migration of New England merchants and families, and, perhaps above all, the successful cultivation of highly prized long-staple Sea Island cotton and the development of the cotton gin near Savannah lit the fuse. An explosion of wealth launched Beaufort's heyday. It was a time of building

A place that ever was lived in is like a fire that never goes out. It flares up, it smolders for a time, it is fanned or smothered by circumstance, but its being is intact, forever fluttering within it, the result of some original ignition. Sometimes it gives out glory, sometimes its little light must be sought out to be seen, small and tender as a candle flame, but as certain.

—*From* The Eye of the Story: Selected Essays and Reviews *by Eudora Welty (New York: Vintage International, 1944, 1990)*

houses and churches in town and developing cotton plantations and plantation households on the islands.

A visitor can see the legacies of this period throughout Beaufort, particularly in a neighborhood called The Point, an astonishing collection of houses and gardens embowered by live oaks. Standing in Beaufort's Waterfront Park, it is easy to imagine a 19th-century scene come to life as dozens of schooners, bateaux, and cottonbox barges, brimming with crops, timber, mail, cotton, animals, passengers, produce, and the latest in English fashion and furniture, load or unload goods. There was a lot of activity, for like other societies made newly rich, Beaufort's had a taste for luxury and indulged it.

That changed abruptly. In another time and place, the shelling of a nearby federal fort (in this case Fort Sumter), and the federal response to it, might have produced a shred of hesitation as to the wisdom of the secessionist rebellion. Not so in Beaufort: With great surprise on November 7, 1861, white residents took flight—leaving hot food on the table, the story goes—from Yankee troops who had swiftly demolished the Confederate port defenses at Bay Point.

Thus the occupation began. Soon the grand old houses were being used as hospitals and headquarters. The area was under military command. Pickets were

Sea Island cotton planters also kept homes in Beaufort to use during the hot summer months. Peter Loftus

There is something very sad about these fine deserted houses. Ours has Egyptian marble mantels, gilt cornice and centre-piece in parlor, and bath-room, with several wash-bowls set in different rooms. The force-pump is broken and all the bowls and their marble slabs smashed to get out the plated cocks. . . . Bureaus, commodes, and wardrobes are smashed in, as well as door panels, to get out the contents of the drawers and lockers, which I suppose contained some wine and ale, judging by the broken bottles lying about. The officers saved a good many pianos and other furniture and stored it in the jail for safe-keeping. But we kindle our fires with chips of polished mahogany, and I am writing on my knee with a piece of flower-stand across them for a table, sitting on my camp bedstead.

—*Edward S. Philbrick* to his wife in Brookline, MA. Written from Beaufort, Mar. 9, 1862 (from Letters from Port Royal 1862–1868, *Elizabeth Ware Pearson*, ed. *[New York: Arno Press, 1969])*

posted at the outskirts of town and along creeks and boat landings: Some on guard duty watched the smoke of rebel campfires across the water. Plantations were turned over to regiments who appropriated the livestock and horses, the liquor, the furniture, the wagons, and the food crops.

By April 1862, the first wave of Northern abolitionists had arrived with a mandate to live in and manage the plantations and teach the former slaves to read and write, to "prepare them for freedom." Their enterprise, which was funded by private missionary societies in the North and carried out with the approval of the federal government, came to be called the Port Royal Experiment. In a sense this was an old-time Peace Corps, in which idealistic, mostly young men and women volunteered to assist a cause they believed in under conditions of definite hardship. Their efforts had an impact on lives of freedmen that resonates today, in particular at Penn Center on St. Helena Island, still an important institution for education and empowerment.

In the years following the Civil War, promises made were usually promises broken. Some former slaves were given land; some bought tracts communally; some worked the old fields under a new owner. A nascent phosphate mining industry provided jobs for a while, but it eventually collapsed. The terrible hurricane of 1893, in which some 5,000 islanders died, soured Sea Island soil for fine cotton plants. The scourge of the boll weevil in the 1920s dimmed the last hope of large-scale cotton production. Commercial truck farming and a seafood processing industry eventually took its place. Photographs from the early 1900s and those taken even as late as 1936 by employees of the Farm Security Administration—Walker Evans and Marion Post Wolcott among them—showed islanders dressed in rags and living in shacks with matted palmetto fronds for roofs, and the large houses in town on the far side of shabby gentility. These were the years of unpaved roads and bare feet and few cars, when white people were "too poor to paint, too proud to whitewash." In 1969, Beaufort County was still one of the poorest counties in the United States, the focus of a Hunger Tour by several U.S. senators.

It is hard to believe that today's downtown Beaufort ever suffered reverses.

The paint doesn't dare peel. It has been discovered, but retains a small-scale charm and an ongoing, robust dialogue among residents about the twin goals of growth and preservation. At the heart of the matter is how to develop new homes and small-scale commercial areas by filling in parts of the old downtown contained in the 304-acre National Historic Landmark District. Beaufort has become a laboratory for the ideas of New Urbanism and is now a destination not only for tourists interested in history but also for planners from around the country trying to understand how to invent new places on the scaffolding of the old without causing gentrification and displacement in historic African American neighborhoods or sacrificing open space to increased density.

The nearby village of Port Royal (www.portroyal.org or www.oldvillageport royal.com) retains its open feel where the main thoroughfare, Paris Avenue, runs from Ribaut Road to the now-shuttered port of Port Royal, where a left turn at its end leads to The Sands, a public beach that attracts fishermen and hunters of fossilized shark teeth. There is also a wooden viewing structure that offers excellent views of Battery Creek and Parris Island. Walking trails of historic sites and the Cypress Wetlands path are easily accessed—parking is widely available—and worth spending an hour touring, followed up by visiting the town's several boutiques and restaurants. The websites have a useful interactive map and schedule of annual events, which are still delightfully funky, including free street concerts.

The area has also had its Hollywood moments: Two of native son Pat Conroy's novels have been filmed here, *The Great Santini* and *The Prince of Tides*, as well as *The Big Chill, Forces of Nature,* and (on the islands) *Daughters of the Dust* and Ron and Natalie Daise's acclaimed TV series for children *Gullah Gullah Island.*

A new arts and cultural app with all the features of a classic guide—including GPS maps and links to recommended reading and pictures, all cross-referenced to cost, geography, and activities—is available from iTunes. Search for BeaufortSC 365. Its author is Lisa Annalouise Rentz, an artist and educator who works for ARTworks, the local nonprofit arts council. And even if you're doing more exploring than cooking, you can pick up coffee, juices, or finger foods at two excellent weekly farmers' markets in downtown Beaufort (Wednesday afternoons) and Port Royal (Saturday mornings).

GETTING THERE

Beaufort is 65 miles from Charleston, 45 miles from Savannah, and 30 miles from Hilton Head. The easiest route by air is via the Savannah/Hilton Head International Airport (912-964-0514; www.savannahairport.com), which is served by American Airlines, Delta, Jet Blue, United Express, and US Airways, and all major car rental agencies. From Charleston, access Beaufort from US 17 to US 21; from Savannah (and other points north and south) via well-marked exits on I-95; from Hilton Head, via US 278 to SC 170. Amtrak (1-800-872-7245; www.amtrak.com) passes through Yemassee, about 30 miles north of Beaufort. One northbound and one southbound train stop each day. For cab transportation to Beaufort, contact Yellow Cab (1-866-319-9646), Happy Taxi Cab Co. (843-575-5000), or ADR Taxi (843-726-5191). Rates are about $80, and it's best to schedule in advance. Greyhound (1-800-231-2222) stops in Beaufort several times a day. Rental cars are available in Beaufort. For more detailed information, see Chapter Five, *Information.*

The beautiful Beaufort Inn at night. Beaufort Regional Chamber VCB (Banker Optical Media)

Lodging

Best places to stay in Beaufort, and what you'll find nearby . . .

The WPA Guide to the Palmetto State, first published in 1941, indicates the presence of three hotels in Beaufort and a number of "tourist homes" where guests could stay. Then the preferred season was spring, although beginning in the 1920s, there was an informal "winter colony" of artists, playwrights, and others who liked the laid-back town. Fall brought sportsmen from the north who hunted and fished in several vast private preserves, which by the 1940s claimed up to one-third of the acreage in Beaufort County.

Today, the visitor in the next room might be a painter, a fly-fisherman, a honeymooning couple, or a member of a wedding party. There are luxury inns and several topnotch B&Bs to choose from—quite a selection for a small town—but do ask ahead about children as guests, rules about pets, and cancellation policies. Smoking is generally permitted outside and wireless Internet connections are common. Beach chairs and bicycles are available for your outings. If you are visiting for a week or more, the website www.vrbo.com lists homes and villas for rent by owner. The regional visitor bureau hosts its own pages at www.beaufortsc.org and is the best place to start your research.

Beaufort Inn (843-379-4667 or 1-888-522-0250; www.beaufortinn .com), 809 Port Republic St., Beaufort, SC 29902. Expensive–Very expensive. Trimmed in vines and rimmed with trees and flowering shrubbery, this Victorian clapboard building with jutting bays and porches owns its busy corner.

There's nothing but luxury inside: long hallways covered in plush carpet, chandeliers, and a vivid decorating style characterized by antiques, patterned wallpapers, draperies and soft curtains, and carefully hidden modern amenities. There are several adjoining cottages with suites, with more on the drawing board in 2014, and a new loft space increases your options. A good choice for a family or larger groups. Southern Graces Bistro, a catering company based at the inn, is noted for its indulgent Sunday brunch.

Beaufort's stylish City Loft Hotel.
Courtesy City Loft Hotel

Beaulieu House at Cat Island (843-770-0303 or 1-866-814-7833; www.beaulieuhouse.com), 3 Sheffield Crt., Beaufort, SC 29907. Expensive. Vibrant Caribbean pinks and greens distinguish this property, including a main house and a cottage that sleeps five on Cat Island, about a 10-minute drive from Beaufort overlooking the Intracoastal Waterway and adjacent to Sanctuary Golf Club.

City Loft Hotel (843-379-5638; www.citylofthotel.com), 301 Carteret St., Beaufort, SC 29902. Expensive. A boutique lodging with 23 rooms on two floors, a fitness center, magazine stand and coffee shop, and attentive concierge service. It's the hippest lodging in town, with elegant details like foam memory beds, flat-screen televisions (even in the bathrooms), walk-in showers, and sleek workstations. Located one block from the Beaufort River and within shouting distance of three excellent restaurants, City Loft is a sophisticated departure from its peers. Guests have golf, tennis, and pool privileges at Sanctuary Golf Club at Cat Island. Pets are welcome in some rooms.

Cuthbert House Inn (843-521-1315 or 1-800-327-9275; www.cuthberthouseinn.com), 1203 Bay St., Beaufort, SC 29902. Expensive–Very expensive. The Cuthbert House has seen its share of excitement, and its architecture tells the tale. It was moved from its original site in 1810, embellished with fine Federal-period woodcarving, served as headquarters of Union General Rufus Saxton during the federal blockade, and then enlarged with Victorian additions (sunporches and bays). Guest rooms (nine in all) include two one-bedroom suites on the ground level and parlor suites. Its great site on the Beaufort River bluff makes the full Southern breakfast, afternoon tea, evening coffee, or simply lounging a pleasure.

Greyhound Flats (843-379-4667 or 1-888-522-0250; www.greyhoundflats.com), 210 Scott St., Beaufort SC 29902. Expensive–Very expensive. Beaufort natives, whose family jewelry and fine china store is a popular Bay Street business, converted the old bus station into two ingeniously designed suites that manage to fit two queen beds and two foldout single beds which double as chairs in a comfortable living area, along with a kitchen nook, access to a washer/dryer, and bathrooms with roll-in showers. Tucked away in the core downtown district.

North Street Inn (843-986-1126; www.northstreetinn.com), 1411 North St., Beaufort, SC 29902. Moderate.

Three guest rooms in a restored 1910 Queen Anne home located a block from the Beaufort River in the Historic District. Queen beds with private baths and a full gourmet breakfast. Rhett House Inn (843-524-9030 or 1-888-480-9530; www.rhetthouseinn .com), 1009 Craven St., Beaufort, SC 29902. Expensive–Very expensive. This is Beaufort's gold standard for inns, started by a couple who left their careers in New York's fashion business, but brought their taste and attention to detail with them. The main house, circa 1820, is only steps from the waterfront and full of sunlight and breezes. Furnished with antiques and comfortable chairs, prints, and vases of fresh flowers, flanked in the back by a garden and on the side by a courtyard fountain. Many of its 10 rooms have fireplaces or Jacuzzi tubs. The upstairs and downstairs porches are dreamy places to read or have afternoon tea and pastries. The seven annex rooms have private porches and entrances, and are just as inviting. Full breakfast, including homemade breads and muffins, is included, as are evening hors d'oeuvres. Guest privileges are also extended to Sanctuary Golf Club.

Sea Island Inn (843-522-2090 or 1-800-528-1234; www.sea-island-inn .com), 1015 Bay St., Beaufort, SC 29902. Moderate. Conveniently located on Beaufort's main street, the 43-unit Best Western has a pool, exercise room, and outdoor patio tables. Continental breakfast is served in the lobby.

Two Suns Inn (843-522-1122 or 1-800-532-4244; www.twosunsinn .com), 1705 Bay St., Beaufort, SC 29902. Expensive–Very expensive. Facing the Beaufort River at one of its prettiest points, just as it turns the bend and heads away from town, this former residence—now a six-room inn—dates from 1917. The room's decor reflects Victorian, Oriental, and country themes. Rates include a full breakfast.

National chain motels are well represented in Beaufort. A list of some of them follows. It's a good idea to make reservations in advance, as they are often booked by family members of the graduating classes (many each year) of "boot camp" recruits from the Parris Island Marine Corps Recruit Depot.

Best Inn (843-524-3322), 2448 Boundary St., Beaufort.

Days Inn (843-524-1551), 1660 Ribaut Rd., Port Royal.

Hampton Inn (843-986-0600), 2342 Boundary St., Beaufort.

Hilton Garden Inn (843-379-9800), 1500 Queen St., Beaufort.

Quality Inn at Town Center (843-524-2144), 2001 Boundary St., Beaufort.

FARTHER AFIELD IN THE BEAUFORT AREA

Fripp Island Resort (843-838-1558 or 1-888-741-8974; www.frippislandresort .com), 2119 Sea Island Pkwy., Harbor Island, SC 29920. Fripp is a private, 3,000-acre island bordered by an ocean beach about 35 minutes by car from downtown. It's a low-key residential community with several golf courses, tennis facilities, biking trails, pools, informal restaurants, and a marina. Activity programs in the summer keep children busy. Rental properties are rated in four categories, from deluxe on down, and vary in price from single family homes to townhouse units, in locations on the ocean, marsh, and internal sites. Weekly rates in the summer range from $1,700 to $5,000. Rentals through the resort enable renters to use resort facilities. If you rent properties privately, your access to amenities may be limited.

Harbor Island Rentals (843-838-4800 or 1-800-553-0251; www.harborisland-sc.com), 2123-B Sea Island Pkwy., Harbor Island, SC 29920. Harbor Island is a small gated community with a pool, tennis courts, and 3-mile beach. Oceanfront homes start at $3,000 for a week in summer; homes with a view of the marsh or creek from $1,850.

Palm Key (843-726-6524; www.palmkey.com), 330 Coosaw Wy.,
Ridgeland, SC 29936. The idea at Palm Key is to enjoy the outdoor, nonoceanfront life of the Lowcountry—crabbing, fishing, kayaking, hiking, fossil-hunting, bird-watching—by slowing down and taking notice, either with a guide or on your own. No television or telephones; attractive, fully equipped one- to five-bedroom cottages cost $165 to $675 per night. Families welcome; handicap access in four cottages and pets allowed in five.

Dining
Taste of the town . . . local restaurants, cafés, bars, bistros, etc.

For a town of about 11,000, there are some very good restaurants as well as several moderately priced or more informal ones with outdoor seating overlooking the river. Chefs tweak the South's favorite dishes, starting with fresh shrimp, fish, and oysters, and have become ardent consumers of locally grown greens and other produce from island farms that operate nearly year-round. Tomatoes are a prominent cash crop in late spring and early summer, and are widely featured at that time, but it's also possible to find traditional ingredients used at the peak of the season, like shad roe from the Edisto River, strawberries, blueberries and melons, Carolina dove, venison, and pork BBQ.

If you find something you especially like, look for the recipe in *Sea Island Seasons*, a cookbook published by the Beaufort County Open Land Trust, a local nonprofit land preservation group. It is available in stores, or by contacting the trust at P.O. Box 75, Beaufort, SC 29902. Within its covers you'll find out how to make such Lowcountry

specialties as Frogmore Stew (sausage, corn-on-the-cob, potatoes, and shrimp in broth); shrimp paste (a spread that retains the delicate, sweet flavor of fresh shrimp); bread-and-butter pickles; and lemon chess pie (the secret ingredient is cornmeal).

Breakwater (843-379-0052; www.breakwatersc.com), 203 Carteret St. Open Mon.–Sat. for dinner. Expensive–Very expensive. Executive chefs Gary Lang and Elizabeth Shaw have nurtured and expanded their restaurant from its original storefront to a few stunning, modern rooms and a beautiful bar that is the most interesting night scene in town. The atmosphere is sophisticated without being stuffy, so it makes sense that the menu is, too. You can create an informal meal from tapas plates, or go the distance with quail or filet mignon. Local farmers and fishermen supply Breakwater, which has encouraged a locavore movement. Reservations are recommended, but it's also possible to drop by for dessert and a glass of wine from their lengthy list.

11th Street Dockside (843-524-7433; www.11thstreetdockside.com), 1699 11th St. W., Port Royal. Open daily for dinner. Moderate–Expensive. A casual family restaurant on Battery Creek in the old village of Port Royal, where shrimp boats tie up and the sunsets pour color into the sky. The menu offers fried, steamed, and broiled seafood specialties, as well as steak and pasta. No reservations, so expect a wait. Dinner begins at 4:30 PM. Lady's Island Dockside (843-379-3288; www .11thstreetdockside.com), 71 Sea Island Pkwy., Lady's Island, is its sister restaurant just over the downtown Beaufort bridge on Factory Creek.

Emily's Restaurant and Tapas Bar (843-522-1866; www.beaufort restaurant.com), 906 Port Republic St. Open daily for dinner. Expensive. The tapas menu changes daily and can be as simple as seafood with a light sauce or a cold vegetable plate with a Middle Eastern dip. The small restaurant is narrow, dark, and cozy, attracting local businesspeople for drinks or informal meals, as well as boaters cruising through on the Intracoastal Waterway. A busy bar scene makes it a good place for a light, late meal.

Griffin Market (843-524-0240; www.griffinmarket.com), 403 Carteret St. Open for lunch and dinner (until 9 PM) Tues.–Sat. and dinner on Sun. Very expensive. Seasonal offerings in the Northern Italian style with four courses, served in a quiet, modest setting where the food is the star. For lunch, try the pumpkin lasagna, white bean soup, or kale pasta. Primi offerings for dinner include the roasted cauliflower soup with black truffle and porcini mushroom cream; for your Secondi, shrimp poached in a tomato, caramelized onion, and pancetta sauce over polenta. Don't miss the hazelnut cake for dessert. Reservations a must.

Old Bull Tavern (843-379-2855), 205 West St. Dinner Tues.–Sat. 5 PM–

Beaufort's Bay Street and its waterfront restaurants are the heart of this small town.

Saltus River Grill in Beaufort. Beaufort Regional Chamber VCB (Banker Optical Media)

midnight (very lively late-dining scene) Moderate–Expensive. The favorite pub of Beaufort's growing arts community and anyone who enjoys handcrafted cocktails and menus that change daily, as do various quotes on overhead boards. Its long, narrow layout puts the bar on the right and tables in the remaining space, with a few in the back if you want a quieter experience, but the whole point is friendly congestion and an abundance of regulars and dedicated staff. Duck, lamb, seafood, a renowned burger of local grass-fed beef, and bar snacks like wasabi-deviled eggs and bruschetta or tapenade keep customers coming. Without reservations, you can expect to wait after 6:30 PM, so book early.

Plums (843-525-1946; plums restaurant.com), 904 Bay St. Open daily for lunch and dinner. Moderate–Expensive. Plums is still the most casual and popular place to eat lunch in Beaufort, including taking a spot at the old-fashioned oyster bar. Hot sandwiches like grilled turkey or Reuben, chicken salad, and homemade soups are menu favorites; there's peanut butter and jelly for the kids. A lively 30-ish nighttime crowd spills onto the outdoor porch, nicely heated in chillier months. Live music a couple of times a week.

Saltus River Grill (843-379-3474; www.saltusrivergrill.com), 802 Bay St. Open daily for dinner. Expensive–Very expensive. Located on the Waterfront Park with a spacious outdoor deck and comfortable seating, this big, upscale restaurant takes its cues from urban restaurants housed in repurposed commercial buildings where exposed ductwork meets linen tablecloths. Full sushi and raw bar as well as grilled fish and organic beef.

Wren Bistro (843-524-9463; www.wrenbistroandbar.com), 210 Carteret St. Open Mon.–Sat. for lunch and dinner. There's a nice price range on the menu, from salads and sandwiches at lunch to a fuller dinner menu, and it's one of the few restaurants with several vegetarian options. The food is simply prepared and beautifully presented, and the surroundings, basically an L-shaped room punctuated by alcoves, are a mix of sleekly manufactured materials and fabrics or wall coverings that look as if they came off the beach. It's a sweet spot where a meal feels special but not too expensive. Service can be slow, and reservations are recommended.

RESTAURANTS ON ST. HELENA ISLAND

Whether you're on your way to Hunting Island State Park or the beach resorts—or are touring St. Helena Island, Fort Fremont, and Penn Center—you have good, nontouristy options in all price ranges and unique venues. The emphasis is on local sourcing. They are located on US 21, 7 to 12 miles from Beaufort.

Bella Luna (843-838-3188; www.bellalunacafesc.com), 859 Sea Island Pkwy. Open Mon.–Sat. for breakfast, lunch, and dinner. Moderate. A family-operated restaurant with simple Italian fare, lightly sauced. Blackboard specials reflect what's come in at the docks or from the surrounding farms that day. Warm and unpretentious, it's a good value with friendly staff. Lots of locals order to-go from the bar, especially the thin-crust pizza and Italian wedding soup.

Foolish Frog (843-838-9300; www.thefoolishfrog.com), 846 Sea Island Pkwy. Open daily for lunch and dinner; Sun. for brunch. Moderate–Very expensive. A small, exuberant restaurant with a deck out back (for informal jams and scheduled perform-

ers) as well as an inside performance area (for scheduled performers). It is usually packed. Southern staples like ribs, grilled fish, steak, and shellfish are often prepared with an Asian twist by a veteran chef who is attuned to unusual pairings.

Gullah Grub (843-838-3841; www.gullahgrubs.com), 877 Sea Island Pkwy. Open Mon.–Tues. noon–6; Wed.–Fri. noon–7:30; Sun. 11:30–4:30; hours can be variable in winter, especially. Moderate. Chef Bill Green wears many hats—horseman, trainer of hunting hounds, storyteller—and his love for and appreciation of his native Gullah heritage and culture comes through in his cooking at this tiny place. Even the not-easily-surprised

Creative reuse of existing buildings turned an old post office into a new restaurant, Foolish Frog.

chef and food provocateur Anthony Bourdain featured him on his television show. Bill's instructional DVDs capture the Gullah way to roast oysters and prepare standards like red rice and greens, and he also hosts cooking classes and has a mail-order business of sauces, rubs, and chowders. His wife Sara Reynolds is, among other things, an organic farmer, educator, and inspirational community leader whose Marshview Farm and Young Farmers of the Lowcountry program provide produce and eggs to the restaurant.

Marsh Tacky's Market (843-838-2041), 2137 Sea Island Pkwy. Open for breakfast at 7 AM and throughout the day, with shortened winter hours. Their motto is "conveniently general and generally convenient" and the offerings bear it out: grilled doughnuts, many kinds of sandwiches, build-your-own subs and paninis, and frozen yogurt—to eat in or to take on a beach picnic at Hunting Island, just down the road. Carolina specialty items like books, boiled peanuts, and Lowcountry-roasted coffee line the shelves, as do craft beers, wine and ice, grills, propane, charcoal, and fresh produce. Ask about fishing charters and equestrian tours.

Shrimp Shack (843-838-2962), 1929 Sea Island Pkwy. Open Mon.–Sat. for lunch and dinner. Inexpensive. Fresh seafood from the family dock—you can see the shrimp boats—accompanied by slaw, red rice, hush puppies, and beans. Deviled crab and shrimp burgers (ground, seasoned shrimp on a bun) are specialties. You can eat upstairs on the screened-in porch or in an adjacent gazebo. The hard work of the Upton family keeps the standards high. Lunch only Nov.–Mar. No credit cards.

Sweetgrass Restaurant and Bar (843-838-2151; www.sweetgrassdataw

.com), 100 Marina Dr., Dataw Island (pick up a visitor pass at the entry gate). Open for dinner every evening except Wed.; Sun. brunch 11:30–5. Moderate–Expensive. The menu changes according to what the local farmers and fishermen bring in, but the atmosphere and view are worth a trip. If the peaches are in season, try the balsamic grilled peach salad. Reservations recommended.

FOOD PURVEYORS

More casual spots are popping up in Beaufort and Port Royal; most have wireless Internet and a relaxed style about surfing online and refilling your mug. WiFi is planned in 2014 to serve the downtown Waterfront Park, opening the option of taking your goodies with you and taking a spot on one of the many benches or low walls overlooking the river.

Bakeries/Coffeehouses

Low Country Produce Market and Café (843-322-1900; www.lowcountry produce.com), 302 Carteret St. Open daily for breakfast and lunch. This was the former Beaufort City Hall and the new owners have renovated it beautifully into a light-filled space. They serve soups, sandwiches, salads, and a daily selection of locally made sweets and breads. There's also a gourmet market selling wine and cheese, handmade and handpacked goods, oils, herbs and spices, jellies, unusual linens, and pretty paper products.

Magnolia Bakery Café (843-524-1961), 703 Congress St. A small, friendly restaurant with limited outdoor dining specializing in homemade bread and soup, desserts, and snacks. Breakfast and lunch. Vegetarian-friendly. Beer and wine available.

Palm & Moon Bagel Co. (843-

Gathering and Corn-Shelling, St. Helena Island

When they go into the field to work, the women tie a bit of string or some vine round their skirts just below the hips, to shorten them, often raising them nearly to the knees; then they walk off with their heavy hoes on their shoulders, as free, strong, and graceful as possible. The prettiest sight is the corn-shelling on Mondays, when the week's allowance, a peck a hand, is given out at the corn-house by the driver. They all assemble with their baskets, which are shallow and without handles, made by themselves of the palmetto and holding from a half a peck to a bushel. The corn is given out in the ear, and they sit about or kneel on the ground, shelling it with cleared corn-cobs. Here there are four enormous logs hollowed at one end, which serve as mortars, at which two can stand with their rude pestles, which they strike up and down alternately. . . . They separate the coarse and fine parts after it is ground by shaking the grits in their baskets: the finest they call corn-flour and make hoe-cake of, but their usual food is the grits, the large portion, boiled as hominy and eaten with clabber.

—Harriet Ware, a young abolitionist and teacher from Boston who lived and taught at Coffin Point Plantation, St. Helena Island, to her parents, May 22, 1862 (from Letters from Port Royal 1862–1868, Elizabeth Ware Pearson, ed. [New York: Arno Press, 1969])

379-9300), 221 Scott St. Bagels baked in-house, several coffee blends, sandwiches, and homemade soup every day. Cheerful folks behind the counter and a parade of local businesspeople and families stopping by.

Candy and Ice Cream
Chocolate Tree (843-524-7980; www .thechocolatetree.us), 507 Carteret St. A family-owned, award-winning shop selling many different kinds of chocolates, truffles, and dipped fruits made on the premises, plus candy-making accessories, gift boxes, jelly beans, cards, and gifts.
Southern Sweets Ice Cream Parlor (843-379-0798), 917 Bay St., in the Old Bay Marketplace. Looks like an old-fashioned soda fountain with a long counter, and serves the Greenwood brand, a rich South Carolina ice cream.

Yo Yo's (843-548-0300; www .beaufortfrozenyogurt.com), 722 Bay St. Add toppings such as fruit, nuts, or candy to frozen yogurt to create your own treat or indulge in smoothies and other chilled refreshments. Eat in or in the adjacent Waterfront Park.

Delis and Faster Food
Alvin Ord's Sandwich Shop (843-524-8222), 1415 Ribaut Rd., Port Royal. Known for its home-baked bread (French or whole wheat) and delicious sandwiches. Limited indoor and outdoor seating and very crowded at lunch, but you can call ahead to order. Open until 8 PM during the week; Sat. until 6 PM.
Blackstone's Café (843-524-4330; www.blackstonescafe.com), 205 Scott St. Best breakfast in town, and nice to sit here engrossed in the morning paper. Lunch is served until 2:30.

Outpost (843-838-2508), Dataw Island Marina. Open 8–5 every day except Wed. Gourmet coffees, baked goods, gourmet-to-go items, grocery staples, beer and wine. A convenient stop for boaters.

Suzara's Kitchen (843-379-2160; www.suzaraskitchen.com), 1211 Newcastle St. Open for breakfast and lunch Mon.–Fri. Eat in or take out. House-made breakfast pastries, soups, salad, and quiches. Their market sells tea, coffee, cheese, bread, and wine.

Yes! Thai Indeed (843-986-1185; www.yesthaiindeed.com), 911 Boundary St. Perfectly simple, traditional Thai food that's inexpensive and served in a one-room restaurant that caters to local families, people coming in after the early movie, and downtown residents who forgot to food shop. Small but not a hole-in-the-wall, and they happily offer vegetarian and a range of spicy options.

Touring
Fun in the Historic District and beyond.

Several companies offer narrated tours of Beaufort's Historic District and the Sea Islands. Buggy and walking tours last 45 to 90 minutes. Guided driving tours may last two hours. CDs for self-guided tours are available at the visitor center (713 Craven St.) or The Spirit of Old Beaufort (1001 Bay St.). General information can be found at the Chamber of Commerce's website: www .beaufortsc.org.

Port Royal sands boardwalk. Beaufort Regional Chamber VCB (Banker Optical Media)

BY CARRIAGE

Sea Island Carriage Company (843-525-1821) and the cleverly named Southurn Rose Buggy Tours (843-524-2900; www.southurnrose.com) depart from the Downtown Marina parking lot daily from 10 AM to 5 PM; Sun. tours depart at noon. Tours last about an hour. Adults $18, children $7.

BY FOOT

The Spirit of Old Beaufort (843-525-0459; www.thespiritofoldbeaufort .com), 1001 Bay St. Guided walking tours covering slightly different paths last about two hours and include a lantern tour at dusk. You must make reservations Mon.–Sat. to depart at 10 AM, 2, and 7. Prices start at $18 for adults, children $9.

Jon Sharp (843-575-5775; www .jonswalkinghistory.com) blends knowledge of history with storytelling skills to make Beaufort come alive on his two-hour tours. Tours cost $25 and start at 11 AM Tues.–Sat. in spring, fall, and winter.

ON ST. HELENA ISLAND

Gullah-N-Geechie Mahn Tours (843-838-7516; www.gullahngeechietours.net) run Mon.–Sat. at 9:45 AM and 1:45 PM. Adults $25, children $20. Reservations required. The Spirit of Old Beaufort (under "By Foot") also offers van tours of St. Helena that include visits to a praise house and a view of a plantation house at the end of a 0.5-mile avenue of oaks. Adults $35, children $18.

If you can tear yourself away from the seductions of "the built environment," you will be rewarded by views of marshes and marine life that exist in such a pristine state in only a few places in the United States. For detailed information on tours by boat—small or large—see the Recreation section below, specifically listings under "Boat Tours" and "Canoeing and Kayaking."

Culture

Great places to see and things to do.

As Beaufort has grown, so have its cultural activities, both indigenous and imported. A recent addition is an international, juried film festival in February (www.beaufortfilmfestival.com).

The museums and annual house tours have gained a professional thoroughness; the University of South Carolina at Beaufort has an active exhibition and theater schedule as well as a chamber-music series and The Metropolitan Opera Live in HD on many Saturdays (www.uscbcenterfor

An island praise house.

thearts.com); and a dozen downtown art galleries coordinate open houses monthly. It may be enough to sit and watch the tide go out on a Friday night, but you don't have to.

For information about cultural organizations, self-guided tours of artists' studios and galleries, or upcoming events, contact The Arts Council of Beaufort County (843-379-2787; www.beaufortcountyarts.com), 2127 Boundary St., Beaufort, SC 29901. Annual tours of local homes and plantations in October and March are sponsored by the Historic Beaufort Foundation (843-379-3331; www.historic beaufort.org) and St. Helena Episcopal Church Women (843-524-0363; www .sthelenas1712.org).

FILM

Hwy. 21 Drive-In (843-846-4500; www.hwy21drivein.com), US 21 at Parker Dr., about 2 miles north of Beaufort.

Plaza Stadium Theatre (843-986-5806), Beaufort Plaza, SC 170. A multi-screen complex offering current releases, including those in 3-D.

University of South Carolina Beaufort Center for the Arts (843-521-4145; www.uscbcenterforthearts.com), 801 Carteret St. Presents films drawn from the best of independent and foreign sources, and the Metropolitan Opera Live HD performances, throughout the year. It is also the setting for the Beaufort International Film Festival in February, a juried showcase with several days of screenings including features, shorts, animation, and student films as well as a popular screen-writers workshop and table read. Information at www.beaufortfilmfestival.com.

HISTORIC HOMES, GARDENS & RELIGIOUS SITES

Baptist Church of Beaufort (843-524-3197; www.bcob.org), 601 Charles St. This is an 1844 Greek Revival beauty. The ceiling plasterwork and ornamented cornices seem to match—in their absolute, solid mass of decoration—the abundant self-confidence of the prosperous little town of Beaufort in its heyday.

Chapel of Ease, Land's End Rd., St. Helena Island. The ruins of this planters' church, built in the 1740s to serve worshippers far from town, are of brick and tabby, a construction material that blends oyster shells with lime, sand, and water. The site is a wonderful place for photographs—spooky in the fog or at dawn, mellow and ageless at dusk.

John Mark Verdier House Museum (843-379-6335; www.historicbeaufort .org), 801 Bay St. Tours are every 30 minutes Mon.–Sat. 10–4.The showcase property of the Historic Beaufort Foundation, saved from demolition in 1945, was built according to the Adam-influenced decoration and floor plans of the day for a local merchant around 1805. It includes a formal parlor and ballroom, ornamental fireplace friezes, carved moldings, and antiques that are original both to the family and to the period of the house. Ongoing research and an exhibit area on the ground floor provide nuanced interpretations of Beaufort and the islands. A small gift shop is on-site. Adults $10, students free.

Penn Center, York W. Bailey Museum (843-838-2474; www.penncenter .com), Martin Luther King Jr. Dr., St. Helena Island. Open Mon.–Sat. 9–4. Founded in 1862 by two Pennsylvania women as a school for the newly freed

Above & right: Tabby ruins of the Chapel of Ease, St. Helena Island, where planters worshipped in the 19th century.

slaves, Penn has remained a vital institution to promote education, self-sufficiency, and cultural expression among native islanders. In the days of segregation, it was one place where blacks and whites could meet together, as they did when the Rev. Martin Luther King Jr. planned his March on Washington. The York W. Bailey Museum holds a collection of cultural artifacts, African objects, and paintings, and sells sweetgrass baskets, quilts, and books on Gullah culture and history. The entire campus is a National Historic Landmark. Adults $5, children $3. Call for schedule of events.

Old Sheldon Church Ruins, Secondary Rd. 21, 1.7 miles north of the intersection of US 17 and US 21. Beautiful brick columns, fragile arches, and sill slabs remain from a church that was burned twice, first by the British in 1779 and then by the Union Army in 1865. It's a little temple in the woods. There's a small shaded picnic area on-site.

St. Helena's Episcopal Church (www.sthelenas1712.org), 507 Newcastle St. Open Tues.–Fri. 10–4; Sat. 10–1. This church, built of brick from England in 1724, is adorned inside with graceful columns, upstairs galleries, and tall, multi-paned windows with deep sills on which rest buckets of blossoming magnolia, daffodils, or narcissi in season. Its shaded, walled churchyard makes for a lovely stroll. See the website for information about noontime organ concerts and tours of the church and grounds.

Frissell Hall, Penn Center, St. Helena Island, where community sings and meetings celebrate a history of education and empowerment for African Americans.

The brick columns and arches of the Old Sheldon Church Ruins.   SC Lowcountry Tourism Commission

Tabernacle Baptist Church, 907 Craven St. A striking, white clapboard building with bell tower. In its churchyard lies the grave—and stands a fine bust—of Robert Smalls, who was born a slave, engineered a daring ship capture during the Civil War, and was later a congressman and significant figure in Beaufort's Reconstruction period.

MILITARY MUSEUMS & SITES

Fort Fremont Historical Park (www.fortfremont.org), Land's End, St. Helena Island. Built in 1899 to protect the coast during the Spanish-American War, the 15-acre site was recently listed on the National Register of Historic Places and an active volunteer group is working with Beaufort County to create a self-guided tour of its ruins overlooking Port Royal Sound. The view is spectacular and the natural vegetation is a classic maritime forest of oaks, palmetto, magnolia, and myrtle. Follow US 21 about 7 miles from Beaufort. Turn right at the traffic light on Martin Luther King Jr. Blvd. (it becomes Lands End Rd.) and proceed 7.75 miles to the entrance on the right.

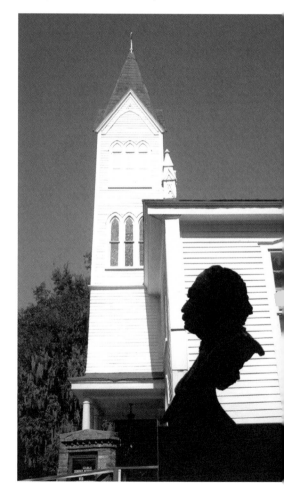

The bust of Robert Smalls outside Tabernacle Baptist Church. SC Lowcountry Tourism Commission

National Cemetery 1601 Boundary St., Beaufort. Created by President Lincoln in 1863 for victims of Southern battles, this 29-acre cemetery is the final resting place of some 9,000 Union soldiers and more than 100 Confederates. It is still in service.

Parris Island Museum (843-228-2951; parrisislandmuseum.com), Marine Corps Recruit Depot, 111 Panama St., Beaufort, SC 29902. Open daily 10–4:30; hours extended on graduation and family days. The museum showcases the history and development of the area on which the famous "boot camp" stands, from its earliest settlement through contemporary recruit training. (Artifacts on display have been recovered from the Spanish village of Santa Elena, circa 1566; from Charlesfort, a French outpost established by Jean Ribaut in 1562; and from Fort San Marcos, circa 1576. Excavation continues at these sites, located near the depot golf course.) Exhibits of uniforms, personal items, weapons, drawings, and documents

Near Fort Fremont at Land's End. SC Lowcountry Tourism Commission

trace the history of the Marine Corps in its worldwide engagements. You can also consult Platoon Books for listings of Marines. Self-guided driving tour maps are available. If you're interested in observing morning colors or a graduation (held on Fridays), contact the Douglas Visitor Center (843-228-3650; www.mcrdpi.usmc .mil). Basic hours are Mon. 7:30 AM–noon; Tues.–Thurs. 7:30 AM–4:30 PM; Fri. 7:30 AM–3 PM; extended hours during recruit graduation. You may also picnic in designated areas or have an inexpensive meal at a base restaurant, including the Officer's Club. This is an active military base. At the entrance gate be prepared to show identification, vehicle registration, and proof of vehicle insurance, and state your desire to visit the museum and visitor center. Free.

MUSIC

Hallelujah Singers (www.hallelujahsingers.com or for updated concert information see their Facebook page) Under the direction of Marlena Smalls, a superior vocalist who has earned a national reputation for her singing and acting (she was Bubba's mother in the movie *Forrest Gump*), the group performs throughout the year, often in a downtown church at the time of annual house tours; weekly during the summer at various sites.

Penn Center Community Sing (843-838-2432), P.O. Box 126, St. Helena Island, SC 29920. Community groups, quartets of senior citizens, gospel choirs, spur-of-the-moment vocalists, and soloists who deacon out lines of spirituals to the audience perform at 7:30 PM on the third Sunday of every month, Sept.–May, in Frissell Hall on the historic Penn Center campus. Call ahead or check website to confirm times. The popularity of the sings and the feelings of dignity and fellowship that characterize them are a moving testament to the pride Sea Islanders share in their culture and heritage. Contributions are welcome.

Recreation

Active pursuits in and around Beaufort.

The reliable bounty of land and sea has nourished Lowcountry residents for more than 250 years. The region's temperate weather makes pleasure of work, even digging for clams in January. These days the sportsman, the naturalist, and the Sunday painter rub elbows outdoors, and visitors can explore by powerboat, kayak, sailboat, or bicycle; with fishing pole, crab net, paintbrush, or binoculars.

Beaufort, in particular, claims the advantage over Charleston and Savannah of having its rural recreational opportunities close at hand. Informally, residents and visitors can fish or throw cast nets for shrimp at bridges and county boat landings, from the Waterfront Park, and on the marsh boardwalk at Hunting Island State Park off US 21, about a 35-minute drive from town. At the north end of Hunting Island is the Fishing Pier (843-838-7437), the state's longest at 1,120 feet, and a Nature Center open Tues.–Sat. year-round. The fee to use the pier—$5 adults, $3 children—also gets you access to the park and the nature center.

There are dozens of public boat landings within easy reach. Launching is free, and so is parking, but you're on your own—no attendants, telephones, or

View of the downtown bridge   Beaufort Regional Chamber VCB (Banker Optical Media)

restrooms. For locations, including piers and ramps, see www.bcgov.net; to see about chartering your own boat, inquire at the Downtown Marina (843-524-4422), 1006 Bay St.; sporting goods stores; or contact the Lowcountry Resort Islands and Tourism Commission (1-800-528-6870; www .southcarolinalowcountry.com), P.O. Box 615, Yemassee, SC 29945. If your recreational pursuits require clothing or equipment you didn't bring with you, see the shops listed under "Sporting Goods and Clothing" in the Shopping section.

The Port Royal Sound Foundation (www.portroyalsoundfoundation.com) is a conservation and education group that is opening a new Maritime Center on Lemon Island in 2014 which will feature exhibits and interactive programs about the natural history surrounding this huge river basin and salt marsh ecosystem. Perhaps the most significant resource for those who love the outdoors and savor its hidden beauty is the Ernest F. Hollings ACE Basin National Wildlife Refuge (843-889-3084; www.fws.gov/acebasin/), 8675 Willtown Rd., Hollywood, SC 29449—a consolidation of some 350,000 acres of marsh, creek, and forest to the north, east, and west of Beaufort. This crescent of landscape encompasses the forested, inland shore of the Ashepoo, Combahee, and Edisto Rivers and their small tributaries, and the vastness of St. Helena Sound. Not all the activity is on the water, either: From points on dry land, birders have identified more than 250 species of resident and migratory birds. To access the ACE and reach its headquarters, take SC 174 from US 17, about midway between Beaufort and Charleston, continue east through Adams Run and follow the signs to Grove House. It is open year-round from dawn to dusk. You may park and walk in; good maps are available online. Several options for visiting the ACE Basin are listed under "Boat Tours" below and its website has many ideas for nature tourism.

Hunting Island Lighthouse offers impressive views of the Atlantic and St. Helena Sound.
Beaufort Regional Chamber VCB (Banker Optical Media)

BEACH ACCESS

Hunting Island State Park (843-838-2011; www.southcarolinaparks.com/hunting island) Open daily 6–6 (until 9 during daylight saving time); adults $5, children $3. (See also entry under "Camping.") Hunting Island is eroding, and as the water reclaims it, it has taken on a haunting, wild aspect, with fallen palmettos and uprooted oaks trailing tangled roots across the beach. Parking is plentiful; there are picnic areas and bathhouses, and miles to walk at the ocean's edge. About 8 miles of bike paths and foot trails thread through its maritime forest. The 19th-century Hunting Island Lighthouse offers an expansive view of the confluence of the Atlantic Ocean and St. Helena Sound from a height of 132 feet. Lighthouse open daily 10–4:45 Mar.–Oct., until 3:45 in Nov. Admission $2. The lighthouse is subject to closure without notice for repairs.

BICYCLING

Local bicycle enthusiasts have developed cue sheets and maps for enjoyable day trips on the emerging network of linked trails from Hunting Island State Park to the ACE Basin. The trips can be from 25 to 60 miles long, and wind through scenic, rural areas and by Revolutionary War sites and movie locations. The Spanish Moss Trail (www.spanishmosstrail.com) is being developed along an old railbed of about 10 miles and winds along marshes and creeks in Beaufort, with designated access points for parking. Low Country Bicycles (843-524-9585; www.lowcountry bicycles.com), 102 Sea Island Pkwy., is a good first stop for equipment, repairs, or trail information. Barefoot Bubba's Surf Shop (843-838-9222; www.barefoot bubbasurfshop.com) 2135 Sea Island Pkwy., Harbor Island, offers rentals near the state park entrance.

The blue heron, a shy Lowcountry icon.
SC Lowcountry Tourism Commission

BIRD-WATCHING

Excellent bird-watching is available at the Bear Island Wildlife Management Area (843-844-8951), Bennett's Point Rd. off US 17 near the village of Green Pond, about 35 minutes north of Beaufort. For general birding information, visit www.carolinabirdclub.org.

BOATING

Boat Tours
A&B Fishing and Eco-Tours (843-812-1722; www.abfishcharters.com) Run by a Beaufort captain who will guide you through the marshes and rivers, or to uninhabited barrier islands. Rates are for up to six passengers: three hours $300.
   Captain Dick's River Tours (843-524-4422; www.beaufortrivertours .com) Offers cruises on the Beaufort River at 2 PM every day except Tue., with sunset cruises Tue. and Sat. at

5:45. The tour leaves from the Downtown Marina (1010 Bay St.) and lasts about 90 minutes, plenty of time to see the old houses from a different perspective and experience the sky, wind, and tidal action that define the landscape. Adults $20, children $12. More personalized trips also can be arranged (call the captain directly at 843-812-2804).

Lowcountry Wildlife Photo Tours (843-524-3037; www.southernlight.biz) Join Eric Horan, a professional photographer/master naturalist, in a group of six (maximum) to photograph the amazing array of wildlife, from waterfowl to deer, that the marsh, beach, sky, and forest offer. A two-hour tour is $130 and is scheduled according to wind, weather, and tides.

Vintage Voyages Yacht Tour (855-266-2533; www.beaufortvintagevoyages .com) Departs from the Downtown Marina (1010 Bay St.). A 1930 Elco Cruisette motors along the Beaufort waterways. Maximum six passengers at $59 per person. Departures vary seasonally, call for schedule.

Canoeing and Kayaking

Trail guides and other good information about regional paddling in the ACE Basin and nearby rivers are available at www.southcarolinalowcountry.com. The Southeast Coast Saltwater Paddling Trail (www.secoastpaddlingtrail.com) connects 800 miles of waterway from the Chesapeake Bay to the Georgia/Florida border through sections in South Carolina. Beaufort has its own 12.6-mile round-trip, self-guided trail (www.beaufortblueways.info) that runs along the Beaufort River. You can rent single or tandem kayaks—sit-on or cockpit-style—from Higher Ground (843-379-4327; www.highergroundbeaufort.com) 2121 Boundary St., Beaufort, and the Port Royal Landing Marina (843-525-6664; www.portroyal landingmarina.com), at the foot of the McTeer Bridge, Port Royal. Daily rates start at $50.

Beaufort Kayak Tours (843-525-0810; www.beaufortkayaktours.com) Half-day trips in and around Beaufort, on the barrier islands, and in the ACE Basin are suitable for beginners to experts. Adults $40, children $30. Call for times and reservations and for information on the paddling club (if you bring a kayak).

Lands End Tours (843-243-4684; www.beaufortlandsendtours.com) As you travel on US 21 to the beach you'll see, about 10 miles from town, a fanciful cottage with outdoor sculpture and stacked boats for rent by the hour, day, or weekend. Design a tour with the guides or a camping expedition, or pick up a kayak and go for the day, $30.

The Kayak Farm (843-838-2008; www.thekayakfarm.com) Guided open-sea kayaking tours launch from the beach, boat landings, and Hunting Island State park, instruction included. Trips in the rivers and marshes last about two hours and fees start at $50 per person. Single and tandem kayaks can be delivered to your vacation rental, with fees beginning at $40 for a half-day. One-hour lessons start at $30. Reservations required to manage small groups.

CAMPING

Hunting Island State Park (843-838-2011 or 1-866-345-7275; www.southcarolina parks.com/huntingisland), 2555 Sea Island Pkwy., Hunting Island, SC 29920, on US 21 about 30 minutes from Beaufort. RV and tent sites, nature trails, picnic areas, showers and dressing rooms, a store, water, and electrical hook-ups. RV sites from $23–25; $17–19 for tent sites. Reserve in advance.

Tuck in the Wood Campground (843-838-2267; www.tuckinthewood.com), 22 Tuc In De Wood Ln., St. Helena Island, SC 29920. Eighty RV and tent sites with water, electricity, cable television connections, WiFi, and shower/restroom facilities. Call for seasonal rates.

FISHING

Fishing is thickly woven into the fabric of local life. Anthropologists note its folkways—cooking, storytelling, skills, and field ingenuity—but a Lowcountry angler is best defined by his or her passion for getting on the river; getting to the river towing a boat behind a beloved, rusted fishing car; or capturing a precious invitation to spend time at one of the area's rustic fishing camps where family traditions reign. A book written in 1856, *Carolina Sport by Land and Water* by Beaufortonian William Elliott, can be read as a nearly modern account.

Today's enthusiast can choose freshwater or saltwater sites; fish from piers, bridges, boats, banks, or the beach; or troll an artificial offshore reef. Saltwater fly-fishing is a popular specialty. The catch can range from small bream, porgy, and spot—of the family commonly known as "sailor's choice"—to flounder and big game fish like wahoo, drum, shark, and cobia. In general, the best part of the season extends from April through November, but small panfish remain active beyond those dates. You may also fish in the lagoon on Hunting Island by using light tackle with shrimp and worms for bait.

Licenses are required for freshwater fishing and for saltwater fishing under certain conditions. Most visitors interested in recreational fishing will not need one. For information on licenses and size and catch limits, see the South Carolina Wildlife and Marine Resources Department website (www.dnr.sc.gov).

For a comprehensive map indicating recreational fishing facilities in the Lowcountry, including marinas, boat landings, bridges and catwalks, shellfish grounds, and offshore reefs, contact the Lowcountry Resort Islands and Tourism Commission (1-800-528-6870; P.O. Box 615, Yemassee, SC 29945) or visit www.beaufortusa.com.

Awesome sunsets are common in summer.
SC Lowcountry Tourism Commission

A sport-fishing charter can take you to the Gulf Stream or to any of the dozen or so artificial reefs offshore. More than 150 years ago, the first artificial reefs used in this area were approximately 6-foot-high, log, hutlike structures that were sunk to attract sheepshead. Today's reefs are far more elaborate affairs built of tires, concrete debris, and cast-off military machinery that attract dozens of species. Given that much of the sea floor off the coast is sandy, these reefs provide the hard substrate necessary to create a "live bottom" of invertebrates, small fish, coral, crabs, and sponges. They are active feeding stations for the big fish, and experienced guides know them well. Trips of this sort generally take a full day. Trips closer to shore, in smaller boats, can be easily enjoyed by the half-day.

A listing of some of the many charter boat services available follows. Rods, reels, bait, and tackle are provided; lunch or snacks are usually available, but you should check in advance; boats are equipped with safety equipment and licenses; all but the smallest have heads. It is wise to bring sunscreen, windbreakers, and a towel.

Many charters will design a trip to suit your particular interest or prepare a boat for a fishing tournament. If stormy weather is forecast, call ahead to confirm that the trip is on. Also check reservation, deposit, and cancellation policies.

Bay Street Outfitters (843-524-5250; www.baystreetoutfitters.com), 825 Bay St. Visitors who are experienced in the art of fly-fishing, as well as those who are rank beginners, can find experienced guides, instruction (Redfish School one-day seminars cost $200 per person; private fly casting lessons are $50/hour), and a full line of Orvis outfits, accessories, and specialty rods here. Guided inshore charters (fly and light tackle) for up to two people, from four to eight hours, cost $400–550 and $50 for an extra angler. Licenses are not required on the charters; drinks and

Sport-fishing charters can be found at many local marinas. Beaufort Regional Chamber VCB (Banker Optical Media)

equipment are provided. Keep up with news and photos of the big catches by reading a local guide's blog (beaufortflyfishing.blogspot.com).

Capt. Eddie Netherland (843-838-3782; www.fishingcapteddie1.com) Off-shore and inshore trips by the day and half-day on a 17-foot boat for two passengers, or a 27-foot boat for six. Offshore rates for four passengers begin at $480 per half-day. Half-day inshore trips start at $300 and two-hour shelling trips to barrier islands start at $200. Trips to the Gulf Stream are $1,400. Charters leave from the Fripp Island Marina. No credit cards.

Cast Away Fishing Charters (843-322-1043; www.beaufortcastawaycharter .com) A 19-foot Carolina Skiff is the classic inshore craft that leads you to cobia, flounder, and redfish. The captain practices catch-and-release, but you can have it cleaned for taking home. Rates start at $350 for three anglers, with $50 for a fourth.

Sea Wolf VI (843-525-1174; www .seawolfcharter.com) Retired Army Major Wally Phinney Jr. is your guide. Deep-sea fishing or cruising, by the day or half-day, aboard a 35-foot boat motoring from 10 to 50 miles offshore. For five people, rates are from $545–1,250. He has more than 60 years of experience in local waters. Passengers are asked not to smoke.

Retired Army Major Wally Phinney Jr. will be your fishing guide on *Sea Wolf VI*.
SC Lowcountry Tourism Commission

FITNESS, WELLNESS, AND SPAS

Aqua Med Spa and Salon (843-522-9179; www.aquamedspaandsalon.com), 2206 Mossy Oaks Rd., Port Royal. Full salon services as well as facials, deep massage, and body wraps.

Dancing Dogs Yoga (843-263-5856; www.dancingdogsyoga.com), 1211 Newcastle St. Call ahead to inquire about class level and per-visit fees.

Omni Health and Fitness Center (843-379-2424; www.omniofbeaufort.com), 1505 Salem Rd. Full range of exercise equipment and programs in a new facility. Day passes available.

Wardle Family YMCA of Beaufort County (843-522-9622; www.ymca beaufortcounty.com), 1801 Richmond Ave., Port Royal. Pool, gym, classes. Membership in another YMCA allows guest registration.

GOLF

The Lowcountry probably has more golf courses per person than any other region in the country, and more with holes offering views of the ocean or marsh, or of deer, heron, and the occasional alligator. Weather allows for year-round play and late-afternoon starting times in the summer. The high-season months are in fall and spring, so it is wise to schedule your playing time well in advance.

Carts are required at peak playing times on some courses. Special prices are often posted for midday tee times in the height of summer. Resort play at Dataw, Callawassie, and Spring Island is usually limited to overnight guests. Golf packages that include lodging are numerous, so ask about them. Club rentals and instruction are available at all courses. Greens fees/cart rentals reflect 2013 prices.

Public and Semiprivate Courses

Fripp Island (1-855-602-5893; www.frippislandresort.com), Fripp Island. Two courses on the rim of the Atlantic and Fripp Inlet. Ocean Point Course, a links-style par 72, is a George Cobb course with five sets of tees. The Ocean Creek Course, the first designed by Davis Love III, is a par 71 that winds through the marshes and interior wetlands. Yardage from 4,884 to 6,613. Walking is an option at both courses. Since they lie within a gated community, you must be a resort guest or renting property of a club member to play.

Gifford's Golf (843-521-9555), 30 Grober Hill Rd., Burton. A friendly, nine-hole course with driving range and pro shop. Fees start at $10.50 for nine holes.

Legends at Parris Island (843-228-2240; www.thelegendspi.com), Marine Corps Recruit Depot, Parris Island. Par 72 course redesigned by Clyde Johnston in 2000, now ranked among top 10 military courses. Tees from 5,700 yards to 6,900 yards. Cart or walk, $30–44 for visitors.

Sanctuary Golf Club at Cat Island (843-524-0300; www.sanctuarygolfcat island.com), 8 Waveland Ave., Beaufort. George Cobb's original design, refined by

Alligators like to be left alone on the golf course or in the swamp. Peter Loftus

Jeff Brauer in 2008. Par 71 with four sets of tees: 4,970 yards to 6,625 yards. The
Grill & Pub is open for lunch and dinner daily. Green fees for nonresidents are
$60, with lower rates for afternoon and twilight play.

BEAUFORT, EDISTO & BLUFFTON

HORSEBACK RIDING

Camelot Farms (843-838-3938; www.camelotfarmshorses.com) Located on a
60-acre farm on St. Helena Island, offers coastline and plantation rides that last
up to two hours ($50–75 per rider) along sandy roads and the beach overlooking
St. Helena Sound and the Atlantic Ocean.

TENNIS

Public courts, some of which are lit for night play, are located on Boundary Street
across from the National Cemetery; at Battery Creek Road and Southside Boulevard; and in the Port Royal Park on Paris Avenue in the village of Port Royal. Free.
No reservations required.

Shopping

Shops and markets
that will pique your interest.

ANTIQUES

Antiques and Such (843-322-0880),
802 Bay St. Two local businesswomen
have enlarged a popular store with
antique furniture (from sets to individual pieces), reproductions, glassware
and silver, and the odd whatnot.

Collector's Antique Mall (843-524-2769), 102C Sea Island Pkwy. A large
space is apportioned to dozens of vendors who sell everything from buttons to
bureaus. Just across the Beaufort River on Lady's Island.

What's In Store (843-838-7473), 853 Sea Island Pkwy., St. Helena Island.
Large-scale furniture and vases, garden ornaments, with some English pine furniture and antique reproductions.

BOOKS

Beaufort Bookstore (843-525-1066; www.beaufortbookssc.com), 2127 Boundary
St. A large selection and wide variety of books, from best-selling fiction and non-
fiction to military and Lowcountry favorites.

McIntosh Book Shoppe (843-524-1119), 917 Bay St. New and used books on
South Carolina you'll find nowhere else. Civil War albums, rare and antique volumes, as well as local writers and local history.

CLOTHING

Beaufort Clothing Co. (843-524-7118), 723 Bay St. Everything men and women
need for a casual Friday or clean-cut preppy look. Features cotton sweaters,
Hawaiian shirts, pastel polo shirts, and accessories.

Grace and Glory (843-521-4050), 1029 Boundary St. Women's apparel, jewelry, home décor, and gifts.

Sugarbelle (843-379-4141), 1440 Ribaut Rd., Port Royal. Women who like to be comfortable and a little sassy in their look can get great guidance and good choices in this little shop which took off with a bang in 2013.

Sweetgrass Ladies Apparel (843-379-3307), 707 Bay St. Linens and light jackets, stylish but informal.

Talbot's (843-322-8040), 1029 Boundary St. A branch of the national store with small sizes and enough to choose from if you need to get dressed up at the last minute.

CRAFTS

Carolina Stamper (843-522-9966), 203 Carteret St. Rubber stamps, supplies, and lots of ideas for making stationery and artwork.

The Craftseller (843-525-6104; www.craftseller.com), 818 Bay St. Local and regional artists' work, including jewelry, benches made of recycled wood from local buildings, fabric art, handmade paper, and wind chimes.

Sweetgrass baskets made by local artists can be found on St. Helena Island on US 21, on the porch at the Gullah Grub restaurant, at the Red Piano Too Gallery, and at other roadside stands. The baskets, which incorporate palmetto frond, pine needle, and rush with the pale grass, come in many shapes and sizes, with individual variations inspired by the utilitarian shapes used in the past. They require enormous amounts of labor and skill, and are useful as well as beautiful.

GALLERIES

Arts Council of Beaufort County (843-379-2787; www.beaufortcountyarts.com), 2127 Boundary St. Featuring exhibits by local artists.

Atelier on Bay (843-470-0266; www.atelieronbay.com), 203 West St. Home to more than a dozen working artists' studios where you can chat with the artist and view and purchase artwork. It's on the second floor of a simply renovated department store that faces Bay St., a beloved institution that was in business for more than 100 years.

Bay Street Gallery (843-522-9210; www.baystgallery.com), 719 Bay St. Original works by Lana Hefner, including impressionistic views of marsh and cloud scenes, as well as the best collection of Sea Island baskets outside of Mount Pleasant. Probably the most sophisticated gallery in Beaufort.

Beaufort Art Association Gallery (843-521-4444; www.beaufortartassociation .com), 913 Bay St. Original works including pottery, prints, jewelry, sculpture, photography, and acrylics by some 75 member artists. New exhibits every six weeks.

Charles Street Gallery (843-521-9054), 914 Charles St. Original works including bronze sculpture, paintings, and etchings. Full-service framing and regularly scheduled gallery shows.

Garden Studio Gallery (843-522-8911; www.sandrabaggette.com), 1908 Lenora Dr., Port Royal. Oil paintings and watercolors of flowers from Sandra Baggette's garden are stunning. Her studio, open by appointment, is located near the base of the Bell Bridge that crosses Battery Creek on the way to Parris Island.

Bay Street   Beaufort Regional Chamber VCB (Banker Optical Media)

Indigo Gallery (843-524-1036), 813 Bay St. Limited and open editions of many of the best-known Lowcountry artists, as well as serigraphs, original art, and framing.

I. Pinckney Simons Gallery (843-379-4774; www.ipsgallery.com), 711 Bay St. Features work in jewelry, sculpture, paintings, and more by a well-known regional artist.

LyBensons Gallery & Studio (843-525-9006), 211 Charles St. A large, bright gallery specializing in art from Africa and from African American artists in a variety of media, including verdite stone sculptures. Photographs depicting the Gullah culture by the Rev. Kenneth Hodges, too.

The Red Piano Too (843-838-2241; www.redpianotoo.com), 870 Sea Island Pkwy., St. Helena Island. Located about 15 minutes from Beaufort, this gallery has an eclectic and renowned assortment of folk art and outsider art by individuals from this area and throughout the South, as well as baskets, books, jewelry, African objects, and prints. Fine framing is available.

Rhett Gallery (843-524-3339; www.rhettgallery.com), 901 Bay St. Prints and watercolors of the Lowcountry by Nancy Ricker Rhett as well as antique first-edition prints and maps, Civil War and nautical materials, and hand-colored engravings.

GIFTS

Lulu Burgess (843-524-5858; www.luluburgess.com), 917 Bay St. An engaging blend of imaginative gifts such as jewelry, stationary, tableware, totes, and decorative accessories. Opened by a young Beaufort native who has brought her good taste back home.

Monkey's Uncle (843-524-6868; www.monkeysuncletoys.com), 808 Bay St.

The Red Piano Too Gallery on St. Helena features traditional crafts and folk art.

Toys, puzzles, books, and games in a cheerful space where kids can try things out and adults can take a breather.

Rossignol's (843-524-2175), 817 Bay St. Fine china patterns, silver and gold jewelry, stationery, and expensive stemware—all suitable for wedding gifts—as well as platters, picture frames, and tea towels—many with Lowcountry themes—that would make good house-warming presents.

John Mark Verdier House Gift Shop (843-379-6335), 801 Bay St. Located in the basement of the historic house museum, it features a collection of books, ornaments, prints, toys, and note cards with sketches of Beaufort's old homes.

GOURMET SHOPS

Cravings by the Bay (843-522-3000 or 1-800-735-3215; www.cravingsbythebay .com), 928 Bay St. Savor Lowcountry flavors and memories by ordering soups, condiments, sauces, and specialty books by mail. Shrimp, oysters, clams, scallops, and soft-shell crab can be delivered overnight. Drop by for more information.

Herban Marketplace (843-379-5550; www.herbanmarketplace.com),1211 Newcastle St. An organic grocery with a upscale, urban feel that delights locavores, vegans, and visitors who might have special food needs.

Olive the Above (843-379-2000), 821 Bay St. Dozens of varieties of infused olive oils and vinegars and kitchen accessories.

HOME FURNISHINGS/KITCHENWARE

Finishing Touches (843-522-1716), 917 Bay St. Tucked away down a passage in the Old Bay Marketplace you'll find cotton rugs, tableware, linens, and even "Tom's" shoes.

In High Cotton (843-522-1405), 903 Bay St. Fine linens and home furnishings.

Le Creuset Manufacturer's Outlet Store (843-589-6650), Yemassee at exit 38 off I-95. Cast-iron cookware, utensils, pottery, and storage pieces from the French manufacturer are available at significant discount from overstock, discontinued, and cosmetically flawed inventory.

Lowcountry Store (843-838-4646; www.lowcountrystore.com), 736 Sea Island Pkwy. A family-run emporium housed in a refurbished tomato packing shed that features jars of regional delicacies like chow-chow, relishes, and jams; artwork, jewelry, and Gullah crafts; and locally made furniture (built on-site) such as joggling boards, rocking chairs, tables, and benches made from reclaimed wood. Examples of the work can be seen online; at the Wren Bistro, the downtown Beaufort restaurant; and in Charleston's Mercury Bar. The café provides picnic provender (sandwiches, wraps, hot dogs) as well as a popular selection of pies made daily. Otis Daise, a local farmer, also runs an outdoor stand with the freshest selections from the field.

Octopuses (843-838-0005; www.sainthelenaislandshops.com), 800 block of Sea Island Pkwy. One of two little pastel cottages that are utterly whimsical, and this one in particular sells useful household items with seashore themes.

SPORTING GOODS AND CLOTHING

Barefoot Bubba's Surf Shop (843-838-9222; www.barefootbubbasurfshop.com) 2135 Sea Island Pkwy., Harbor Island. The latest in surf wear, surfboards, skimboards, rafts, and toys for the beach. They also have a location at 828 Bay St. in Beaufort.

Bay Street Outfitters (843-524-5250; www.baystreetoutfitters.com), 825 Bay St. A full line of high-end sportswear from Orvis and Barbour, as well as fishing gear, reels, binoculars, and books.

Buck, Bass, 'N' Beyond (843-524-2825), 2127 Boundary St. A store for the serious hunter with specialized clothing lines, an indoor archery range, and high-tech gear for those in pursuit of deer, pig, fish, and other game.

Higher Ground (843-379-4327; www.highergroundbeaufort.com), 2121 Boundary St. Surfboards, kayaks, climbing gear, clothing, and camping accessories. You can rent surfboards, too.

EDISTO ISLAND

It takes some time to get to know Edisto. What remains of its "Golden Age," the period between the Revolutionary

Local herbs and spices create a distinctive Gullah flavor in gumbos, boils, and fish stews.

and Civil Wars, is mostly hidden, tucked away along secondary roads that wind through fields and patches of scrub oak, and meander by the North and South Edisto Rivers and their tributaries. Historic sites that are listed on the National Register of Historic Places (27 so far) include some churches, but consist primarily of private plantation homes and gardens that are not open to the public. Orient yourself through the Edisto Chamber of Commerce (843-869-3867 or 1-888-333-2781; www.edistochamber.com), P.O. Box 206, Edisto, SC 29438.

Edisto Beach, where there are rental accommodations, is lively in the summer but quiet the rest of the time. That's what attracts visitors. It's a great spot for family reunions, punctuated by beachcombing, a good meal, and a kayak or boat tour. A few years ago, a sickly loggerhead turtle washed up. It was nursed to health, and when the time came to release it back into the ocean, more than 300 people showed up to watch, cheer, and take pictures. They found out by word of mouth, Edisto-style.

The island lies about 45 miles south of Charleston by road, and about 75 miles from Beaufort—of course far less by water. From US 17, take SC 174 and follow it east for about 20 miles, threading your way through the country. It's a hike to travel from Charleston or Beaufort just for dinner, but fine for a day trip. Cab and car rental services are limited. Original sections of the King's Highway, laid out in the early 18th century, are still in use today. The main road dead-ends at the Atlantic Ocean.

An old pier on Edisto Island.

For an overview of the island's history, visit the Edisto Island Museum (843-869-1954; www.edistomuseum .org), SC 174 at Chisolm Plantation Rd. Open Tues.–Sat. noon–5; admission $4, free to children 10 and younger. Baskets, clothing, farm tools, letters and documents, uniforms, and furniture are displayed as well as haunting old photographs. The little gift shop sells a variety of natural history items for kids and excellent reprints of booklets you're not likely to find anywhere else. They include *Edisto Island in 1808, Indigo in America, Gullah,* and *She Came to the Island,* the Edisto diary of Mary Ames, a Northern abolitionist whose account of teaching and living among the newly freed slaves during the Civil War is among the most poignant of the genre.

Since Edisto's old homes are not open to the public, one way to get a closer view is by taking a 2½-hour tour. Reserve through Pink Van Tours (843-869-1110) or Tours of Edisto (843-869-1984). Adults $20, children $10. Annual Tours of Edisto take place the second Saturday in October. Contact the Edisto Island Historic Preservation Society (843-869-1954; www.edistomuseum.org), 8123 Chisolm Plantation Rd., P.O. Box 393, Edisto Island, SC 29438. Tickets generally cost $45.

For an education on the subject of the region's reptile life, visit the Edisto Island Serpentarium (843-869-1171; edistoserpentarium.com), 1374 SC 174, where more than 500 reptiles are on display in natural habitats. Feeding and presentations occur every hour. Hours and days of operation change monthly; closed Nov.–Feb. Adults $14.95, children $10.95.

One of Edisto's best places to eat is the Old Post Office Restaurant (843-869-2339; www.theoldpostofficerestaurant.com), 1442 SC 174, a cozy place that serves creative Southern cuisine—this is not fried food—with entrées like steak, pork, and the best local fish and shellfish. Open Nov.–Feb., Wed.–Sat. 5:30 PM–10 PM; Mar.–Oct., Tues.–Sat. 5:30 PM–10 PM. They close for the month of January. Po Pigs Bo-B-Q (843-869-9003), 2410 SC 174, is a family-run dining room with a huge buffet and a cheerful atmosphere. It's Southern with a twist, offering curried rice with sun-dried fruit as well as country ham. The price is inexpensive to moderate. Open for lunch and dinner, but you should call ahead for operational hours. The Seacow Eatery (843-869-3222; www.theseacoweatery.com), 145 Jungle Rd., offers a varied breakfast menu, from standard bacon and eggs to shrimp and eggs. At lunch you can order the veggie melt, deli sandwiches, or a shrimp po' boy. Their dinner menu features your choice of fried or grilled seafood, steaks, and chicken, and there is a kids' menu. Open Mon. 7 AM–3 PM; Tues.–Sun. 7 AM–9 PM. Whaleys (843-869-2161), 2801 Myrtle St., is open Mon.–Sat. 11:30–2:30 and 5–10; Sun. 5–10. This is an old filling station that has been turned into a beachy café, serving crabcakes, fresh seafood, steaks, wings, pork chop sandwiches, and the "Big Ugly" burger. Call restaurant to confirm their in-season and off-season hours.

Edisto has several art and craft galleries, with local and regional work represented informally. With These Hands (843-869-3509; www.withthesehandsgallery .com), 1444 SC 174, and The Edistonian Gift Shop (843-869-4466), 406 SC 174, are two shops where you might find a treasure.

For books it's the Edisto Bookstore (843-869-1885; www.theedistobookstore .com), 547 SC 174.

Continuing across Edisto Island brings you to Edisto Beach (www.edisto beach.com), the curve of land that faces the Atlantic, then turns to embrace the inner marsh and St. Helena Sound. For years it has been the summer destination of South Carolina families. They take up residence in the plain, raised, two-story houses that line the boulevards for about three-dozen blocks and spill across adjacent avenues. There's nothing fancy: It's full of kids riding bikes (good bike lanes here, and watchful drivers) and minivans parked in the sand. A high point of the day is watching the shrimp boats come in. Plentiful beach access, too.

Many of these houses rent by the week, and several agencies list them. The market is organized by location: beachfront, second row (across the street from the beach, usually with an ocean view); beach walk (easy access but on a side street); condos; and homes with docks (deep water, tidal creek, or other access, which may not be near the beach). It is common for houses to accommodate 10 to 16 people, so the range of prices for a week in the summer can be from $795 to $4,000. Rental specs also include amenities like "fish-cleaning sink," "hot and cold outside shower," grills, and cribs. For information contact:

Atwood Vacations (843-869-2151 or 1-866-713-5214; www.atwoodvacations .com).

Edisto Rentals (843-869-2527 or 1-866-856-6538; www.edistorealty.com).

Kapp/Lyons Co. (1-800-945-9667; wwwkapplyons.com).

A small resort, Wyndham Ocean Ridge (1-888-743-2687 or 1-877-296-6335 (rentals); www.wyndhamoceanridge.com), 1 King Cotton Rd., Edisto Island, SC

29438, offers rentals. Its 300-acre layout includes tennis, golf (Plantation Course, 843-869-1111) swimming, boating, and beach access. The accommodations are more rustic at the 1,255-acre Edisto Beach State Park (843-869-2156; www.south carolinaparks.com), 8377 State Cabin Rd., Edisto Island, SC 29438. There's a 111-site camping area with water and electricity for tents and RVs (some are designated for handicapped visitors), a smaller section for tents only, and seven cabins. Restrooms near the sites offer hot showers. Nightly fees for tent sites begin at $21; full hook-ups start at $38. The cabins are furnished, heated, air-conditioned, and have access to a dock for crabbing and fishing. Nightly rates are $80–166. Reservations are highly recommended. Call 1-866-345-7275 directly or make them online. The park includes 1.5 miles of beachfront, open marsh, a forest with nature trails, a general store, boat-launching access to Big Bay Creek, and interpretive programs. The beach is a wonderful place to hunt for fossils and shark teeth. Admission is $5 for adults, $3 for children.

In a moment of exceedingly wise land stewardship, the state of South Carolina obtained Botany Bay Plantation (843-869-2713; www.dnr.sc.gov/mlands) a pristine, 4,687-acre tract of undeveloped wetlands, and opened it to the public for visitation daily during daylight hours. You first obtain a day pass at the main gate off Botany Bay Road. Check their website for a schedule. Cultural resources on Botany Bay include outbuildings from the Bleak Hall Plantation. The pristine and primitive beach, monitored by friendly volunteers, is not to be missed.

Because of its location at the confluence of the North and South Edisto Rivers, the Atlantic, and St. Helena Sound, Edisto Beach offers probably the easiest access to the basin and all sorts of fishing, boating, and water sports. For maps and information about sight-seeing and bird-watching, contact the ACE Basin National Wildlife Refuge Headquarters (843-889-3084; www.fws.gov), 8675 Willtown Rd., Hollywood, SC 29449, or the South Carolina Department of Natural Resources (843-844-8957; www.dnr.sc.gov), 585 Donnelly Dr., Green Pond, SC 29446. The website www.scnhc.org tracks things to see and do along a newly developing coastal heritage trail, and has good links.

If you want to tour the ACE Basin by water, stop by Edisto Watersports & Tackle (843-869-0663; www.edistowatersports.biz), 3731 Docksite Rd. Captain Ron Elliott's Edisto Island Tours (843-869-1937) provide boat trips to offshore islands for shelling, island river tours, and inshore fishing. You may also tour by canoe and kayak with him. He is a passionate naturalist and a font of Edisto lore. Rent bikes, boats, kayaks, golf carts, and beach gear at Island Bikes and Outfitters (843-869-4444; www.islandbikesandoutfitters.com), 140 Jungle Rd.

BLUFFTON

Historic Bluffton village, now branded Old Town Bluffton, is one of the Lowcountry's last cul-de-sacs. There are a couple of "Historic" this-and-that signs nailed up, but what you thought it ought to be and whether or not it ever becomes that scrubbed-up, idealized version of itself is of no concern. It has all the charm of a barefoot kid. An hour or two spent walking along its quiet streets, looking through the bramble and old fences at some of its 19th-century frame houses, visiting the church on the bluff, browsing in a few shops and art galleries—that about does it for Bluffton. Visitor information can be found at www.oldtownbluffton.com.

Flocks of birds gather to feed on the saltwater edge of the ACE Basin. Peter Loftus

Don't be confused by Bluffton addresses. In the past five years, the town has annexed so much adjacent land that all but the old village is being taken over by sprawl. The most luxurious addition to greater Bluffton, indeed the entire area from Charleston to Savannah, has been Palmetto Bluff (1-800-501-7405; www .palmettobluff.com), 476 Mount Pelia Rd., Bluffton, SC 29910, one of the largest and last unspoiled tracts in the area and one of the nation's top luxury resorts. You can dine at the Inn at Palmetto Bluff's River House (843-706-6542), its luxury venue, or in a slightly less formal though equally stylish restaurant, Buffalo's (843-706-6630). Cottage accommodations (in several configurations but with kitchens and porches) run from $650–1,100 per night in the high season of March through May, October, and November. Rental houses are more expensive. Call 1-866-706-6565 for reservations or secure them online. There's a par-72 golf course for guests, as well as tennis, swimming, boating, and other amenities. It's incredibly beautiful, on the May River, and low-key with fierce determination. Located about 30 minutes from the Savannah airport.

Visiting Bluffton

From Beaufort (about 40 minutes), follow SC 170 and continue as if you were going to Hilton Head, across the Broad River Bridge. About 8 miles ahead, exit right at the sign to Hilton Head and loop around. You are now on US 278 (William Hilton Parkway), the main Hilton Head road. After a couple of miles, you will see SC 46 marked as a right turn. Take it into Bluffton. From Hilton Head (about 30 minutes), follow US 278 across the Graves Bridge, turn left on SC 46, and follow it to Boundary Street.

Bluffton was a summer community of island planters, and in 1863 it was nearly burned to the ground by Union troops. Ten antebellum buildings remain; another 16 or so houses were built after the Civil War. Taken together, they give a view of classic Lowcountry village life. Far from extravagant, they are nonetheless suffused with a sense of form appropriate to the landscape and to their function as seasonal dwellings. It is worth the trip alone to see the Church of the Cross (843-757-2661), 110 Calhoun St., an unpainted building (circa 1857) with beautiful interior detailing, original pews, and Gothic-style windows. Docents are on-site Mon.–Sat., 11–2.

Start your tour at the town's historic center, the Heyward House (843-757-6293; www.heywardhouse.org), 70 Boundary St., an 1840s Carolina farmhouse and slave cabin. It's open Mon.–Fri. 10–5; Sat. 10-4. Tours are $5 for adults, $2 for students. Walking tours of the village originate here Thursdays at 9 AM or by appointment; cost is nominal. Then pick up a self-guided walking tour or biking map. Houses are marked by plaques, but not all are visible from the street. One book will help you appreciate them: *No. II: A Longer Short History of Bluffton, South Carolina and Its Environs,* produced by the Bluffton Historical Preservation Society (843-757-6293), P.O. Box 742, Bluffton, SC 29910. The society may have copies of the out-of-print book for you to look at. It includes historic essays and descriptions of homes, a map, and wonderful photographs.

Bluffton's mid-19th-century Church of the Cross, one the the the few buildings in the village to survive the Civil War.
Courtesy of the Hilton Head Island Visitor & Convention Bureau

If you are biking, Bluffton is well situated for longer treks in rural areas. Local cyclists have created maps for enjoyable day trips from 25 to 60 miles that take you to historic sites and churches, remote boat landings, and lovely vistas. You can rent bikes at Sports Addiction (843-815-8281; www.sportsaddiction.us), 200 Okatie Village Dr.

Bluffton—Calhoun Street in particular—has emerged as a center for working artists. Every third Friday there are street parties, and gallery walks are regularly scheduled. These are just a few places to visit: Pluff Mudd (843-757-5590; www .pluffmuddart.com), 27 Calhoun St., features paintings and crafts by local artists. The Society of Bluffton Artists Gallery (843-757-6586; www.sobagallery.com), corner of Church and Calhoun Sts., includes work of 82 Lowcountry artists in a remodeled gallery space. The working studio of potter Jacob Preston (843-757-3084), 10 Church St., between Boundary St. and Calhoun St., inside a converted church is open Tues.–Sat.10–5 or by appointment. Outdoor sculpture consisting of remodeled bikes and motorcycles and painted furniture beckons you inside. Fantozzi's Wrought Iron Design (843-301-9855), 41 Calhoun St., features functional and funky ironwork, from garden gates to candlesticks.

Bluffton's stores are no less unique. Eggs 'N' Tricities (843-757-3446), 71

The Bluffton Farmers' Market. SC Lowcountry Tourism Commission

Calhoun St., which is located in an old filling station, has funky furniture outside and inside, and sells everything from 1940s-era lamps and linens to clothing and contemporary tableware. The Store (843-757-3855), 56 Calhoun St., covers some of the same ground with similar esprit and also has wine, beer, and gourmet snacks. Stock Farm Antiques (843-757-8046; www.stock farmantiques.com), 1263 May River Rd., offers prints, porcelain, silver, rugs, and furniture—some American, some English—chosen with a sense of what fits in the big new houses at the resorts as well as the real old ones. There are also several consignment shops and thrift stores in the area that offer bargains and maybe a treasure. Ask about them. Corks Wine Company (843-815-5168; www.corkswinecofbluffton .com), 14 Promenade St., has small plates to sample and a large wine and beer selection. The Cottage Café, Bakery, and Tea Room (843-757-0508), 38 Calhoun St., serves breakfast, lunch, and dinner Mon.–Sat., and Sun. brunch in a charming setting.

If Time Is Short

What to do on a quick visit.

The Rhett House Inn (843-524-9030; www.rhetthouseinn.com), 1009 Craven St., Beaufort, or City Loft Hotel (843-379-5638; www.citylofthotel.com), 301 Carteret St., Beaufort, will pamper you with concierge service, and by staying there you have access to golf, swimming, tennis, and the fitness center at the Sanctuary. Visit Hunting Island State Park (843-838-2011 or 1-866-345-7275; www .southcarolinaparks.com/huntingisland) for a long walk on the beach, or drop by the John Mark Verdier House (843-379-6335), 801 Bay St., part of a leisurely walk down Bay St. with another stop at the Waterfront Park or one of the restaurants where you can sip a drink on the patio. Then stroll through The Point neighborhood or visit St. Helena's Episcopal Church and grounds. Penn Center (843-838-2432; www.penncenter.com), St. Helena Island, was the nation's first school for freed slaves. Try an eco-tour, shelling expedition, or kayak adventure to get on the water (see Recreation) and, depending on your budget, choose Breakwater or Griffin Market for an elegant meal, Old Bull Tavern for gastropub atmosphere and bistro food, or Suzara's Kitchen for breakfast.

On Edisto Island, the Old Post Office Restaurant (843-869-2339), 1442 SC 174, is the best place for dinner; Po Pigs Bo-B-Que (843-869-9003), 2410 SC 174, for lunch. Edisto Beach State Park (843-869-2156) is a well-known spot to find fossilized shark teeth. The Edisto Island Museum (843-869-1954) is a little gem.

4

Hilton Head

COURTS, COURSES, SAILS & SAND

UNLIKE THE REST of the Lowcountry, Hilton Head is a place of condensed and organized pleasures. The island is 12 miles long and 5 miles wide, fronts the Intracoastal Waterway, the Atlantic, and Port Royal Sound, and is laced by creeks. The commercial districts are discreetly screened from view, and even the busiest thoroughfare, US 278 (William Hilton Parkway), lacks neon signs. Summer is the busiest time, when the year-round population of about 37,000 sees a turnover of 10,000 visitors a week; more than 2.5 million visitors come every year.

Until 1955, when the first bridge linked Hilton Head to the mainland, the island's history resembled that of its Sea Island neighbors. Slaves worked on 16 or so plantations until the Civil War, when it became a federal base defending the entrance to Port Royal Sound and the railways and Confederate strongholds further inland. Unlike other islands, Hilton Head's native islanders remained rural and self-sufficient well into the mid-1960s. The African American families farmed and fished; the visitors who came were gentleman hunters, millionaires from the north. Packet steamers, sailboats, and barges supplied transportation, and more often than not, their market destination was Savannah, for Hilton Head is the southernmost area of Beaufort County.

Harbour Town at dusk.
Courtesy of the Hilton Head Island Visitor & Convention Bureau and the Harbour Town Lighthouse at Sea Pines Resort

Years of scholarly research have yielded new information about Mitchelville, considered the first self-governing African American community in the country, established as a result of the federal occupation and liberation of the plantations. See below for tours and ongoing restoration projects.

Resort development led to the modern "plantation" layout that orders the

LEFT: Hilton Head is a boater's paradise.

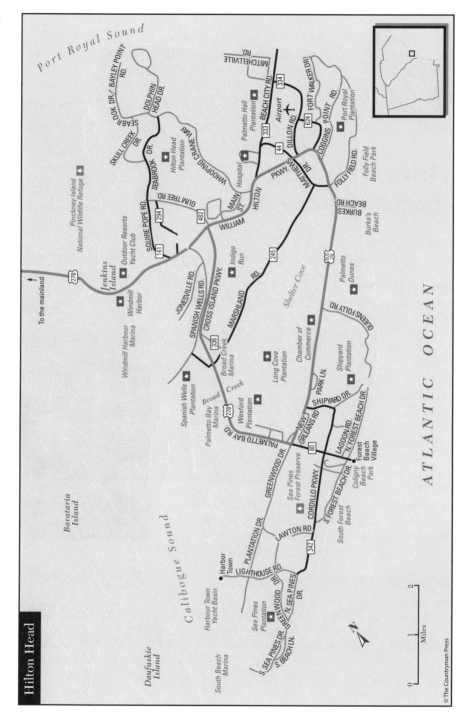

Hilton Head

© The Countryman Press

Port Royal Sound

ATLANTIC OCEAN

Calibogue Sound

Barataria Island

Daufuskie Island

To the mainland

MITCHELLVILLE RD.

SEABROOK DR. / BAYLEY POINT RD.

DOLPHIN HEAD DR.

SKULL CREEK DR.

SEABROOK DR.

SQUIRE POPE RD.

GUM TREE RD.

WHOOPING CRANE WAY

Hilton Head Plantation

Pinckney Island National Wildlife Refuge

Outdoor Resorts Yacht Club

Jenkins Island

Windmill Harbour

Windmill Harbour Marina

Palmetto Hall Plantation

BEACH CITY RD.

Airport

DILLON RD.

FORT WALKER DR.

COGGINS POINT RD.

Port Royal Plantation

Folly Field Beach Park

MAIN ST.

Hospital

HILTON

MATTHEWS DR.

HEAD PKWY.

FOLLY FIELD RD.

BURKE'S BEACH RD.

Burke's Beach

WILLIAM

JONESVILLE RD.

SPANISH WELLS RD.

CROSS ISLAND PKWY.

MARSHLAND RD.

Indigo Run

Shelter Cove

Palmetto Dunes

QUEENS FOLLY RD.

Spanish Wells Plantation

Palmetto Bay Marina

Broad Creek

Broad Creek Marina

Long Cove Plantation

Chamber of Commerce

Shipyard Plantation

PARK LN.

SHIPYARD DR.

Wexford Plantation

PALMETTO BAY RD.

NEW ORLEANS RD.

LAGOON RD.

N. FOREST BEACH DR.

S. FOREST BEACH DR.

Coligny Plaza

Forest Beach Park

Forest Beach Village

GREENWOOD DR.

Sea Pines Forest Preserve

CORDILLO PKWY.

South Forest Beach

LAWTON RD.

PLANTATION DR.

Harbor Town

Harbour Town Yacht Basin

LIGHTHOUSE RD.

S. SEA PINES DR.

GREENWOOD DR.

N. SEA PINES DR.

S. BEACH LN.

Sea Pines Plantation

South Beach Marina

N

0 1 2

Miles

141

294

482

278

336

278

80

342

245

278

295/278

44

333

334

624

island's geography, the main ones being Sea Pines Plantation, Shipyard Plantation, Palmetto Dunes, Port Royal Plantation, and Hilton Head Plantation. Within and around them are the dozens of golf courses, tennis courts, and marinas that define island recreation. Stores and restaurants are usually gathered in mall clusters and shopping pods, like the Village at Wexford or Coligny Plaza. Many smaller residential areas lie scattered across the island, some of them "gated" communities, others not.

As the island's topography has changed (much of it sculpted into golf courses), so has its population. Census figures categorize residents by race (90 percent white) and by age (some 30 percent over 60 years old). Spillover development into greater Bluffton has blurred the "Hilton Head" brand, meaning a restaurant may actually be off-island. The listings in this chapter are located on Hilton Head Island with a few exceptions.

If you mostly want to play golf or tennis or stay near the beach, look for options in the Lodging section for "stay-and-play" packages. If you're traveling with friends or family, you may want to rent a house or villa unit. If you decide upon a resort, you may not need a car—most resort amenities are within walking and biking distance, and you will be provided with airport transportation. For touring without a car, rent a bike and explore the island's bike trails.

The high season starts in March, when families come on spring vacation, and lasts through October. When the island is crowded, expect traffic congestion.

GETTING THERE

Savannah/Hilton Head International Airport (912-964-0514; www.savannah airport.com) and the smaller Hilton Head Airport (www.bcgov.net) are gateways. Flights to Hilton Head are lightly served by a regional carrier; Savannah is the major hub. Rental car service is available at both locations, as are courtesy shuttles if you are staying at a resort. K Shuttle (1-877-243-2050; www.kshuttle.com) and Palmetto Taxi (843-683-4279; www.palmettotransportation.com) serve Hilton Head. Shared rate fares from Savannah are about $45 one-way. By car, take exit 8 from I-95 to US 278, the link to Hilton Head. It's about 25 minutes by car from the exit to the north end of the island and Bluffton locations, although count on an hour to get to the island's south end. Amtrak (1-800-872-7245; www.amtrak.com) serves Savannah twice each day.

Lodging
Best places to stay in Hilton Head, and what you'll find nearby . . .

There are more than 3,000 hotel and motel rooms and 6,000 rental units on Hilton Head, including cottages, houses, and villas scattered across the island, from sites on or near the beach to those around golf courses, marinas, lagoons, in residential subdivisions or low-rise housing complexes, even on the main highway. Another 1,000 units are dedicated to "time-share" arrangements and may be available for rent, too. Your accommodations may be elegant or simple; offer as much or as little privacy as you wish; come with or without kitchens; and lie within walking distance, or not, from the beach and recreational amenities.

Rates vary from as little as $60

per night (off-season) for an economy motel room to $6,500 per week for an oceanfront home with a swimming pool. The range reflects differences in size and location—oceanfront is premium; resort privileges add to the price—and also the time of year. Rates are highest during the vacation seasons, March through April and June through mid-August. The shoulder seasons of late April and May, then September and October bring ideal golfing conditions, so prices stay high, though not at the seasonal peak. In the winter months, rates can be half what they are in the high season.

Like many resort areas, Hilton Head adds an accommodations tax to lodging bills, and some establishments place a surcharge on credit card payments. Ask for an estimate of your total bill when you are booking and inquire about special rate packages or coupons offered for restaurants. Many hotels have discounts for golf and tennis; some have family plans, including activities for kids. In larger hotels, children often stay for free. Access to the Internet via WiFi is widely available; however, cell phone service can be spotty although it is improving all the time.

The easiest way to make reservations in a hotel or motel is by phone or website. To inquire about home and villa rentals, call a property management company listed under "Vacation Property Rentals." Central reservation agencies can give you a sense of the big picture, and they may be especially helpful in designing a package tailored to your specific interests. The Hilton Head Island–Bluffton Chamber of Commerce (843-785-3673 or 1-800-523-3373; www.hiltonhead.org) is a good place to start. If you're interested in camping, look into the recreational vehicle parks listed later in this section.

If you're staying on a boat, see "Marinas," also in the Recreation listings. The following rates are for one night's stay, per person, double occupancy. They do not include taxes, surcharges, or any special recreation/entertainment discounts. Prices quoted are for high season accommodations. Note that the rates for luxury accommodations are at least in the "very expensive" category: They can easily run to $329 per night. Villa and home rentals generally run from Saturday to Saturday during peak season. Three kennels provide places for your cat or dog to stay: Brooke's Bed & Biscuit (843-757-7387, www.brooksbedandbiscuit.com); Evergreen Pet Lodge (843-681-8354 or 1-866-680-8354; www.evergreenpetlodgehhi.com); and Southpaw Pet Resort (843-342-7200; www.southpawpetresort.com). They allow you to pick up your pet during the day, while also providing boarding, care, and grooming. Note that from Memorial Day to Labor Day pets are not permitted on the beach between 10 AM and 5 PM, and at other times are required to be on a leash.

HOTELS AND LARGER INNS

Hilton Head Marriott Resort & Spa (843-686-8400 or 1-888-511-5086; www. marriott.com), 1 Hotel Circle, Palmetto Dunes. Very expensive. The largest hotel on the island, with 512 rooms, indoor pool, Olympic-sized outdoor pool, and children's pool. Health club, tennis courts, three golf courses, sailboat and bicycle rentals, and lots of beachfront. Four restaurants, including casual poolside dining. A children's program (for an additional fee) is available weekends year-round, daily during the summer.

Inn at Harbour Town (843-363-8100 or 1-800-732-7463; www.seapines.com), 32 Greenwood, Sea Pines

Lowcountry pleasures can be found on Hilton Head. Peter Loftus

Plantation. Very expensive. Renovated in 2012, this 60-room inn is in the Harbour Town complex, a Mediterranean-style marina village whose lighthouse is the best-recognized symbol of Hilton Head. The inn is situated just off the water, in a quieter location by the golf courses. It's more thoughtfully designed than the functional fun-and-sun architecture or the low-slung Tahiti-roof look of Sea Pines, and its focus on service and serenity seem to suggest another way to enjoy the resort experience: to be in it, but not of it.

Omni Oceanfront Resort & Spa (843-842-8000 or 1-800-843-6664; www.omnihiltonhead.com), 23 Ocean Ln., Palmetto Dunes. Very expensive. Renovated in 2013, a luxury 323-room hotel that claims the largest rooms on the island—550 square feet each—with private balconies and kitchenettes. At the oceanfront setting there's an adults-only pool and a family pool,

whirlpools, a fitness center, 25 tennis courts, and three golf courses. There is biking, canoeing, and kayaking on the 11-mile lagoon system. In the summer months, activities for kids ages 4 to 16 can be arranged for an additional charge. Restaurants and nightclubs within the complex.

Sonesta Hotel (843-842-2400 or 1-800-766-3782; www.sonesta.com /HiltonHeadIsland), 130 Shipyard Dr., Shipyard Plantation. Expensive. A 340-room oceanfront hotel renovated in 2013, with full concierge service, two restaurants, and a popular lounge for evening entertainment. Two pools on-site, golf courses within a mile and accessed by complimentary shuttle, nearby tennis courts and a day spa, and sailing and water sports by arrangement. On-site bike rentals and a kids' program for a fee.

Westin Hilton Head Island Resort and Spa (843-681-4000 or

1-800-937-8461; www.westinhilton head.com), 2 Grasslawn Ave., Port Royal Plantation. Very expensive. Recently upgraded. Considered the most luxurious of the island's ocean-front resort hotels, with 416 rooms and 32 suites. The Westin is praised for its spa, the elegant decorations, and rooms with balconies. Guests may play golf on three Port Royal courses and tennis on hard and clay courts. Heated, covered pool and two outdoor pools. Six on-site restaurants, from elegant to casual, including a poolside café and several bars.

SMALLER LUXURY INNS

The Beachhouse: A Holiday Inn Resort (843-785-5126 or 1-800-465-4329; www.thebeachhousehhi.com), 1 S. Forest Beach Dr. Expensive. A popular public-access beach is at your doorstep, plus a poolside restaurant and the only volleyball courts on the beach, where there is most always a pickup game available. The Tiki Hut bar is a great place for people-watching. Kids, who stay free, will enjoy nearby Coligny Plaza with its touristy gift and T-shirt shops, informal restaurants, and movie theater. The inn tends to attract bargain-minded international guests and young people; it can be noisy, but has an upbeat, friendly vibe and underwent a significant makeover in 2013.

Park Lane Hotel and Suites (843-686-5700 or 1-877-247-3431; www.hiltonheadparklanehotel.com), 12 Park Ln., Central Park. Expensive. An all-suite hotel with rooms that are larger than average and feature a fully equipped kitchen; some have wood-burning fireplaces. A recreation area includes basketball and tennis courts, pool and Jacuzzi hot tub, and jogging trails and a playground.

South Beach Marina Inn (843-671-6498 or 1-800-367-3969; www .sbinn.com), 232 S. Sea Pines Dr., Sea Pines Plantation. Moderate–Expensive. Part of a New England–style marina village in Sea Pines Plantation, this 17-room inn sits above waterfront shops and restaurants. The rooms are condominium suites, with living and dining areas and kitchenettes over-looking the courtyard or marina. With tennis, water sports, restaurants, and the beach close by, you could pretend you're on Cape Cod . . . with much warmer water.

BUDGET CHOICES

Each of these national chain motels of approximately 100 rooms has a swim-ming pool and is close to inexpensive restaurants or shopping areas. They tend to be several blocks from a beach access point.

Comfort Inn (843-842-6662 or 1-800-522-3224; www.comforthilton head.com), 2 Tanglewood Dr.

Hampton Inn (843-681-7900 or 1-800-426-7866; www.hamptoninn .com), One Dillon Rd.

Quality Inn (843-681-3655 or 1-877-424-6423; www.qualityinn.com), 200 Museum St.

Red Roof Inn (843-686-6808 or 1-800-733-7663; www.redroof.com), 5 Regency Pkwy.

RESORTS AND RENTALS

Most vacation rental properties are concentrated on the south end of the island in Sea Pines Plantation, Shipyard Plantation, South Forest Beach, and Palmetto Dunes Resort. Several villa rental complexes are located midisland on or near Folly Field Beach. The northern half of the island is geared mainly to permanent residents; the

End of the day in the Lowcountry. Peter Loftus

for cleaning services. If you have special needs such as handicapped-accessible rooms, or will be renting cots, cribs, bicycles, or beach chairs, alert the agent from the start. The agencies listed below are just some of many.

Beach Properties of Hilton Head (1-800-671-5155; www.beach-property .com) A variety of deluxe and non-oceanfront properties and villas, many available by the night with a three-night minimum.

Hilton Head Vacation Rentals (843-689-3010 or 1-800-232-2463; www.800beachme.com) A selection of more than 300 homes and villas in all areas of the island.

Palmetto Dunes Resort (843-785-1138 or 1-866-310-6014; www .palmettodunes.com) Manages villas and homes throughout Palmetto Dunes, including Shelter Cove Marina condominiums.

Resort Rentals of Hilton Head Island (843-686-6008 or 1-800-845-7017; www.hhivacations.com) More than 200 properties in Sea Pines, South Forest Beach, North Forest Beach, Shipyard Plantation, and Palmetto Dunes.

Sea Pines Resort (1-866-561-8802; www.seapines.com) One- to six-bedroom accommodations in private homes and villas in the island's most exclusive and well-known resort.

Vacation Time of Hilton Head (1-800-845-9500; www.vthhi.com) Oceanfront accommodations in efficiencies or one-, two-, and three-bedroom villas.

Wyndham Vacation Rentals (843-842-3006 or 1-800-448-3412; www.wyndhamvacationrentals.com) Representing some of Hilton Head's high-end properties, as well as the best in the moderate range, in five island communities.

island's other private communities do not generally permit short-term rental programs.

Villas and homes usually rent by the week. The least expensive summer rates are about $1,000 per week, which can buy you a small unit outside a plantation more than 0.5-mile from the beach. In 2013, about $7,000 per week in the summer would secure an oceanfront home. From November to February, rates drop substantially.

Most rental companies manage properties in a variety of sizes, shapes, and locations. A desirable vacation rental would offer free swimming, free or discounted tennis, discounts on golf, and should be within walking distance of the beach. Before you sign a rental agreement, make sure you understand policies regarding deposits, refunds in the event of cancellation, times of arrival and departure, and charges, if any,

RECREATIONAL VEHICLE PARKS/CAMPING

Hilton Head Island Motor Coach Resort (843-785-7699 or 1-800-722-2365; www.hiltonheadmotorcoach resort.com), 133 Arrow Rd. Full hook-ups, 401 sites, six tennis courts, pool, artificial lake, shuffleboard, horseshoes, basketball, playground, dog park, WiFi, laundry, and bathrooms with tubs and saunas.

Hilton Head Harbor RV Resort & Marina (843-681-3256 or 1-800-845-9560; www.hiltonheadharbor.com), 43 Jenkins Rd., north end of Hilton Head. Full hook-ups, 200 RV sites, bathhouses, two pools, three tennis courts, laundry, WiFi, exercise room, sauna, and whirlpool.

Dining

Taste of the town . . . local restaurants, cafés, bars, bistros, etc.

These are just some of the 300 places to eat or relax and listen to music. There are selections in every price category. Where you go may depend on whether you're traveling with children (if you're at a resort, ask the concierge about babysitting services or specifically family-friendly restaurants); if you're on a guy's golf weekend or with the ladies for spa treatments; celebrating in a quiet way; or if you seek a later-night bar scene. The price categories are the same as described elsewhere in the guide, and represent per-person expenses estimated without tax, tip, or bar beverages. In general, dining out is more expensive on Hilton Head than in similar restaurants elsewhere, although there are savings to be found in eating before the crowd (early-bird specials) or on a particular evening when the restaurant has an advertised special. Taxi service for night owls 24/7 is Yellow Cab (843-686-6666; www .yellowcabhhi.com).

Charlie's L'Etoile Verte (843-785-9277; www.charliesgreenstar.com), 8 New Orleans Rd. Open Mon.–Sat. for dinner and lunch. Expensive–Very expensive. For 30 years, Charlie's has been welcoming locals and return visitors with consistently delicious and creative French cuisine. The menu changes daily based on the freshest seafood, and it also features such favorites as rack of lamb and filet mignon. Charlie's is known for its extensive wine list and cozy atmosphere and is often considered the island's best fine dining restaurant.

CQs (843-671-2779; www.cqs restaurant.com), 140 Lighthouse Rd. Open daily for dinner. Expensive. When Hilton Head was a lot smaller, CQs was kind of a clubhouse tucked into Sea Pines. It still has that feel, with its murals, memorabilia, and heart-pine floors. The cuisine is much upgraded to steaks and seafood specials and local treats like South Carolina BBQ chicken. The early seating features an inexpensive tasting menu, about $20 apiece; you can pick and choose from small-portion samplings at The Chef's Table; or select from about a dozen entrées on the dinner menu paired with wine by the glass. The patio, with its tables shaded by live oaks, is popular in spring and fall.

Daniel's Restaurant and Lounge (843-341-9379; www.danielshhi.com), 2 N. Beach Dr. Open daily for dinner. Moderate–Expensive. Small tapas plates featuring the cuisines of Asia, India, and the Americas. Hearty steaks and local seafood and late night bottle service. Reservations for dining recommended. It pushes back the chairs at night and becomes a dance club. A local favorite bar scene.

Hilton Head Diner (843-686-2400; hiltonheaddiner.com), 6 Marina Side Dr. Open 24 hours a day for breakfast, lunch, and dinner. Inexpensive. An update on the classic American roadside eatery. Breakfast is served all the time—but there are big sandwiches, dinner entrées (with potato, salad, and vegetable), and beer and wine available. Desserts from the cold case.

Hudson's on the Docks (843-681-2772; www.hudsonsonthedocks.com), One Hudson Rd., just off Squire Pope Rd., north end of the island. Open daily for lunch and dinner. Moderate. Large, informal family restaurant, one of the first on the island, in a rustic setting overlooking the Intracoastal Waterway and the shrimp trawlers and fishing boats docked at Skull Creek. Known for its sunsets, with plenty of seating on the deck. Classic entrées include fried local seafood platters, but there are blackened and boiled options. No reservations—go early on a summer night or risk waiting two hours to be served.

Market Street (843-686-4976; www.marketstreetcafe.com), 1 N. Forest Beach Dr. Open daily for lunch and dinner. Inexpensive. If on a starry summer night you've decided to walk the beach near the Coligny Beach access and hear Greek music, you must be nearby. Enjoy informal grill food— gyros, pita wraps—or Greek specialties like moussaka, dolmathes, and spanakopita. Locals come for the homemade soups and vegetarian options.

Michael Anthony's (843-785-6272; www.michael-anthonys.com), 37 New Orleans Rd. Open for dinner nightly except Sun. Expensive. Family owned and run, the kitchen elaborates on northern Italian classics like homemade gnocchi, osso buco, and veal tenderloin. Seasonal additions include game in the fall and specialty mushrooms and truffles when available. An elegant room, divided lengthwise by a curving, granite bar illuminated by pinpoint lights on one side, and a dining area accented by walls the color of terra-cotta and pale wood furnishings. The work of the pastry chef attracts diners for nightcaps, wine by the glass (for which they are noted), and dessert in the bar.

Red Fish (843-686-3388; www .redfishofhiltonhead.com), 8 Archer Rd. Open Mon.–Sat. for lunch, daily for dinner. Expensive–Very expensive. Red Fish is popular because of its creative menu of spiced seafood (like the Cajun shrimp and lobster burger) and steak, although you can order entrées simply grilled with oil and lemon. A stunning dining room feels like an art gallery on South Beach. The attention to its wines, and an on-site wine market with more than 1,000 bottles from which you may select for your meal, has garnered national recognition. Dining indoors or out. Reservations are a good idea.

Skull Creek Boathouse (843-681-3663; www.skullcreekboathouse .com), 397 Squire Pope Rd. Expensive. Casual. Open daily for lunch and dinner. No reservations, but there are lots of places to sit or walk around if you have to wait, and room for restless kids to play. Its outdoor bar and wine list have been awarded nationally in "best of" lists. Live music. Soups, salads, sandwiches, steaks, seafood, pasta, and chicken.

Truffles Café (843-671-6136; www.trufflescafe.com), 71 Lighthouse Rd., Sea Pines Center. Open daily for lunch and dinner. Inexpensive–

Moderate. Casual atmosphere, home-made soups, huge salads, French-bread sandwiches and wraps, burgers, fresh vegetables, and grilled entrées. Light meals like the potpie are inexpensive, and you can order them at any time. The market is full of gourmet items, and take-out is available. It's a cross between a fern bar and a wine bar, with a bistro menu.

Vine (843-686-3900), 1 N. Forest Beach Dr. Expensive. Open daily for dinner. A tiny, casual European bistro that takes its farm-to-table philosophy seriously but without any pretension.

Excellently curated wine list. It's not at all typical Hilton Head—much more intimate on a Greenwich Village scale and anonymously located right off the busiest beach access at Coligny.

Wise Guys (843-842-8866; www.wiseguyshhi.com), 1513 Main St. Dinner nightly until midnight, later on weekends. Known for its mixed sea-food grill entrees and a hefty cowboy ribeye with brandied peppercorn sauce as well as other serious chops and cuts. But they bow to gluten-free tastes and pork, veal, and lamb, too. The look is cool, urban, and sleek.

Nightlife
After-hours attractions and activities

The beat goes on and on at Hilton Head, especially in summer, when crowds jam the dance floor or couples find quieter music in lounges or late-night eateries. Check ahead for cover charges or drink minimums. The legal drinking age is 21.

Big Bamboo (843-686-3443; www.bigbamboocafe.com), upstairs at Coligny Plaza. Live music and dancing in a pretend World War II–era South Pacific retro setting. Check website for music listings.

Char Bar (843-785-2427), 33 Office Park Rd. Open Tue.–Sun. 12–10. Casual. Place for late-night specialty burgers. Music and outdoor bar.

The Electric Piano Bar (843-785-5397; www.electricpianohhi.com), 33 Office Park Rd. A late night venue where the customers are as much a part of the show as the performers—sing-along and dancing. Not for youngsters, this scene can get raucous. Live music Wed.–Sat.

Jazz Corner (843-842-8620; www.thejazzcorner.com), Village at Wexford. National and regional jazz artists perform here nightly. Check the schedule to find your favorites: big band, swing, rhythm and blues, and classic jazz. Shows start at 8. In addition to being a grown-up place to hear great music, it has a wonderful menu that in the past couple of years diners are raving about. This is dinner and a show that can compare to the big city. Reservations strongly recommended.

Kingfisher (843-785-4442; www.kingfisherseafood.com), Shelter Cove Har-bour. Live music and dancing beginning at 6:30 PM Wed.–Fri., including big bands, jazz combos, and acoustic guitarists. Bar menu or full meals (steak, pasta, seafood) served.

Quarterdeck (843-842-1999; www.seapines.com), Harbour Town. Laid-back waterfront lounge, an island classic since 1970. Late-afternoon beach music, folk rock, or steel drums outside daily (5–9 PM); after sunset on Fri. and Sat., the music rocks harder and moves inside until midnight.

Though it's known for its beaches, golf courses, and boating, Hilton Head has a vibrant night-life as well.

Reilley's North (843-681-4153; www.reilleyshiltonhead.com), 95 Mathews Dr., and Reilley's South (843-842-4414), 7D Greenwood Dr. Reilley's has been an island institution for 27 years, with the feel of a true Boston pub. Both locations offer nightly specials and happy hour.

The Salty Dog (843-363-2198; www.saltydog.com), South Beach Marina Village. Waterfront dining and bar with nightly music. They also offer a children's magic show Wed.–Fri. from 7–8 and pre-dinner kids' concerts.

Wild Wing Café (843-785-9464; www.wildwingcafe.com), 72 Pope Ave. Live music Thurs.–Sat. and weekly trivia contests. Happy hour specials every day.

XO Lounge (843-842-8000; www.xohhi.com), Omni Oceanfront Resort in Palmetto Dunes. Live entertainment nightly in a swanky, recently renovated club where champagne flights and an appetizer menu are served into the wee hours.

Touring

Fun in and around Hilton Head's historic sites..

The towns of Bluffton and Beaufort are easy day trips. (For detailed information on these destinations, see Chapter Three, *Beaufort, Edisto & Bluffton.*) Each has a historic area of old houses, shops, galleries, and restaurants. Savannah is about an hour away, and you could tour the historic district, wander around and have at least one meal, and be back in time for sunset. A trip to Charleston requires a bit more time and planning, including approximately four hours by car, round-trip.

An excursion to Daufuskie Island, which is not linked to the mainland or Hilton Head Island, is not only easier than ever but a few more touring options have emerged. For a sense of its history before you go, and if you're deciding on a day trip, contact the local historical foundation (www.daufuskieislandhistorical foundation.org). A small part of the island has luxury homes but it remains in proud isolation—with two art galleries and restaurants, and a limited tour business including site visits to cemeteries and slave cabins, churches and schools. The Daufuskie Conservancy (www.daufuskieconservancy.org) is a nonprofit organization that offers guided history tours by bus (not for children under 12).

Calibogue Cruises (843-342-8687; www.daufuskiefreeport.com) provides transport, leaving from Broad Creek Marina on Hilton Head. A day visit is $59 per person and includes ferry ticket, lunch or dinner at the Old Crab Company, and either a 2½ hour self-guided tour via golf cart or a 2-hour guided history tour.

Chapels of ease like this one were built for those who could not reach the main church.

SC Lowcountry Tourism Commission

Outside Daufuskie (843-686-6996; www.outsidedaufuskie.com) offers private charters and customized trips.

From Savannah to Daufuskie, contact the Bull River Marina (912-897-7300; www.bullrivermarina.com) where a trip costs $225 for six passengers to the south end and $275 to the north end, where the resort at Haig Point is located. Marshside Mama's Café (843-785-4755; www.marshsidemamas.com), 15 Haig Point Rd., is a small tin-roofed shack with most dining outside, a full bar, and dogs in the yard. Funky and country. It serves lunch and dinner on a seasonal schedule.

For additional information on canoeing, kayaking, and eco-tours, which may include dolphin-watching, see the Recreation section below.

Camelot Limousine and Tours (843-842-7777; www.hiltonheadlimo .com) On- and off-island transportation and personalized tours.

Coastal Discovery Museum at Honey Horn (843-689-6767; www .coastaldiscovery.org), 70 Honey Horn Dr. The museum offers nine tours by boat, trolley, and on foot. Most tours suitable for all ages, including tours with historic, wildlife, marine, and landscape themes. Tours last from one to two hours. Make reservations on their website.

Gullah Heritage Tours (843-681-7066; www.gullaheritage.com) Two-hour tour departs from the Coastal Discovery Museum, Tues.–Sat., 10 AM and 2 PM; $32 adults, $15 children under 12. This narrated tour visits ten Gullah communities and usually is led by a native islander. Specialized tours and lunches may be arranged.

Low Country Adventures (843-681-8212; www.lowcountryadventures.com) Island and off-island tours in a tour van or bus, including day trips with a guide to the historic areas of Charleston, Savannah, and Hilton Head Island.

Vagabond Cruise (843-363-9026; www.vagabondcruise.com), Harbour Town Marina, Sea Pines. Vessels take you to Savannah's River Street and pick you up four hours later. A good way to avoid the driving/parking hassle and get a sense of place: why Savannah was and is such a significant port. You may also arrange for a cruise to Daufuskie Island on a Wed. from 9 AM–1 PM. Call for reservations and rates.

Culture

Great places to see and things to do.

As Hilton Head has grown, so has its arts community. Check the Arts & Entertainment section of *The Island Packet* (www.islandpacket.com) for listings. The largest venue for performances is the Arts Center of Coastal Carolina (843-842-2787; www.artshhi.com), 14 Shelter Cove Ln., which features nationally touring performers, regional orchestras, dance, theater, children's theater, and gallery space. It is active all year long, booking high-quality traveling shows. Performances by local gospel choirs and storytellers celebrating Gullah heritage in the Sea Islands occur once a season.

ART

The Art League of Hilton Head and Walter Greer Gallery (843-681-5060; www .hhal.org), in the Arts Center of Coastal Carolina, 14 Shelter Cove Ln., has shows by local artists and national visual artists nearly every month and features more than 500 members. They offer off-site exhibits in various locations on the island. (See "Galleries" in the Shopping section in Chapter Three for more art information and gallery listings for Bluffton, which is more invested in artists and an art scene than Hilton Head.)

FILM

Cinemark Bluffton (843-706-2888; www.cinemark.com), 106 Buckwalter Pkwy., Bluffton. A multiplex with the latest releases and a classics series of old films for kids and adults.

Coligny Theatre (843-686-3500; www.colignytheatre.com), Coligny Plaza. Showing independent and art house films.

Northridge Ten Cinemas (843-342-3800; www.southeastcinemas.com), 435 William Hilton Pkwy.

Park Plaza Cinemas (843-715-0479), 33 Office Park Rd.

Several sites dating to the time of Native American settlements and covering the plantation and Civil War period and after are accessible to visitors. For more information and location maps, contact Coastal Discovery Museum at Honey Horn (see address and hours below) and ask about Gullah Heritage Trail Tours, which include visits to praise houses and cemeteries, and to Mitchelville, the first freed African American township in the country. The Heritage Library Foundation (843-686-6560; www.heritagelib.org), 852 William Hilton Pkwy., offers a unique opportunity to research families, not just sites. Hundreds of books and periodicals and access to genealogy subscription websites form the core of an African American research collection. Open Mon., Tues., Thurs., and Fri. 10–3, but call to confirm.

Baynard Ruins within Sea Pines Plantation. The remains of a plantation house and outbuildings first constructed circa 1800 can be seen on a short, self-guided walk at the site. The ruins are made of tabby, a popular homemade Lowcountry building material that resulted from burning oyster shells (to make lime), which were then mixed with whole shells, sand, and water. This is one of few sites where you can still see it. $5 gate fee to access Sea Pines.

Coastal Discovery Museum at Honey Horn (843-689-6767; www.coastal discovery.org), 70 Honey Horn Dr. Located at the north end of the island. Archaeological digs have yielded a collection of artifacts related to the island's history and culture, and these are on display along with models, dioramas, and explanatory

Tabby ruins on Daufuskie Island.   SC Lowcountry Tourism Commission

panels and videos on the area. Oral history interviews capturing the decades of small farming, fishing, oystering, and timbering industries are ongoing. The gift shop offers an excellent selection of books on the Lowcountry as well as maps, field guides, and activity kits for kids. The museum offers many tours of the marsh, beach, other natural areas; and historic sites, including the Steam Cannon, Mitchelville, and Fort Walker. Fees vary; reservations suggested. Museum hours are Mon.–Sat. 9–4:30, Sun. 11–3.

Fish Haul Plantation off Beach City Rd. Only the chimneys of slave dwellings remain at what was once a thriving Sea Island cotton plantation. Federal troops camped here from the time of Union occupation in November 1861.

Fort Howell, Beach City Rd. A large earthwork built by the Union troops in 1864 to strengthen the defense of Mitchelville.

Fort Mitchel, Hilton Head Plantation. An earthwork fortification, circa 1862, constructed as part of the island's defense system. For a guided tour, call the Heritage Library Foundation (843-686-6560).

Indian Shell Ring, Sea Pines Forest Preserve. Native Americans occupied Hilton Head and other sea islands some 4,000 years ago, and left their mark in huge rings and shell middens. It is thought that this site represents the refuse of oyster shells piled behind each of many huts that stood in a small circle.

Zion Chapel of Ease, William Hilton Pkwy. at Mathews Dr. A small chapel, built circa 1786 for the convenience of worshippers who lived too far from the Episcopal church at Beaufort, once occupied this site. The circa 1846 Baynard Mausoleum within its cemetery is the largest antebellum structure extant on the island.

MUSIC

The Hilton Head Symphony (843-842-2055; www.hhso.org) In its 32nd season, the Hilton Head Symphony offers a variety of concerts throughout the year. Check the website for their calendar of events.

THEATER

South Carolina Repertory Company (843-342-2057; www.hiltonheadtheatre.com), 136 Beach City Rd., near the airport. The diverse troupe often collaborates with other regional companies to produce professional-quality plays, mostly for the spring season.

Recreation

Active pursuits in and around Hilton Head.

Hilton Head's reputation as a place to pursue golf, tennis, fishing, water sports, and touring, or to simply enjoy the beach, is well deserved. The following listings offer some sense of the range of activities the island has to offer. There are seven public beach access points (with metered parking) and 60 miles of pathways for bikers, in-line skaters, and runners. View pathways information and maps at www.hiltonheadislandsc.gov.

BEACH ACCESS

Twelve miles of gently sloping beaches define the island's ocean edge. They can be as wide as 600 feet at low tide, providing a hard surface for fat-tire bicycles. Although most entry points to the beach are restricted—behind private resort plantation gates—the most popular public ones are: Coligny Beach Park (located at the end of Pope Ave.), Folly Field Beach Park (off Folly Field Rd.), Dreissen Beach Park (off Bradley Beach Rd.), Burkes Beach and Chaplin Community Parks (off US 278), Alder Lane (off S. Forest Beach Dr.), Fish Haul Creek Park (284 Beach City Rd.), and Mitchelville Beach Park (off Beach City Rd.). Islander's Beach Park (off Folly Field Rd.) is a local spot with less parking, where you could have someone drop you off or ride your bike. Others offer metered parking spaces (50 cents to $1 per hour), and Coligny and Dreissen have long-term lots.

On some nights (May through October), you can watch the amazing logger-head turtle, an endangered species, crawl ashore and lay its eggs in nests it digs on the beach, or see hundreds of loggerhead hatchlings make their way back to the ocean. Volunteer groups monitor the beach and sometimes move the eggs to higher ground or protected sites, away from tides and hungry raccoons. The turtles are slow moving and docile, but chary: Do not disturb them with light or touch the nests. Just seeing these huge creatures is magical.

Dogs are not permitted on the beach from 10 AM to 5 PM from the beginning of Memorial Day weekend through Labor Day. Motor vehicles, alcohol, glass con-

There are more than 12 miles of oceanfront beach in Hilton Head, with many points of public access and multiple places to rent bikes or beach chairs.
Courtesy of the Hilton Head Island Visitor & Convention Bureau

tainers, and nudity are not allowed. Fishing, boating, surfing, ball-playing, and similar activities are prohibited in designated swimming areas. The beaches are patrolled by sheriff's deputies; lifeguard stations are posted.

BEACH ACTIVITIES

If you haven't brought your beach equipment with you, stock up at the Coligny Kite Company (843-785-5483), Coligny Plaza, or rent larger items such as boogie boards, chairs, umbrellas, and floats on the beach. The shops at Coligny Plaza, at the end of Pope Avenue near the beach access point, offer the best selection of beach accessories on the island.

Coastal Discovery Museum at Honey Horn (see entry above under "Historic Sites" in the Culture section) offers guided walks several days per week on the island's beaches, and, on some evenings, a turtle tour to see the loggerheads nesting or hatching. Each tour lasts about 90 minutes and explains the island's ecology, flora, and fauna. Children will like learning about shells and hunting hermit crabs.

Palm trees are everywhere on Hilton Head.

BICYCLING

Bikes are easy to come by, and you can expect island-wide pickup and delivery. If you're traveling with youngsters, you'll be able to get baby-carriers, helmets, bikes with training wheels, hook-on "trailers," and jogging strollers. Ask about in-line skate rentals. Local enthusiasts have created maps for rides of 22 to 60 miles (www.hiltonheadisland.org.) Bike paths extend from the tip of North Forest Beach to the end of South Forest Beach, along Pope Avenue, and up William Hilton Parkway to Squire Pope Road, and take detours to the beach and marsh. Bike paths also thread through the private plantations. At low tide, ride on the beach. Rental charges for bicycles start at $15 per day and $20–30 per week for a simple cruiser model.

AAA Riding Tigers (843-686-5833; www.aaaridingtigers.com).

Bike Doctor (843-681-7532; www.bikedoctorhhi.com) can also repair your bike.

Hilton Head Bicycle Company (843-686-6888; www.hiltonheadbicycle.com).

Island Cruisers (843-785-4321; www.islandcruisersbikerentals.com).

Pedals (843-842-5522; www.pedalsbicycles.com).

BIRD-WATCHING

Hilton Head still has some quiet places for birds to nest and feed. According to the island's Audubon Society chapter, some 200 species of birds regularly visit, and in the past 10 years, more than 350 species have been sighted. Among the most distinctive "frequent flyers" are the snowy egret, great blue heron, white ibis, and osprey. Catch a glimpse of them for yourself during daylight hours at the following sites, where paths and boardwalks can accommodate hikers, bikers, and joggers.

Audubon Newhall Preserve, Palmetto Bay Rd., 0.75 mile from Sea Pines Circle. A 50-acre sanctuary open daily from dawn to dusk that preserves the Lowcountry environment for plants and animals. Trees and plants are labeled for self-guided walks on woodland trails, and lists of bird sightings are posted on a bulletin board at the entrance. Interpretative walks are offered in the spring and fall. To arrange a group tour, contact the local Audubon organization through their website (www.hiltonheadaudubon.org).

Coastal Discovery (843-689-6767; www.coastaldiscovery.com) Offers guided walks in the Sea Pines Forest Preserve and has a birding exhibit on display at its museum headquarters. For nearby, off-island sites, see "Nature Preserves" in the Recreation section of Chapter 2, *Savannah*.

Pinckney Island Wildlife Refuge (912-652-4415; www.fws.gov/pinckney island), 0.5 mile west of Hilton Head Island on US 278. Open daily dawn–dusk. This pristine 4,035-acre landscape features the best bird-watching during the spring and fall and an easy 4 mile bike trail to White Point, site of an early Native American settlement.

Sea Pines Forest Preserve (843-842-1979; www.seapines.com), enter at Greenwood Dr. and Lawton Dr. in Sea Pines Plantation. This 400-acre site with a shell ring and old rice field offers a self-guided walking tour, which takes one to two hours. $5 fee to enter Sea Pines Plantation.

Whooping Crane Pond Conservancy (www.hhilandtrust.org), Hilton Head Plantation. Features a boardwalk and self-guided nature trail.

BOATING

For sailboat charters and bareboat rentals, contact the companies listed below and also check the "Marinas" section. If you want to nurture a wilder streak, look into waterskiing or kneeboarding, floating with a parasail, riding a WaveRunner, or "sledding" on a rubber tube. Some companies have special lessons/day programs for kids.

Commander Zodiac (843-671-3344; www.commanderzodiac.com), South Beach Marina. Visit the dolphins in engine-powered rubber rafts. Small sailboats for rent, private lessons, and rides.

H20 Sports Center (843-671-4386; www.h20sports.com), Harbour Town Marina, Sea Pines. Rentals for, and instruction in, parasailing, waverunning, kneeboarding, paddle boarding, and waterskiing.

Jarvis Creek Water Sports (843-681-9260; jarviscreekwatersports.com), 104A William Hilton Pkwy. The hydrobikes look like sleek bicycle assemblies mounted on even sleeker rowing shells, pedal-powered by one or two people. They also offer kayak and canoe rentals.

Hilton Head is a major recreational port for local and visiting boaters.

Palmetto Bay Water Sports (843-785-2345; www.palmettobaywatersports
.com), Palmetto Bay Marina. If you want more than paddle or wind power, you
can rent a variety of watercraft by the hour: about $105 for single WaveRunners;
$235 for a 19-foot motorboat for 2 hour minimum rental.

UFO Parasailing (843-686-4386; www.flyufoparasail.com), Palmetto Bay
Marina. For $69 you can hold your breath and rise 500 feet in the air; double
parasails available.

Canoeing and Kayaking

Amid the opportunities to play golf and tennis or be a spectator in a beautifully
manicured and maintained resort landscape, a visitor can forget that Hilton Head
has in its own backyard world-class, low-tech, low-impact recreational options.
They are found in the creeks and on the perimeter that makes Hilton Head an
island, after all.

Today you can explore miles of waterways in a canoe or kayak, on your own
or with a guided tour, by the half-day, the day, at sunset, by moonlight, or on an
overnight expedition. No experience is necessary, all safety equipment and basic
instruction is provided, and kids are welcome. You may end up paddling out to
a sandbar, fishing, taking a birding tour, or winding through the maze of coastal
marshlands, pristine rivers, and nature preserves.

Some outfitters offer extended-day programs for teens. For paddlers who
feel comfortable going out on their own, day-rate rental charges for kayaks start

at $55 for a single, $65 for a double, and kayaks may be rented for as long as six days. Two-hour guided tours of local waters like Broad Creek, where you are likely to see lots of birds and fish in action, start at $40 per person, $30 for kids 12 and younger. Longer tours run about $125 per person, depending on the arrangements. Customized trips and overnight camping/biking expeditions are available, just ask. Reservations suggested for tours.

Hilton Head Outfitters (843-785-2449; www.hiltonheadoutfitters.com), 80 Queens Folly Rd. Guided tours of the Palmetto Dunes lagoon system.

Native Guide Tours (843-816-4538; www.nativeguidetours.com), 8 Second St. For kayakers. Tours include the May River and coastal regions between Hilton Head and Savannah.

Outside Hilton Head (843-686-6996; www.outsidehiltonhead.com), 32 Shelter Cove Ln., Suite H. This longtime island business and outfitter offers clinics, teen camps, weekend retreats, and lessons as well as tours. Trips vary in length and season, but always include two-hour and daylong excursions.

Water-Dog Outfitters (843-686-3554; www.waterdogoutfitter.com), 10 Simmons Rd. Paddling in Broad Creek is easy enough for families, and Pinckney Island is challenging enough for intermediates. Bike/kayak excursions are also offered.

If you're on your own with a kayak, here are public landings. Note that while you can park for free, the spaces fill quickly.

Broad Creek Boat Ramp (Helmsman Way, under the Charles Fraser Bridge)
C. C. Haigh, Jr. Landing (off US 278 at Pinckney Island)
Marshland Road Boat Ramp (Marshland Road)

Cruises

Adventure Cruises (843-785-4558; www.hiltonheadisland.com), Shelter Cove Harbour. Dolphin-watch nature cruises lasting nearly two hours as well as sunset cruises. Adults $16, children $8.

Dolphin Nature Tour (843-681-2522; www.hiltonheadtours.com), Broad Creek Marina. Narrated environmental tours (90 minutes) aboard the 16 passenger *SS Pelican,* a restored Navy Motor Whaler with canopy, or the *Island Queen,* which holds up to 40 passengers. Adults $20, children $11. Advance purchase recommended.

Flying Circus and Pau Hana (843-686-2582; www.hiltonheadisland.com /sailing), Palmetto Bay Marina. *Flying Circus* is a fast catamaran offering two-hour daylight and sunset cruises for a maximum of six passengers. *Pau Hana,* a larger catamaran, can carry 49 passengers. Call for reservations and rates.

Lowcountry Nature Tours (843-683-0187; lowcountrynaturetours.com), departs from Shelter Cove Marina. Another good option for children to see the dolphins and birds up close for two hours. Maximum six passengers.

FAMILY FUN

Beachcombing, bike-riding, flying a kite, sunset concerts, and fireworks displays are part of the Hilton Head package. Outside Hilton Head (843-686-6996; www .outsidehiltonhead.com) offers kayak camps for kids as young as 7, as well as teen activities. Playgrounds are located at Harbour Town in Sea Pines ($5 admission),

Shelter Cove Harbour, and the Island Recreation Center, 20 Wilborn Rd. at the north end of the island. Bristol Sports Arena Skate Park is located off Arrow Rd. on the island's south end. The rec center features a handicapped-accessible area with a swing for wheelchairs. Check *The Island Packet* to confirm schedules or find special family-oriented events. Some of the following listings may be of help on a rainy day, or for older kids who might prefer arcades.

Adventure Cove Family Fun Center (843-842-9990; www.adventurecove .com), Folly Field Rd. and US 278. Miniature golf and arcade.

Island Recreation Center (843-681-7273; www.islandreccenter.org), 20 Wilborn Rd. A year-round activity center with camps, clinics, and sports programs organized by the day, week, and month for children, teens, and adults. Check to see if events like water carnivals or craft classes (among others) might coincide with your visit. Call ahead; registration may be required.

Zipline Hilton Head (843-682-6000 or 1-888-283-6084; www.ziplinehilton head.com), at Broad Creek Marina Adventures, 33 Broad Creek Marina Wy. Eight ziplines, up to 75 feet high, course above the marsh and sound. Up to eight zipliners can join a group, zipping with two guides. For ages 10 and up, a two-hour eco-tour is $89 per person and a 900-foot zip ride is $20 per person.

Summer Concerts: In the evening, family entertainers gather large audiences for free shows. Check the local paper for listings, and plan to arrive early to secure parking. In Sea Pines Plantation (under the Liberty Oak at Harbour Town; Sea Pines gate pass $5), singers and guitarists perform from 8 to 10 nightly except Saturday. The audience sits on benches and kids are encouraged to participate. Family sing-alongs also take place Monday through Friday at Shelter Cove Harbour, and Tuesday nights there are fireworks. Various musicians, puppeteers, and clowns also turn up at Coligny Plaza (off Pope Avenue) Monday through Friday nights to entertain families. At South Beach Marina (Sea Pines Plantation) you can enjoy music while the sun sets over the docks.

FISHING

There are many options, too numerous to define here, but the diversity indicates the number of customized possibilities: size of the boat, length of the day, level of challenge, location, number of anglers, type of catch, and, of course, the probability of success. (All but the last can be provided.) Fly-fishing is also available. Boats are fully equipped with tackle, etc., and depart from several marinas for inshore waters, flats, artificial reefs, and the Gulf Stream. Potential catches include tarpon, marlin, and sailfish; amberjack, shark, king mackerel, and bluefish closer to shore; and flounder, red drum, sea trout, and sheepshead in the coastal flats. Prices for four to six passengers for a half-day of fishing run from about $425 to $700. A Gulf Stream expedition (about 14 hours) starts at about $2,300 for six passengers.

Atlantic Fishing Charters (843-671-2704; www.seapinesresort.com), Harbour Town Yacht Basin. Five boats (25 to 38 feet long) rigged with fish-finding equipment; catch and release fishing at night for shark.

Blue Water Bait & Tackle (843-671-3060; www.bluewaterhhi.com), 232 S. Sea Pines Dr., South Beach Marina. Trophy fishing and taxidermy services. Five boats, 17–32 feet long, fishing offshore and inshore.

Capt. Hook (843-785-1700; www.hiltonheadisland.com/captainhook), Shelter Cove Harbour. A good family choice: 70-foot boat with enclosed cabin and restrooms, food on board.

Palmetto Bay Marina Charter (843-785-7131; www.palmettobaymarinahhi .com), Palmetto Bay Marina. Book a boat and captain for a half-day of offshore fishing for six passengers, or inshore fishing to the flats for four passengers.

FITNESS, WELLNESS, AND SPAS

Major resorts such as the Westin and Hilton have in-house spas. Reservations are highly recommended at all locations. If you want to continue your yoga practice on a daily basis while visiting, contact the businesses listed—who can steer you in the right direction or suggest a personal trainer.

Body Pilates by Jenni (843-842-5562), 26 Palmetto Bay Rd.

Esmeralda's Pilates Studio and Massage Therapy Center (843-785-9588), 14 New Orleans Rd.

The European Spa (843-682-3915; www.european-spa.com), 5 Grasslawn Ave. Serving men and women, featuring aromatherapy massage, facials, and foot and leg massages for athletes.

Hilton Head Health Institute (843-785-7292; www.hhhealth.com), 14 Valencia Rd. A full-service spa where you can also go for extended visits to embark on a personalized program of fitness, diet, and a healthier lifestyle.

Le Spa (843-363-6000; www.lespahiltonhead.com), 71 Lighthouse Rd., Sea Pines Plantation. A wide selection of massages is available, long and short, shiatsu, hot rock, deep tissue, reflexology, or any combination.

The Sanctuary (843-842-5999; www.sanctuaryeurospa.com), 217 Park Plaza. A full-service spa for men and women where you can spend an hour or a day.

Seeds of Calm Spa (843-686-5525; www.seedsofcalmspa.com), 18 Executive Park Rd. You can detoxify your body with a wrap, rejuvenate with an herbal rub, undergo deep massage therapy, and have a vegetarian meal brought to you.

GOLF

Golf culture has shaped life here physically and in many ways determined Hilton Head's identity (changing somewhat in 2013, with a civic committee examining the branding of Hilton Head as a tennis mecca). Today there are some 30 courses in the Hilton Head area (on and just off the island), and more than half of them are open for public play. The remainder serve resort guests or members. Golf is expensive, and Hilton Head is no different—anywhere from $95 to $250 for prime time, with the average about $125 including cart and fees. Early morning or later afternoon play costs less, as do resort packages or packages sold by bundling brokers. Public course play starts at about $95. (Walking is permitted on several courses—check ahead for caddie help.) During the low season—winter months—prices can drop by 40 percent. A good source for information on many courses is www.lowcountrygolfcourseownersassociation.com.

For courses in and around Beaufort—within an hour's drive of Hilton Head—check Chapter Three, *Beaufort, Edisto & Bluffton*. For information and central reservations, contact Hilton Head Golf Island (www.hiltonheadgolfisland.com).

Reservations to secure tee times are essential—some courses accept reservations from nonresort guests up to 90 days in advance, others just 30 to 60 days in advance. (It gets crowded—800,000 rounds of golf are played annually at Hilton Head.) Unless noted, all courses are 18 holes. Appropriate dress calls for shirts with collars for men and no blue jeans, gym shorts, or jogging shorts. At Sea Pines, nonmetal spikes are required. If you're looking to improve your game, inquire about clinics, private instruction, and programs from half a day to three days at Golf Academy at Sea Pines (843-785-4540; www.seapines.com) or Palmetto Dunes Golf Academy (843-785-1138; www.palmetto dunes.com).

Hilton Head's dozens of golf courses draw year-round visitors and PGA tournaments. Courtesy of the Hilton Head Island Visitor & Convention Bureau

Hilton Head Plantation

Country Club of Hilton Head (843-681-4653; www.hiltonheadclub.com) Par 72; 5,373-yard ladies course to 6,919-yard champion course. Designed by Rees Jones.

Oyster Reef Golf Club (843-681-1700; www.oysterreefgolfclub.com) Par 72; 5,288-yard forward course to 7,005-yard champion course. Designed by Rees Jones.

Indigo Run

Golden Bear Golf Club (843-689-2200; www.goldenbear-indigorun.com) Par 72; 4,965-yard forward course to 7,014-yard champion course. Designed by Jack Nicklaus. Four-star rating from *Fodor's Golf Digest*.

Palmetto Dunes Resort

Arthur Hills Course (843-785-1140; www.palmettodunes.com) Par 72; 4,999-yard forward course to 6,651-yard champion course. Designed by Arthur Hills. *Fodor's Golf Digest* gave it a 4.5-star rating.

George Fazio Course (843-785-1130; www.palmettodunes.com) Par 70; 5,273-yard ladies course to 6,873-yard champion course. Designed by George Fazio. Named one of *Fodor's Golf Digest*'s 100 top American courses.

Robert Trent Jones (843-785-1136; www.playpalmettodunes.com) Par 72; 2,625-yard junior to 7,005-yard champion course. Designed by Robert Trent Jones/Roger Rulewich. Named South Carolina's Golf Course of the year in 2003. Permanent junior tees allow young golfers to play a classic course.

Palmetto Hall Plantation

Arthur Hills Course (843-681-1700; www.palmettohallgolf.com) Par 72; 4,956-yard forward course to 6,918-yard champion course. Designed by Arthur Hills. Four-star rating from *Fodor's Golf Digest*.

Robert Cupp Course (843-681-1700; www.palmettohallgolf.com) Par 72; 5,220-yard forward course to 7,079-yard tour course. Designed by Robert Cupp.

Port Royal Plantation

Barony Course (843-681-1700; www.portroyalgolf.com) Par 72; 5,183-yard forward course to 6,543-yard champion course. Designed by George Cobb.

Planter's Row Course (843-681-1700; www.portroyalgolf.com) Par 72; 5,119-yard forward course to 6,625-yard champion course. Designed by Willard Byrd.

Robber's Row Course (843-681-1700; www.portroyalgolf.com) Par 72; 4,902-yard forward course to 6,675-yard champion course. A Pete Dye renovation of a George Cobb course near what was Fort Walker, a Civil War camp.

Sea Pines Plantation

Harbour Town Golf Links (843-842-8484; www.seapines.com) Par 71; 5,208-yard green course to 7,107-yard "Heritage" course. Designed by Pete Dye. The Heritage is played on this course—rated among the top 75 in the world and among the top 50 in the U.S.—every April.

Heron Point (843-842-8484; www.seapines.com) Par 72; 5,261-yard ladies course to 7,103-yard champion course. Designed by Pete Dye.

Ocean Course (843-842-8484; www.seapines.com) Par 72; 5,325-yard green course to 6,906-yard "McCumber" course. First course on the island, redesigned in 1995 by Mark McCumber to remain challenging but still convey the original beauty that earned it an "Audubon Cooperative Sanctuary" designation.

SHIPYARD PLANTATION

Shipyard Golf Club (843-681-1700; www.shipyard.com) Par 36; 18 holes; 5,240-yard forward course to 6,830-yard champion course. Designed by George Cobb /Willard Byrd. A favorite of the senior PGA Tour.

Off-Island

Crescent Pointe Golf Club (843-706-2600; www.crescentpointegolf.com), US 278, Bluffton. Par 71; four tees from 5,219 yards to 6,772 yards. Designed by Arnold Palmer for "Arnie's Army."

Eagle's Pointe Golf Club (843-757-5900; www.eaglespointegolf.com), US 278, 7 miles west of Hilton Head. Par 71; 5,112 yards to 6,780 yards. Designed by Davis Love III, a five-time Heritage Classic winner. Advance reservations up to six months.

Hidden Cypress Golf Club (843-705-4999), Sun City Hilton Head, SC 170. Par 72; five tees from 4,974 yards to 6,953 yards. Designed by Mark McCumber.

Hilton Head National (843-842-5900; www.golfhiltonheadnational.com), US 278, Bluffton. Par 72; 18 holes; 4,649-yard forward course to 6,779-yard champion course. Designed by Gary Player/Bobby Weed. Advance reservations up to one year.

Island West Golf Club (843-689-6660; www.islandwestgolf.net), US 278, Bluffton. Par 72; 4,948-yard ladies course to 6,803-yard champion course. Designed by Fuzzy Zoeller/Clyde Johnston.

Okatie Creek Golf Club (843-705-4653), Sun City Hilton Head, SC 170. Par 72; 4,741-yard to 6,719-yard tees. Designed by Mark McCumber. The first of the courses at this resort designed for the over-55 crowd. Five sets of tees per hole accommodate the skilled and less-skilled golfer.

Old Carolina Golf Club (843-757-8311; www.oldcarolinagolf.com), US 278, Bluffton. Par 71/72; 9 holes; 2,290-yard ladies course to 3,440-yard champion course. Designed by Clyde Johnston.

Old South Golf Links (843-785-5353; www.oldsouthgolf.com), US 278, Bluffton. Par 71/72; 4,776-yard red tee ladies course to 5,772-yard green tee champion course. Designed by Clyde Johnston.

Rose Hill Golf Club (843-757-9030; www.golfrosehill.com), Rose Hill Plantation, US 278, Bluffton. Par 72; 18 holes; 5,100-yard to 6,961-yard tees. Designed by Gene Namm.

HORSEBACK RIDING

Lawton Stables (843-671-2586; www.lawtonstableshhi.com), 190 Greenwood Dr., Sea Pines. One-hour walking trail rides for adults and kids. Some riding experience

Riding on sandy roads, woodland trails, and the beach allows vistors to slow way down and experience the Lowcountry through five senses at once. Peter Loftus

required on trips through the 600-acre Sea Pines Forest Preserve. Prices start at $55 per person; pony rides for the younger set. Lessons for all levels include preparation of the horse. Check with the stable for lesson pricing. Reservations required.

MARINAS

The Hilton Head area has nine public marinas that offer boat rentals, transient berths, fishing charters, and services such as dry-dock storage, launching ramps, fuel, showering facilities, ship's stores, and repair shops. Rates for berthing vary, from $1–2.50 per foot, or by week/month. Charter fishing boats, small power-boats, sailboats, and yachts as long as 150 feet are berthed side by side, offering a striking example of the many ways residents and visitors choose to enjoy the water.

Broad Creek Marina (843-681-3625), 18 Simmons Rd. Slips accommodating boats up to 100 feet. Ship's store with boat-cleaning supplies and equipment. Charters and sight-seeing, and ZipLine Hilton Head tours in the adjacent maritime forest. Low-tide draft: 16 feet.

Freeport Marina (843-785-8242), Daufuskie Island. The gateway to Daufuskie for large tour boats and the island touring headquarters. Golf-cart rental for transportation; restaurant, cookouts, gift shop, and marina store. Low-tide draft: 15 feet.

Harbour Town Yacht Basin (843-671-2704; www.harbourtownyachtbasin.com), Sea Pines Plantation. Ninety slips accommodating boats up to 150 feet. Marina store, various types of boats for rent, tours, instruction, and cruises available. Extensive dredging will occur in 2014 to increase low-tide draft.

Hilton Head Harbor RV Resort & Marina (843-681-3256 or 1-800-845-9560; www.hiltonheadharbor.com), 43 Jenkins Rd., north end of Hilton Head. More than one hundred slips; maximum boat length 70 feet. Amenities of Hilton Head Harbor RV Resort (see Lodging) as well as charters; Jet Ski, kayak, and paddleboard rentals; ship's store. Low-tide approach depth: 8 feet; 25 feet at dockside.

Palmetto Bay Marina (843-785-3910; www.palmettobaymarinahhi.com), 86 Helmsman Way. One hundred forty slips; maximum length 85 feet. Marina store, boat repair, fishing and sailing charters, and parasailing. Low-tide draft: 20 feet.

Shelter Cove Harbour (843-842-7001; www.palmettodunes.com), Palmetto Dunes Resort. One hundred seventy slips; maximum length 135 feet. Fish and tackle store, charters, cruises, rentals; rod and reel rental, too. In villagelike area of shops and restaurants. Low-tide draft: 8.5 feet.

Skull Creek Marina (843-681-8436; www.theskullcreekmarina.com), Hilton Head Plantation. One hundred eighty slips; maximum length 200 feet. Sailing charters and night fishing, restaurant and lounge, courtesy bike and van transportation. Low-tide draft: 10 feet.

South Beach Marina (843-671-6699; www.sbinn.com), Sea Pines Plantation. One hundred wet slips, twenty dry slips; maximum length 30 feet. Tackle and bait shop, boat and motor repair, rentals, and cruises. Restaurants and shops at the marina village. Low-tide approach depth: 3 feet.

Windmill Harbor (843-681-9235; www.windmillharbourmarina.org), northwest coast of Hilton Head Island on Intracoastal Waterway. Enter via a lock system. About two hundred fifty slips accommodating boats up to 70 feet. Very few transient slips available; reservations a must. Approach draft: 8 feet.

MINIATURE GOLF

A half-dozen courses (par 40 to par 65) feature water hazards, doglegs, and sand traps laid out in realistic settings. Most lit for night play. From $9 per adult.

Adventure Cove (843-842-9990; www.adventurecove.com), William Hilton Pkwy. at Folly Field Rd.

Legendary Golf (843-686-3399; www.legendarygolfhhi.com), 900 William Hilton Pkwy.; (843-785-9214), 80 Pope Ave.

Pirate's Island Adventure Golf (843-686-4001; www.piratesislandgolf .com), William Hilton Pkwy. and Marina Side Dr.

TENNIS

There are more than 300 tennis courts spread through nineteen clubs on Hilton Head. A 2013 study suggested increasing their numbers and the visibility of the sport in a place known best for golf. Seven clubs are open for public play. Call ahead for reservations—the staff may be able to set you up with a game. Pros on-site offer lessons, daily stroke clinics, and intensive camps year-round; fully stocked shops provide stringing services and sales of equipment, clothing, and accessories. Reserved court rental fees range from $20–25 per hour, but some clubs offer reduced walk-on rates for midday play (noon–4 PM) and off-season use. Free exhibitions take place at 5:30 PM Monday through Thursday and Sunday afternoons at different clubs on a rotating basis.

Hilton Head Beach and Tennis Club (1-800-475-2631; www.hhibeach andtennis.com), 40 Folly Field Rd. Ten courts, pro shop, and instruction.

Palmetto Dunes Tennis Center (843-785-1138; www.palmettodunes. com), Palmetto Dunes Resort. Twenty-three clay, two hard courts. Hard courts and eight clay courts are lighted for night play.

Port Royal Racquet Club (843-686-8803), Port Royal Resort. Ten clay, four hard courts.

Sea Pines Racquet Club (843-363-4495; www.seapines.com), Sea Pines Plantation. Twenty-three clay courts.

South Beach Racquet Club (843-671-2215), Sea Pines Plantation. Thirteen clay courts, all lighted.

Van der Meer Tennis Center (843-785-8388 or 1-800-845-6138; www .vdmtennis.com), DeAllyon Rd. Seventeen hard courts. The center is internationally known for its rigorous teaching programs and camps for kids and pros, as well as serious players. The island's top youngsters often train here.

Van der Meer Tennis/Shipyard Racquet Club (843-686-8804), Shipyard Plantation. Twenty courts: thirteen clay, seven hard.

Shopping

Shops and markets that will pique your interest.

Harbour Town, in Sea Pines Plantation, remains the only shopping area with a genuine village character, located around the harbor basin, clustered near the lighthouse. There's a $5 gate fee to enter Sea Pines. You can head toward Harbour Town, or pay your fee, park your car inside the Sea Pines Greenwood Gate, and take a free trolley (every 20 minutes) to Harbour Town. South Beach Marina, a Cape Cod–style village, is also in Sea Pines Plantation.

Main Street Village (north island, just inside the entrance to Hilton Head Plantation—no gate fee) feels like a few downtown blocks in a prosperous suburb, with its specialty boutiques, pubs and restaurants, and "real" stores that sell ordinary things like beer and diapers. Village at Wexford has the most interesting collection of stores, restaurants, and more "artsy" locales, like a gallery, a jazz club, and a clothing store for women who love things made of flax. Coligny Plaza is oriented toward kids and tourists, a good place to find beach toys, souvenirs, and inexpensive resort wear.

Just off the island on US 278 are Target and other big "box stores." At Tanger Outlet Stores 1 & 2 there are bargains in every category: housewares, toys, shoes, eyeglasses, children's clothing, linens, high fashion, and sportswear. Dozens of brand-name manufacturers include Coach, Brooks Brothers, J. Crew, Donna Karan, Dansk, Waterford, and Nike.

ANTIQUES/GALLERIES

Some galleries have limited hours, but welcome visitors by appointment. If you're interested in more than browsing, call ahead to check.

The Art League of Hilton Head Gallery (843-681-5060; www.hhal.org), in the Arts Center of Coastal Carolina, 14 Shelter Cove Ln. Changing exhibits of local and regional work and guest artists.

The Greenery, Inc. (843-785-3848; www.thegreeneryinc.com), 960 William Hilton Pkwy. This full-service landscape design business also has a small and ever-changing collection of antique garden statuary, containers, and accent pieces.

Iron Fish Gallery & Studio (843-842-9448; www.ironfishart.com), 168 Benjies Point Rd., Daufuskie Island. Chase Allen is a self-taught artist who creates metal sculptures of fish in his studio on Daufuskie, where he landed about 15 years ago. A trip to his website might be easier than the ferry ride to Daufuskie, but if you find yourself there, well, there you are. Eccentric and beautiful. The gallery is usually open even if the artist is not around.

J Banks Design Studio & Retail Store (843-681-5122; www.jbanksdesign .com), 35 Main St. Near Hilton Head Plantation. High-end home accents and tableware, not just meant for resort or beach life.

Morris & Whiteside Galleries (843-842-4433; www.morriswhiteside.com), 220 Cordillo Pkwy. American painting and sculpture from the 19th and 20th centuries and contemporary art.

Folk art in all kinds of media takes its inspiration from the region's plants, animals, and Gullah heritage.

BOOKS

Barnes & Noble (843-342-6690), 20 Hatton Place. Check local listings for events that feature readings, demonstrations, and author signings.

Heaven Sent Christian Bookstore (843-837-4727; www.heavensentchristian gifts.com), 1200 Fording Island Rd., Bridge Center Shoppes. Inspirational literature, Bibles, and children's books.

Paperback Exchange (843-842-5614; www.thecourtyardhhi.com), Village Exchange, 32 Palmetto Bay Rd. A wide and constantly changing selection of used books. Books on tape for rent here, too.

CLOTHING

Camp Hilton Head (843-842-3666; www.camphiltonhead.com), Shelter Cove. Beachwear branded with the store's unique logo is ubiquitous here but will stand out at home. Stores also at Harbour Town and Coligny Plaza.

Currents (843-671-1919), Harbor Town. Women's shoes, handbags, resort clothing, and jewelry.

Jamaican Me Crazy (843-785-9006), Coligny Plaza. Wacky resort wear, hip beach accessories.

Knickers (843-671-2291), Harbour Town. Classic outfits in linen, cotton, tweeds, and madras for a slightly updated preppy look. An institution.

Outside Hilton Head (843-686-6996; www.outsidehiltonhead.com), Plaza at Shelter Cove. Top-of-the-line durable sports clothing (Patagonia, The North Face, Teva), footwear, and accessories. They also run camps and tours.

Porcupine (843-785-2779; www.theporcupinestyle.com), Village at Wexford. Designer sportswear for women, lingerie, excellent shoe selection, swimwear. The classiest fashion stop on the island.

S. M. Bradford–Lilly Pulitzer Shop (843-686-6161; www.forlp.com), Village at Wexford. The bright florals for women and children that are the designer's trademark, with accessories and some home goods.

Teagues (843-842-9868), Village at Wexford. Crisp and casual men's clothing and accessories.

CRAFTS

Art Café (843-785-5525), 14 Greenwood Dr. A hands-on pottery studio where you select an unadorned object (mug, plate, bowl, something else), choose the glazes and tools, and decorate it until it's unique. A good family project.

The Island Gift Shop Harbortown (843-671-3643), Harbour Town. One-of-a-kind Lowcountry gifts, much nicer than plain souvenirs, and a selection of wines.

Needlepoint Junction (843-842-8488), Village at Wexford. A boutique with stitchery supplies, thread, yarn, canvas, and kits.

Smith Galleries of Fine Crafts (843-842-2280; www.smithgalleries.com), Village at Wexford. More than 300 American artisans are represented in media such as glass, wood, metal, clay, and textiles.

GIFTS

Forsythe Jewelers (843-671-7070; www.forsythejewelers.biz), Sea Pines Center. MacKenzie-Childs ceramics, designer jewelry, and watches.

The Goldsmith Shop (843-785-2538; www.thegoldsmithshop.com), 3 Lagoon Rd. Gold charms of dolphins, starfish, and boats, many studded with tiny jewels.

Legends Sports Gallery (843-681-4444), Main Street Village. Old and new trading cards, autographed memorabilia, and Ted Williams signature items.

Marina Store (843-842-7002), Shelter Cove Harbour. A shop for the sailor that stocks local charts and a limited offering of nautical accessories.

GOURMET SHOPS

Chocolate Canopy (843-842-4567; www.chocolatecanopy.com), Crossroads Center, Palmetto Bay Rd. Homemade chocolates galore.

The Frozen Moo (843-842-3131), Coligny Plaza. Fun and friendly ice cream shop featuring 92 flavors.

Truffles Market (843-671-6136), Sea Pines Center. Sandwiches, pâté, salads, breads, pastries, and wine.

SPORTING GOODS AND CLOTHING

Outside Hilton Head (843-686-6996; www.outsidehiltonhead.com), 32 Shelter Cove Ln. Equipment for canoeing, kayaking, fishing, and camping. The island standard for outdoor activity and its experienced staff can offer ideas for eco-touring.

Player's World (843-842-5100), Fresh Market Shoppes. Hilton Head's largest sporting goods store. Specializing in tennis equipment and accessories.

Golf etc. (843-341-7000; www.golfetchhi.com), 11 Palmetto Bay Rd. Clubs, apparel, accessories, and club rentals.

Information

PRACTICAL MATTERS & SEASONAL EVENTS

WHAT FOLLOWS is information to make your visit run more smoothly and make planning simpler.

AMBULANCE, FIRE, AND POLICE

The general emergency number is 911, whether you're in Charleston, Beaufort, Hilton Head, or Savannah. Outside the cities, the counties have basic 911 service. Here's a selected listing for emergencies.

First Call for Help (Information and referral service):

Charleston	1-800-922-2283
Beaufort/Hilton Head	843-524-4357
Savannah	912-651-7730

Poison Control

South Carolina	1-800-922-1117 (from within SC)
Georgia	1-800-222-1222 (from within GA)

LEFT: The view from atop Hunting Island Lighthouse.   SC Lowcountry Tourism Commission

Rape Crisis Hotline

Charleston	843-745-0144
Beaufort/Hilton Head	1-800-637-7273
Savannah	912-233-7273

Disaster/Hurricane Emergency Preparedness

Charleston County	843-202-7400
Beaufort County	843-470-3100
Colleton County	843-549-5632
Hampton County	803-914-2150
Jasper County	843-726-7797
Chatham County	912-201-4500

State Police

S.C. Highway Patrol

Charleston Area	843-953-6000
Beaufort/Hilton Head	843-953-6000
Ridgeland	843-953-6000

Ga. Highway Patrol

Savannah Area	912-754-1180

Police (nonemergency):

City of Charleston	843-720-2402
Town of Edisto Beach	843-869-2505
City of Beaufort	843-322-7900
Town of Port Royal	843-986-2220
Town of Hilton Head (sheriff)	843-255-3300
Town of Bluffton	843-706-4550
Town of Hardeeville	843-784-2233
Tybee Island	912-786-5600
City of Savannah	Dial 311 or 912-651-6675

AREA CODES, TOWN GOVERNMENT, AND ZIP CODES

Area Codes

The area code for the South Carolina Lowcountry is 843, with the occasional use of 803. The area code for Savannah, Georgia, and its metropolitan region is 912.

Town Halls

Charleston, Beaufort, Hilton Head, and Savannah are governed by a mayor and city/town council; their outlying lands are controlled by county government. Charleston, Beaufort, Walterboro, Ridgeland, Hampton, and Savannah are the region's county seats. For general information call:

Charleston County	843-958-4000
Beaufort County	843-255-2000
Colleton County	843-549-5221
Jasper County	843-717-3690
Hampton County	803-914-2103
Chatham County	912-652-7878

There are also smaller, scattered municipalities governed by smaller councils. For general information, contact the following town/city hall offices:

Town	Address	Telephone
Beaufort	1911 Ribaut Rd., 29902	843-525-7000
Bluffton	20 Bridge St., 29910	843-706-4500
Charleston	80 Broad St., P.O. Box 652, 29402	843-724-3729
Edisto Island	2414 Murray St., 29438	843-869-2505
Folly Beach	21 Center St., 29439	843-588-2447
Hilton Head	1 Town Center Crt., 29928	843-341-4600
Isle of Palms	1207 Palm Blvd., 29451	843-886-6428
Port Royal	700 Paris Ave., 29935	843-986-2211
Ridgeland	1 Town Sq., 29936	843-726-7500
Savannah	2 E. Bay St., P.O. Box 1027, 31402	912-651-6444
Tybee Island	401 Butler Ave., 31328	912-786-4573
Walterboro	42 Hampton St., P.O. Box 709, 29488	843-549-2545

CLIMATE, WEATHER, AND WHAT TO WEAR

There is something in bloom year-round in the Lowcountry, from April jessamine to late-summer mums to camellias to paperwhite narcissus, which scent the air at Christmas. This comes as a result of the semitropical to subtropical climate and the ever-present breezes that characterize the coastal region. There are also microclimates—as small as a yard, as wide as an acre—which make it possible to cultivate plants that are used to a warmer zone, like oranges and freesia. Rarely do days pass in succession without sunshine. The annual rainfall for the region is about 51 inches.

Lowcountry winters are mild, while summers are hot and humid. SC Lowcountry Tourism Commission

The winters are generally mild—maybe nine days of frost and a half-dozen hard freezes. Spring comes early. Farmers generally break ground on February 1. In the old days, the cotton crop was finished by "lay-by time" in late August, when slaves, temporarily released from heavy field work, would tend to their cemeteries and families.

By May 1, it's hot, and that heat will penetrate until the end of September. The mean summer temperature in the Lowcountry runs around 88 degrees, but with the humidity factored in it feels much hotter. The water temperature reaches the high 80s in summer, and stays in the mid-70s through October. Be prepared to move slowly, wear a hat, use sunscreen, and drink plenty of liquids. Take extra precautions if you're planning athletic pursuits: The tennis court is no place to be at midday. The wild cloudbursts that drench the region in summer, and the often-spectacular thunder and lightning shows that accompany them, may cool things off a bit. More likely, they'll just bring mosquitoes.

Then there are the gnats, also known as flying teeth. Just when you're enjoying a beautiful autumn day, they find you. Insect repellent can be effective, as is staying out of the shade or standing in a breeze.

The seasons each bring their color, their migratory birds, their harvest of fish or shellfish, duck or deer. And twice a year it seems as if there's a whole new shipment of air—in late October, when the marsh has turned golden and the clouds pull themselves into exquisitely defined cumuli; and again in late February, when the prevailing northeast winds of winter start to shift south and southwest.

But perhaps the best quality of Lowcountry weather is its subtlety and contradiction: the warm day in January that you were not expecting, the roaring fire in October that banishes the morning chill, but by late afternoon seems an inferno.

For clothing, pack more cotton shirts than you think you'll need. Take comfortable shoes for touring (high-heeled shoes are often forbidden in house museums and on tours) and a light sweater or windbreaker. An overcoat or parka may be too much in winter; sweaters and shells work better.

The hurricane season lasts from June to November, with most recent devastating storms having come between late August and October. If you're traveling then, make sure you are aware of evacuation routes, and keep alerted to local media for hurricane watch and warning announcements. The National Weather Service (www.erh.noaa.gov/chs) provides excellent coverage of the South Carolina and Georgia area on its website.

GETTING THERE, GETTING AROUND

The Lowcountry is mostly water. Perhaps this is why the old houses of the region's cities and towns—and the dense feeling of permanence they exude—are so venerated, above and beyond their architectural and historic status. They appear— now, as in the past—literally to triumph over their surroundings, as if daring wind, water, and the harsh storms of hurricane season to teach them the lessons of frailty.

The tides, which cast the riches of sea life toward shore and offered planters the possibility of power to operate rice dikes, bestowed on the Lowcountry an abundance of marine and bird life. Flat-bottomed plantation barges loaded with rice, bales of cotton, and farm produce plied the rivers and creeks to the city

Edisto Island

The only thoroughfare by Land between Beaufort and Charleston is the "Shell Road," a beautiful avenue, which, about 9 miles from Beaufort, strikes a ferry across the Coosaw River. War abolished the ferry, and made the river the permanent barrier between the opposing picket lines. For 10 miles, right and left, these lines extended, marked by well-worn footpaths, following the endless windings of the stream; and they never varied until nearly the end of the war. Upon their maintenance depended our whole foothold on the Sea Islands; and upon that finally depended the whole campaign of Sherman.

—*From* Army Life in a Black Regiment *by Thomas Wentworth Higginson (New York: W. W. Norton, 1984. First published in 1869.)*

harbor. Eight-oared bateaux, made on the plantations and navigated by slaves, clove the marsh from one plantation to another, carrying news, goods, and passengers. The Savannah River offered both protection to an English colony in the Southern wilderness and a commercial avenue.

Quite often, what roads existed were hardly distinguishable from the water. Highways could be covered with washed-up shells, sponges, and seaweed, brought and removed by the tides each day. As time went on, people of the Lowcountry took nature one step further: They made roadbeds of oyster shell, fashioning a crown at the "center line" to facilitate drainage. These were the best roads around, and in towns like Beaufort they were in use well into the 20th century. An unimproved road common today on the Sea Islands is plowed through fine sand, perhaps a foot deep, rutted and banked. More than one elderly resident can tell a tale of pushing a Model T Ford through this sand, or of watching the ice melt through the sawdust when the iceman got stuck.

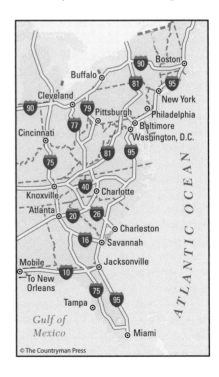

Perhaps as a result of the reliance on water travel, as well as the sheer isolation of the plantations and their rural dependencies, a thickly veined series of land transportation routes never really developed in the Lowcountry. Instead there evolved a fleet of small steamers that made their way from island to island, picking up passengers, mail, produce, and cotton to deliver to Charleston and Savannah. And ox-drawn carts, horses, or marsh "tackies" (diminutive horses, something like a Shetland pony) serviced them. When, in 1894, historian Henry Adams visited St. Helena Island, he traveled first by train, then by carriage over a sand road, then on a shell road, then by foot to the ferry crossing, then over the river to board the steamer *Flora*, which carried him to his destination. These days travel is easier, but there are still plenty of unlit, two-lane roads flanked by drainage ditches that require extra time and careful driving. Directions to specific areas are noted near the beginning of each chapter.

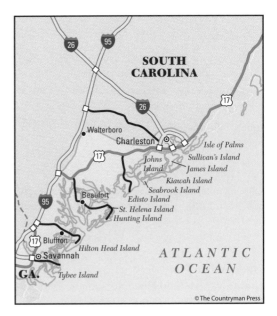

By Car

Unless your visit to the Lowcountry is limited strictly to Charleston, Savannah, or a Hilton Head resort, having your own car pays off. The Lowcountry is decentralized; a lot of space separates those "points of interest." What's more, appreciating that very space by finding yourself in it lies at the heart of the Lowcountry experience. That's where you'll find some of the region's subtle treasures: the view of a marsh at sunset, the sight of feeding pelicans as they hit the water, the faded impression of an abandoned oyster-shell road strewn with wildflowers. It is in these very open spaces, in their linked geography, that the sense of times passed and lives abundantly lived will catch up with you and shape your awareness of what the Lowcountry is all about. US 17, one of the region's oldest roads and still perhaps the most direct, threads its way from above Charleston to Savannah (and beyond) through marshes, old rice fields, and bottomland forests. Turnoffs that access the Sea Islands (Kiawah, Seabrook, Edisto, Port Royal, St. Helena, Hilton Head) to the east and the Ashley River plantations (Drayton Hall, Middleton Place, Magnolia Gardens) to the west (along SC 61) are well marked, as are historic sites, parks, and picnic grounds.

From Washington and points north: Travelers from the north can reach the Lowcountry by approaching it on I-95, which roughly parallels the coast. From there, well-marked exits direct you to downtown Charleston (via I-26), to Beaufort (via US 21), to Hilton Head (via US 278), and Savannah (via I-16). The coastal destinations beyond the big cities, such as Kiawah Island, Edisto Island, Beaufort, and Hilton Head, lie approximately 45 minutes east of I-95. Distance from Washington to Charleston: 512 miles; to Savannah: 616 miles.

From Jacksonville and points south: Like visitors from the north, drivers from the south approach on I-95 and then turn east to the coast. Distance from Jacksonville to Charleston: 241 miles; to Savannah: 139 miles.

From Asheville and points northwest: Take I-40 to I-26, then follow I-26

toward Spartanburg and Columbia. About an hour out of Columbia, you meet
I-95. At that point either continue east to Charleston or turn south. Distance from
Asheville to Charleston: 265 miles; to Savannah: 297 miles.

From Charlotte: Take I-77 south to I-20 at Columbia; follow I-20 for a few
exits to link up with I-26 east. Distance to Charleston: 200 miles; to Savannah:
240 miles.

From Atlanta: Take I-75 to I-16. When it crosses I-95, go north for Charleston or continue directly to Savannah. Distance to Charleston: 286 miles; to Savannah: 259 miles.

Lowcountry Access

The approximate distances and driving times to Charleston and selected cities
are given in the charts below. The distance between Charleston and Savannah
is 114 miles, so depending on the direction from which you are traveling, you
should adjust accordingly. If you're touring within the Lowcountry, however, and
stopping along the way between Charleston and Savannah in places like Beaufort,
Hilton Head, Bluffton, Edisto, or Walterboro, this trip easily may take a day. In
general, traveling to specific Sea Island destinations located to the east of the
major cities can add up to an hour to your trip.

To Charleston from:

City	Miles	Hours
Atlanta	286	5
Boston	929	17
Charlotte	200	4
Chicago	906	15.5
Knoxville	395	7
Miami	590	10.5
New Orleans	784	13
New York	768	13
Washington, D.C.	512	8.5

By Bus

Greyhound (1-800-231-2222; www.greyhound.com) serves Charleston, Beaufort, and Savannah, and maintains stations in those cities. It also serves points in
between, but here the stops are less formal—perhaps as simple as a crossroads
store. As a result, if you're planning to do a substantial amount of traveling by bus,
you should consult both a detailed map and the bus schedule. Don't expect to
find a taxi or rental-car stand at every stop.

The service and price to Charleston and Savannah from various points are
roughly equal; in most cases the same bus goes to both cities. Travel times on
longer trips may vary up to three hours, according to the number of stops and the
specific route, so it's wise to ask about arrival times and whether it's a direct trip.

Charleston Greyhound Bus Terminal (843-744-4247; 3610 Dorchester Rd.,
North Charleston).

Savannah Greyhound Bus Terminal (912-232-2135; 610 W. Oglethorpe
Ave).

Beaufort Greyhound Bus Terminal (843-524-4646; 3659 Trask Pkwy.).

By Train

Amtrak (1-800-872-7245; www.amtrak.com) travels the north-south corridor, making daily stops at North Charleston (843-744-8264; 4565 Gaynor Ave.), about 25 minutes from downtown; Yemassee (15 Wall St.), about 30 miles west of Beaufort; and Savannah (912-234-2611; 2611 Seaboard Coastline Dr.), about 20 minutes from downtown. Cabs are available at city depots; for Yemassee you should arrange advance transportation through a Beaufort taxi company. On the long hauls from cities like Boston, New York, Chicago, and Miami, there are generally two trains a day, departing morning and evening and arriving either late the same day or early the following morning. Traveling by night with sleeping accommodations is a nice option for these 10- to 18-hour trips.

By Private Plane

If you're flying on your own, contact the following county or regional airports or services:

Beaufort County Airport (843-770-2003; www.bcgov.net).

Mount Pleasant Regional (843-767-7000; www.airnav.com).

Hilton Head Airport (843-255-2950; www.bcgov.net).

John's Island–Charleston Executive Airport (843-559-2401; www.atlantic aviation.com).

Atlantic Aviation–Charleston International (843-746-7600; www.atlantic aviation.com).

Savannah Aviation (912-964-1022; www.savannahaviation.com).

By Boat

The Intracoastal Waterway winds through creek and river, ocean and sound, from one end of the Lowcountry to the other. In Charleston, Beaufort, and Hilton Head, you can dock at a marina downtown within walking distance of restaurants and sight-seeing. Savannah's marinas are about 20 minutes from downtown. Most provide repair service. If you want to make use of the charter fishing, sailing, or tour services based at marinas, see the Recreation section in the appropriate chapter for some ideas. If your main mode of transportation is by boat, check those listings for details on berthing facilities and services.

By City Transportation

Inexpensive or free shuttle bus service to the historic districts is convenient, handicapped-accessible, and a great alternative to a car. In Charleston, the attractive trolleylike Downtown Area Shuttle (DASH) (843-724-7420; www.ridecarta .com) makes regular stops along three routes in the Historic District and greater downtown area. Board at the Visitor Center (843-724-7174; 375 Meeting St.), where you can purchase your pass and park your car ($16 per day). The DASH maps and schedules are easy to follow and color-coded by route. All-day bus passes cost $6; a three-day pass is $12; there are reduced fares for adults over 55 and disabled passengers; children age 6 and younger ride free. City buses operated by the Charleston Area Regional Transportation Authority (843-747-0922; www.ride carta.com) service destinations like Mount Pleasant, some from the Visitor Center, some from nearby stops. Fares begin at $1.75. Bike racks are available at no charge on most of these routes and take about 10 seconds to operate.

In Savannah, there's Chatham Area Transit (912-233-5767; www.catchacat
.org), a free shuttle bus service within the Historic District with regular stops at
the Visitor Center (912-944-0455; 301 Martin Luther King Jr. Blvd.), downtown
inns and hotels, the waterfront, and many sites of interest. It connects to most bus
routes, with additional fares for regional service throughout Chatham County. For
$7 visitors can buy a 24-hour pass that allows unlimited parking in any city lot or
garage, or overtime at meters. A 48-hour pass costs $12. Passes can also be pur-
chased at Live Oak Public Libraries. Check the website for other locations.

A day pass for Savannah's city bus routes costs $3 and can be purchased on
the bus.

HANDICAPPED SERVICES

Most of the region's accommodations, museums, restaurants, and touring services
provide access and facilities for those with special needs, but call ahead to confirm
details: Problems remain in retrofitting the older historic buildings for complete
handicapped access, and this includes some house museums and inns. Your guides,
hosts, or the visitor center staff in each city will gladly assist you—several offer
handicap-accessibility guides. See Tourist Information & Online Addresses at
the end of this chapter for addresses of city or county offices of tourism and travel.
City buses and trolleys are handicapped-friendly.

HOSPITALS

Beaufort
Beaufort Memorial Hospital (843-522-5200; www.bmhsc.org), 955 Ribaut Rd.

Charleston
Bon Secours St. Francis Hospital (843-402-1000; www.rsfh.com;), 2095 Henry
Tecklenburg Dr.
Medical University of South Carolina (843-792-1414; www.muschealth.com),
169 Ashley Ave.
Roper Hospital (843-724-2000; www.rsfh.com), 316 Calhoun St.
Trident Regional Medical Center (843-797-7000; www.tridenthealthsystem
.com), 9330 Medical Plaza Dr.
Ralph H. Johnson VA Medical Center (843-789-7732; www.charleston
.va.gov), 109 Bee St.

Hilton Head
Hilton Head Medical Center and Clinics (843-681-6122; www.hiltonheadregional
.com), 25 Hospital Center Blvd.

Savannah
Candler Hospital (912-819-6000; www.sjchs.org), 5353 Reynolds St.
Memorial Medical Center (912-350-8000; www.memorialhealth.com), 4700
Waters Ave.
St. Joseph's Hospital (912-819-4100; www.sjchs.org), 11705 Mercy Blvd.
Urgent Care 24/7 (912-234-3714; www.urgentcare247.com), 144 Lincoln St.

The metropolitan areas of Charleston and Savannah, and the resort centers of Hilton Head, stay lit and active well after midnight—especially during the spring and summer—so finding gas or even grits should not be a problem. However, if you're traveling at night, remember that the Lowcountry is largely rural. Unless you plan to gig for flounder and fry them up by the side of the road, it's best to travel with snacks or stop when you can.

Beaufort
Huddle House (food), 2248 Boundary St. 843-524-5891. Open 24 hours.
   Waffle House (food), 2344 Boundary St. 843-770-0080. Open 24 hours.
   Kangaroo Express (grocery and fuel), 290 Robert Smalls Pkwy. 843-525-9156. Open 24 hours.

Charleston
Waffle House (food), 325 Savannah Hwy. 843-766-0717. Open 24 hours.
   Butcher & Bee (food), 654 King St. 843-619-0202. Lunch daily, late night Thurs.–Sat.
   Circle K (grocery and fuel), 737 King St. 1-800-649-0895. Open 24 hours.

Hilton Head
Hilton Head Diner (food, beer, and wine), 6 Marina Side Dr. at US 278. 843-686-2400. Open 24 hours.
   Kangaroo Express (grocery and fuel), US 278 and Arrow Rd. 843-686-4899. Open 24 hours.

Savannah
Circle K (grocery and fuel), 7203 Abercorn St. 912-354-3491. Open 24 hours.
   Parker's Market (grocery and fuel, beer, wine), 222 Drayton St. 912-233-1000. Open 24 hours.
   Waffle House (food), 7301 Abercorn St. 912-354-4333. One of several in the Savannah area, open 24 hours.

NEWSPAPERS AND MAGAZINES

Beaufort and Hilton Head
The Beaufort Gazette/Island Packet (843-706-8100; www.islandpacket.com), 10 Buck Island Rd., Bluffton, SC 29938. Daily. Local coverage, wire-service features, and columns.
   The Gullah Sentinel (843-982-0500; www.gullahnewspaper.net), 909 Bladen St., Beaufort, SC 29902. A biweekly with an African American perspective, local and syndicated columnists.

Charleston
Charleston City Paper (843-577-5304; www.charlestoncitypaper.com), 1049 B Morrison Dr., Charleston, SC 29403. Weekly paper, excellent listings.
   Charleston Magazine (843-971-9811; www.charlestonmag.com), P.O. Box 1794, Mount Pleasant, SC 29465. A glossy monthly featuring stories about the city,

gossip, local politics, development, and some art features. Reviews, columns, and blogs.

The Post and Courier (843-577-7111; www.postandcourier.com), 134 Columbus St., Charleston, SC 29403. The daily paper of Charleston.

Savannah

Connect Savannah (912-238-2040; www.connectsavannah.com), 1800 E. Victory Dr., Suite 7, Savannah, GA 31404. Art and culture listings, reviews weekly.

The Herald (912-232-4505; www.savannahherald.net), 1803 Barnard St., Savannah, GA 31401. Weekly, featuring news of the African American community.

Savannah Morning News (912-236-9511; www.savannahnews.com), 1375 Chatham Pkwy., Savannah, GA 31402. Daily and Sun.

Savannah Tribune (912-233-6128; www.savannahtribune.com), 1805 Martin Luther King, Jr. Blvd., Savannah, GA 31401. Weekly, featuring news of the African American community.

Savannah Magazine (912-652-0423; www.savannahmagazine.com), 1375 Chatham Pkwy., P.O. Box 1088, Savannah, GA 31402. Bimonthly features on local events and people.

REAL ESTATE

If you came to the Lowcountry and couldn't bear to leave without owning a piece, take your place in line. Practically every new resident who has settled here recently was once in your position. The population in Beaufort County alone has increased 40 percent in the past 10 years. The fastest-growing segment of the market is in traditional, single-family homes and in new "walking communities" which try to reproduce the feel of a small town. The trend for urban "in-fill" in Beaufort and Port Royal has enhanced a village look. Gated communities—glorified subdivisions which may or may not be resorts—are continuing to expand in the Bluffton countryside. If you want to be on the water, be certain about rules regarding dock permits and building in the flood zones. Rapidly rising annual insurance rates in these areas should be factored into any purchase.

There are hundreds of real estate agents, many independent, some affiliated with national brokerage firms. One of them might be the proprietor of your bed and breakfast. For starters, pick up the free, widely available real-estate magazines that are published weekly to get a general idea of the market. Resorts usually rely on exclusive sales teams. Walk-ins are welcome, but if you can't find what you're looking for, ask for referrals in other towns.

ROAD SERVICE

Here is a list of some 24-hour towing and emergency road services.

Beaufort
Gur's Wrecker Service (843-522-4285).

Hilton Head
D&M Towing Service (843-681-4636).

Charleston
Craven's Towing (843-556-7676).

Savannah
Hook Towing (912-232-0541).

SEASONAL EVENTS IN THE LOWCOUNTRY

The following list highlights annual events in the Lowcountry. Some of them, like outdoor concerts in a park, offer informal pleasures that you can enjoy on a whim. Others, like house and garden tours, Spoleto performances, or tennis and golf tournaments, require planning. Purchase tickets and book lodgings in advance, especially in the busy spring season. For specific information regarding dates, schedules, performance times, and admission or ticket prices (if applicable), call in advance, or check online or in local media. For lodging and dining suggestions, see specific chapters.

January
Charleston

Lowcountry Oyster Festival (843-577-4030; www.charlestonrestaurant association.com) A huge oyster roast held on the grounds of Boone Hall Plantation in Mount Pleasant. Games, entertainment, and contests for the whole family.

Savannah

First Friday Fireworks on the River (912-234-0295; www.riverstreet savannah.com) Food, crafts, and a festival atmosphere with a backdrop of pyrotechnics. Beginning in March, a First Saturday festival is added.

February
Beaufort

Beaufort International Film Festival (843-522-3196; www.beaufortfilm festival.com), P.O. Box 998, Beaufort, SC 29901. A juried festival that highlights feature films, documentaries, shorts, and animated work made by professionals and students.

Charleston

Lowcountry Blues Bash (www.blues bash.com) Ten days of concerts and films, many free, and often in intimate venues. The series covers every blues style, including electric, acoustic, post-modern, Delta, and Chicago. Tickets are usually pay-as-you-go at the venue, but some advance tickets are sold.

Southeastern Wildlife Exposition (843-723-1748; www.sewe.com), P.O. Box 20635, Charleston, SC 29413. A comprehensive, multisite exhibition of wildlife art in various media, and presentations promoting habitat conservation and wildlife appreciation. A three-day national event that draws collectors, artists, hunters, and bird-watchers. Tickets sell out early.

Hilton Head

Native Islander Gullah Celebration (843-255-7304; www.gullahcelebration .com) A month-long look at island culture and its African roots through concerts, lectures, performances by gospel choirs, storytelling, art exhibits, and tours.

Savannah

Georgia History Festival (912-651-2125; www.georgiahistory.com) A multiday celebration of the founding of Georgia and the Savannah colony which features tours, re-enactments of colonial life, lectures, art exhibits, music, dance, and crafts at various city locations.

March
Beaufort

St. Helena's Episcopal Church Spring Tour of Homes (843-522-1712; www .sthelenas1712. org), P.O. Box 1043, Beaufort, SC 29901. Traditionally held in March or early April, the candlelight

The famous St. Patrick's Day Parade in Savannah. Savannah Area Convention & Visitors Bureau

tours are distinguished by organ concerts in the parish church, a beautiful brick structure built in 1724. The number of tickets sold can be limited by access to private homes, so it's best to reserve early.

Charleston

Festival of Houses & Gardens (843-722-3405; www.historiccharleston .org), 108 Meeting St., Charleston, SC 29401. The Historic Charleston Foundation's tours of private homes, plantations, gardens, and churches usually start toward the end of the month and last four weeks. A tradition for more than 50 years, they will enrich your understanding of the city's unique urban geography. Neighborhood streets and sidewalks are crowded and warmly accommodating, where laughter and conversation drift from gardens and homes. Highlights are the oyster roasts and picnics at Drayton Hall. The Charleston International Antiques Show kicks off the festival.

Hilton Head

WineFest (843-686-4944; www.hilton headislandwineandfood.com) A big and popular event, part of a series of activities which include musical performances and outdoor celebrations, including many for families throughout the month.

Savannah

St. Patrick's Day Parade (912-233-4804; www.savannahsaintpatricksday .com), Parade Committee, P.O. Box 9224, Savannah, GA 31412. Savannah claims a substantial Irish heritage and celebrates it with abandon. Mobs of people turn out to watch the downtown parade, which starts at 10 AM and dominates all other city activity for the day and night.

Savannah Music Festival (912-234-3378; www.savannahmusicfestival .org), 200 E. St. Julian St., Suite 601, Savannah, GA 31401. Fifteen days of jazz, blues, international music, and classical concerts held in the Historic

District. Some 400 performances—a top-notch selection.

Savannah Tour of Homes and Gardens (912-234-8054; www.savannah tourofhomes.org), 321 E. York St., Savannah, GA 31401. Each day of the tour features a different neighborhood to explore at your own pace, with guides and docents on hand to answer questions. You can expect to cover about six sites, including churches and museums, in a three-hour period. Homes and gardens are not handicapped accessible.

April
Charleston
Family Circle Cup Tennis Tournament (1-800-677-2293; www.family circlecup.com), Family Circle Tennis Center at Daniel Island, Daniel Island, SC 29403. A handsome tennis stadium with great sight lines and a relaxed atmosphere attracts the highest-ranked women in the sport. Located about 30 minutes from Charleston.

Hilton Head
RBC Heritage (843-671-2448; www .rbcheritage.com), 71 Lighthouse Rd., Suite 4200, Hilton Head, SC 29928. Falling about a week after the Masters at Augusta, this premier golf tournament brings thousands of people and the top PGA players to the Harbour Town Golf Links at Sea Pines Resort.

Savannah
NOGS Tour: The Hidden Gardens of Savannah (912-447-3879; www .gardenclubofsavannah.org) A small gem, usually featuring fewer than 10 walled gardens, but all treasures, located north of Gwinnett Street.

Walterboro
Colleton County Rice Festival (843-549-1079; www.thericefestival.com),

109 Benson St., Walterboro, SC 29488. Arts and crafts, cooking demonstrations, and rice-husking celebrate the Lowcountry's rice-growing heritage.

May
Beaufort
Gullah Festival (www.gullahfestival .org) Held the weekend before Memorial Day, this event features a big outdoor market with a quirky variety of vendors, dance performances, concerts of spiritual and gospel music, and demonstrations of boat-building, net-weaving, and other skills related to the West African heritage of the Sea Islands.

Bluffton
Bluffton Village Festival (843-815-2277; www.blufftonmayfest.moonfruit .com), Bluffton Town Hall, Bluffton, SC 29910. A small, old-fashioned street festival featuring artisans, food, and entertainment, usually held the second Saturday of May.

Charleston
Confederate Memorial Day Observance (843-722-8638), Magnolia Cemetery Trust, 70 Cunnington Ave., P.O. Box 6214, Charleston, SC 29405. The United Daughters of the Confederacy and other groups sponsor a program honoring the Confederate war dead. (A similar celebration takes place in Savannah.)

Piccolo Spoleto (843-724-7305; www.piccolospoleto.com), Office of Cultural Affairs, 180 Meeting St., Charleston, SC 29401. The more informal aspect of Spoleto highlights regional artists and celebrates art, music, dance, and outdoor events, usually at no charge.

Spoleto Festival U.S.A. (843-722-2764; www.spoletousa.org), 14 George St. Charleston, SC 29401. Beginning in late May and lasting for about 18 days, Spoleto brings the best of international theater; choral, chamber, and symphonic music; art; and dance to Charleston. It's a magical time in the city.

Savannah

Scottish Games and Highland Gathering (www.savannahscottishgames.com), P.O. Box 13435, Savannah, GA 31416. Scottish dancing, pipe bands, and traditional games honoring Scottish heritage, usually held in mid-May.

Tybee Island Beach Bums Parade The official kickoff to summer is a massive water fight between parade participants on floats with water cannons, and spectators lining Butler Avenue, armed with Super Soakers and hoses. Held on Friday, a week before Memorial Day weekend. High-spirited fun, signature Tybee-style.

June

Hampton

Hampton County Watermelon Festival (803-914-2143; www.hcmelon fest.org), Chamber of Commerce, P.O. Box 516, Hampton, SC 29924. The oldest festival in the state celebrating the county's best crop. Held at the end of the month and lasting a week, it features seed-spitting contests, beauty queens, and a big parade.

July

Fourth of July Fireworks take place in several Lowcountry resorts as well as Charleston, Parris Island (Beaufort), Hilton Head, Bluffton, Savannah's riverfront, and the beach at Tybee.

Beaufort

Beaufort County Water Festival (843-524-0600; www.bftwaterfestival.com), P.O. Box 52, Beaufort, SC 29901. A 10-day festival starting in mid-July that features special events each day

and night: croquet, fishing, golf tournaments, a juried art show, antiques show, kids' day, parade, and several outdoor dances with live music. The air shows and acrobatic waterskiing demonstrations are especially fun to watch. It's a reunion for locals who have moved away and maintains a small-town feel.

August

Hilton Head

Celebrity Golf Tournament (843-842-7711; www.hhcelebritygolf.com), P.O. Box 6319, Hilton Head Island, SC 29938. Held over three days at three different courses on the island, this is a tradition that attracts movie stars, professional athletes, and media personalities to raise money for island charities.

Fishing tournaments (Various locations) Check the "Marinas" listings in the Recreation section of Chapter Four, *Hilton Head*, to inquire about tournaments. There are many, for marlin, billfish, and other species.

September

Charleston

Fall Tours of Homes and Gardens (843-722-4630 or 1-800-968-8175; www.preservationsociety.org), The Preservation Society, 147 King St., Charleston, SC 29401. Walking tours of private homes and gardens are offered over a period of about four weeks from mid-September through mid-October by the city's oldest preservation organization.

Moja Arts Festival (843-724-7305; www.mojafestival.com), Office of Cultural Affairs, 180 Meeting St., Charleston, SC 29401. A celebration of the African American and Caribbean heritage in the Charleston area. The influence on Southern culture is traced through music, dance, art, food, stage performances, and more.

Hardeeville

Catfish Festival (803-784-3606; www
.hardeevillechamberofcommerce.
com), Chamber of Commerce, P.O.
Box 307, Hardeeville, SC 29927.
Family entertainment, boat races on
the Savannah River, and, of course,
catfish are the focus of this festival,
which takes place the third weekend
in September.

Savannah

Savannah Jazz Festival (404-997-
3281; www.savannahjazzfestival.
org), Coastal Jazz Association, P.O.
Box 60205, Savannah, GA 31420. All
styles of blues and jazz played for several days throughout the city.

October
Beaufort

Historic Beaufort Foundation Fall
Tour of Homes (843-379-3331; www
.historicbeaufort.org), P.O. Box 11,
Beaufort, SC 29901. A weekend of
candlelight and daytime tours of
homes and gardens in and around
Beaufort; the final day often features
tours of outlying plantations, such as
the rarely seen Auldbrass designed by
Frank Lloyd Wright and meticulously
restored inside and out.

The annual Savannah Jazz Festival brings hundreds of locals and visitors to the waterfront.
Savannah Area Convention & Visitors Bureau

Bluffton
Historic Bluffton Arts & Seafood
Festival (843-757-2583; www.bluffton
artsandseafoodfestival.com) A week-
long fair showcasing local and regional
arts and crafts, historical exhibits and
tours, and steaming fresh fish and
shellfish.

Edisto Island
Edisto Historic Preservation Society
Tour of Homes (843-869-1954; www
.edistomuseum.org), P.O. Box 206,
8123 Chisolm Plantation Rd., Edisto
Island, SC 29438. Daylong tour of
homes which are not usually open to
the public and not often visible from
public roads.

Ridgeland
Gopher Hill Festival (843-726-7500;
www.gopherhillfestival.org), P.O. Box
1776, Ridgeland, SC 29936. A one-day
celebration with arts and crafts, music,
and food. The Ridgeland area was long
known as Gopher Hill, named for the
gopher tortoise, a species that lives a
protected life in the sand hills of Jasper
County.

Savannah
Savannah Film and Video Festival
(912-525-5216; filmfest.scad.edu)
Several days of screenings and lectures
sponsored by the Savannah College of
Art and Design.

Tybee Island
Piratefest (www.tybeepiratefest.com),
P.O. Box 1970, Tybee Island, GA
31328. Usually held on an October
weekend. Thursday is the Buccaneer
Ball with the coronation of the Pirate
King and Queen, featuring live music,
dancing, and wenches with grog. Friday is the street fest with all things
pirate, and the parade is Saturday.
Some of the evening activities are for

adults only, but there's lots for the kids,
too.

November
Bluffton
Music to Your Mouth (www.musicto
yourmouth.com) Held annually at
Palmetto Bluff, this ingenious, expen-
sive, and popular multiday event mixes
Southern music, cooking, and stories.
There are classes and demonstrations,
oyster and pig roasts, storytelling and
art.

Charleston
Holiday Festival of Lights (843-795-
4386; www.holidayfestivaloflights.com),
James Island County Park. See more
than 100,000 holiday lights strung in
the park, a dazzling display in a place
that rarely knows a white Christmas.
Family entertainment and special
events scheduled through Christmas.
   Plantation Days (843-556-6020;
www.middletonplace.org), Middleton
Place, SC 61, Charleston SC 29414.
The spirit of plantation harvest days is
re-created through activities such as
blacksmithing, wool dying and spin-
ning, candle-making, and pottery. Traditional music and crafts in the stable
yards and green at Middleton Place.

St. Helena Island
Heritage Days (843-838-2432; www
.penncenter.com), Penn Center,
P.O. Box 126, St. Helena Island, SC
29920. Held the second weekend in
November on the historic Penn Center campus, Heritage Days celebrates
Sea Island culture in its many forms.
Thursday there is a children's theatre
production on Penn's history followed
by a community sing. Friday features
lectures, an art exhibit, and an old-
fashioned fish fry with musical entertainment. Saturday, there's a parade
and performances that include Gullah

INFORMATION

games and storytelling, dance, music, and demonstrations of traditional crafts and cooking.

December

Beaufort

Christmas at the Verdier House (843-379-6335; www.historicbeaufort.org), 801 Bay St., Beaufort, SC 29902. The late 18th-century planter's home is decorated during Christmas week as it might have been during holidays of long ago.

Night on the Town (843-525-6644; www.downtownbeaufort.com) Join in an informal street party thrown by the downtown merchants, usually the first weekend of the month. There are decorations everywhere, jazz musicians, carolers, and even Santa. The following night, a wonderful parade of boats of all shapes and sizes floats down the Beaufort River, easily enjoyed from the Waterfront Park off Bay Street.

Bluffton

Christmas Parade (843-706-4500; www.townofbluffton.sc.gov).

Charleston

Christmas in Charleston (1-800-774-0006; www.christmasincharleston. com), 423 King St., Charleston, SC 29403. The season brings special tours and holiday events such as open-air marketplaces and displays of boats strung with lights. Many restaurants and hotels offer holiday specials.

Drayton Hall Annual Spirituals Concert (843-769-2600; www.drayton hall.org), 3380 Ashley River Rd., Charleston, SC 29414. The concert has been presented here for decades and takes you back in time when the house was a center of plantation society.

Savannah

Christmas in Savannah (912-644-6400; www.visitsavannah.com), Convention & Visitors Bureau, P.O. Box 1628, Savannah, GA 31402. All month long, Savannah comes alive with special tours, performances, 19th-century-style holiday presentations in old homes, craft shows, and celebrations at the beach and on the river.

Frampton Plantation House, at Exit 33 off Interstate 95, is now the Welcome Center for the region. SC Lowcountry Tourism Commission

For questions you won't find answered anywhere else, look here for websites, overviews, and links. In many cases, booklets, videos, and pamphlets are available at a nominal charge.

Fishing and Hunting Regulations

Licenses, permits, and wildlife stamps, whichever apply, must be in your possession while in the field or on the water. They may be purchased at tackle shops, sporting goods stores, and from the state. Check for links on the websites to maps of boat landings and public hunting preserves.

Georgia Department of Natural Resources Coastal Resources Division (912-264-7218; www.gadnr.state.ga.us), One Conservation Way, Suite 300, Brunswick, GA 31520.

South Carolina Department of Natural Resources (843-953-9300; www.dnr .sc.gov), P.O. Box 12559, Charleston, SC 29422.

Visitor Information

Charleston Area Convention & Visitors Bureau (843-853-8000 or 1-800-774-0006; www.charlestoncvb.com), 423 King St., Charleston, SC 29402. The visitor center is located at 375 Meeting St.

Edisto Island Chamber of Commerce (843-869-3867 or 1-888-333-2781; www.edistochamber.com), P.O. Box 206, Edisto Island, SC 29438. Offices located at 430 SC 174, Edisto Island.

Greater Beaufort Chamber of Commerce and Visitor Bureau (843-525-8500 or 1-800-638-3525; www.beaufortsc.org), P.O. Box 910, Beaufort, SC 29901. A well-designed welcome center is located at 713 Craven St., in the old Arsenal.

Hilton Head Island–Bluffton Chamber of Commerce (843-785-3673 or 1-800-523-3373; www.hiltonheadchamber.org), P.O. Box 5647, Hilton Head Island, SC 29938.

Lowcountry and Resort Islands Tourism Commission (843-717-3090 or 1-800-528-6870; www.southcarolinalowcountry.com), P.O. Box 615, Yemassee, SC 29945. The visitor center is located off I-95 at exit 33 and US 17, 1 Lowcountry Ln., Yemassee, SC 29945.

The Savannah Area Convention & Visitors Bureau (www.visitsavannah.com), P.O. Box 1628, Savannah GA 31402. The visitor center is located at 301 Martin Luther King Jr. Blvd. Its number is 912-944-0455.

South Carolina Department of Parks, Recreation, and Tourism (www .discoversouthcarolina.com), 1205 Pendleton St., Columbia, SC 29201. Visitor information: 803-734-1700; state park information: 803-734-0156.

BIBLIOGRAPHY

Lowcountry life is well documented and bookstores have growing "local history" sections. Many out-of-print volumes are back in circulation; originals may be still found in secondhand bookstores and online. Here is a list of some classics, the books you're likely to find in residents' libraries. Don't overlook self-published histories, for they contain gems of regional lore. And, since the best part of a trip is often reliving it at home, check your local bookstore upon returning. The boxed quotes scattered throughout this book are taken from those included in the list below. The list is by no means complete; think of it as a mere guide to the shelves.

Art & Architecture

Cole, Cynthia, ed. *Historic Resources of the Lowcountry.* Yemassee, SC: Lowcountry Council of Governments, 1979, 2nd. ed. 1990. 202 pp., illus., photos, index, $29.95. The definitive four-county survey of historic houses and sites with fine historical and architectural explanation.

Dugan, Ellen, ed. *Picturing the South: 1860 to the Present.* Atlanta, GA: Chronicle Books, the High Museum of Art, 1996. 213 pp., index, $29.95. Based on a 1996 exhibit at the Photographic Galleries of the High Museum in Atlanta, the selection of pictures (from the Library of Congress Collections, private donors, historical societies, and museums) is honed to perfection and the accompanying essays by several Southern writers of the first rank are excellent. The book is moving without being sentimental.

Green, Jonathan. *Gullah Images: The Art of Jonathan Green.* Columbia, SC: University of South Carolina Press, 1996. 214 pp., $49.95. More than 180 gorgeous color reproductions of paintings by Jonathan Green tell the story of Sea Island life and its rituals and pleasures as he experienced them growing up in Beaufort County, SC. Forward by Pat Conroy.

Lane, Mills. *Architecture of the Old South: South Carolina.* Savannah, GA: Beehive Press, 1984. 258 pp., photos, $75. Exquisite, large-format, black-and-white photos.

———. *Architecture of the Old South: Georgia.* Savannah, GA: Beehive Press, 1986. 252 pp., photos, $75.

Ravenel, Beatrice St. Julian. *Architects of Charleston.* Columbia, SC: University of South Carolina Press, 1992. 338 pp., photos, index, bibliog., $19.95. First published in 1945, a detailed examination of the lives and works of the city's builders, engineers, and architects.

Rosengarten, Dale. *Row Upon Row: Sea Grass Baskets of the South Carolina Lowcountry.* Columbia, SC: McKissick Museum, 1986. 64 pp., photos, $10. A thorough and lovingly documented catalog of a vibrant Sea Island art. It is the authoritative text on the shapes, weaving style, and uses of island baskets.

Severens, Kenneth. *Charleston Antebellum Architecture and Civic Destiny.* Knoxville, TN: University of Tennessee Press, 1988. 330 pp., photos, index, $49.95. A specialized topic explained in clear prose for the interested amateur or professional architect.

Severens, Martha R. *Charles Fraser of Charleston.* Charles L. Wyrick Jr., ed. Charleston, SC: Carolina Art Association, 1983. 176 pp., illus., $14.95. The subject was a miniaturist of the 19th century whose portraits of local gentry, in the collection of the Gibbes Museum of Art, are exquisite and incisive.

———. *The Charleston Renaissance.* Charleston, SC: Robert M. Hicklin Jr., Inc., 1999. 232 pp., illus., $65. A scholarly, beautifully illustrated chronicle of the artists in early 20th-century Charleston who were inspired by the city's heritage and story, and expressed themselves in a variety of media.

Talbott, Page. *Classical Savannah: Fine and Decorative Arts 1800–1840.* Savannah, GA: Telfair Museum, 1995. 320 pp., illus., $24.95. An overview of a period during which Savannah was deeply influenced by English Regency and Continental architecture and interior style.

Vlach, John Michael. *Back of the Big House: The Architecture of Plantation Slavery.* Chapel Hill, NC: University of North Carolina Press, 1993. 236 pp., illus., photos, index, $18.95. A serious, well-written, and fundamental study of the relationship of plantation "spaces"—the outbuildings, the quarters, the "Big House," the allées or avenues, fields, docks, and waterways—to the black and white people who lived there, and to each other. Numerous plantation plans are cited.

Autobiography, Biography, Diaries & Letters

Bartram, William. *Travels through North & South Carolina, Georgia, East & West Florida.* New York: Viking Penguin, 1988. 452 pp., $7.95. The account of an 18th-century trip through the Lowcountry by the famous botanist.

Chesnut, Mary Boykin. *A Diary from Dixie.* Cambridge, MA: Harvard University Press, 1980. 608 pp., $12.95. A classic account with good detail on Charleston society.

Daise, Ronald. *Reminiscences of a Sea Island Heritage.* Columbia, SC: Sandlapper, 1986. 103 pp., photos, $18.95. Archival black-and-white photos accompanied by text and stories of Sea Island Gullah culture. Ronald and his wife, Natalie, were the creators and stars of the TV series for children *Gullah Gullah Island,* and continue to perform nationally.

Egerton, Douglas. *He Shall Go out Free: The Lives of Denmark Vesey.* Madison, WI: Madison House, 1999. 272 pp., illus., $34.95. A complete, well-researched and well-argued account of the failed slave uprising in Charleston in 1822.

Elliott, William, and Theodore Rosengarten. *Carolina Sports by Land and Water, Including Incidents of Devil-Fishing, Wild-Cat, Deer, and Bear-Hunting, Etc.* Columbia, SC: University of South Carolina Press, 1994. Illus., $14.95. A reprint of Elliott's 1850s original, it is still funny, easy to read, and as full of suspense as ever.

Forten, Charlotte L. *The Journal of a Free Negro in the Slave Era.* New York: W. W. Norton, 1981. 286 pp., index, $8.95. The vivid impressions of a Northern teacher who came to the Sea Islands to educate the newly freed slaves.

Georgia Writers' Project, ed. *Drums and Shadows.* Athens, GA: University of Georgia Press, 1986. $11.95. The collection of oral histories first published under the WPA program in 1940. It allows you to hear the voices of the coast.

Higginson, Thomas Wentworth. *Army Life in a Black Regiment.* New York: W. W. Norton, 1984. 279 pp., appendix, index, $6.95. Higginson, a Boston Brahmin, was the white commander of the 1st South Carolina Volunteers, headquartered in Beaufort during the Civil War. Its honest, self-effacing narrative of camp life, countrysides, and skirmishes is invaluable.

Kemble, Frances Anne. *Journal of Residence on a Georgia Plantation in 1838–1839.* Athens, GA: University of Georgia Press, 1984. 488 pp., $11.95. Although the setting is the coastal Georgia plantation of the author's husband, Pierce Butler, her insights into plantation life and the culture of black female slaves make this perhaps the best account of that time.

McTeer, J. E. *High Sheriff of the Lowcountry.* Beaufort, SC: JEM Co., 1995.

101 pp., $19.70. Newly reprinted, it contains the colorful recollections of the author's days as a Lowcountry lawman and his encounters with voodoo and witch doctors, rumrunners, and local scoundrels.

Olmsted, F. L. *A Journey in the Seaboard Slave States.* Westport, CT: Negro Universities Press, 1969. Illus., index, $35. A reprint of the 1856 edition in which the author acutely observes the coastal region and standards of living there.

Pearson, Elizabeth Ware, ed. *Letters from Port Royal, 1862–1868.* New York: Arno Press, 1969. $14. In 1862, dozens of Northern abolitionists flocked to the federally occupied area around Beaufort to educate the newly freed slaves and manage the abandoned cotton plantations. This collection of letters by the Boston contingent is as forceful and moving a commentary on race relations and liberal expectations as exists.

Pennington, Patience. *A Woman Rice Planter.* Cambridge, MA: Belknap Press of Harvard University Press, 1961. The author was a Lowcountry native who managed her father's rice plantations after the Civil War and wrote about the experience for New York newspapers. The illustrations are by Alice Ravenel Huger Smith, a lyrical interpreter of the rural Lowcountry.

Pinkney, Roger. *The Beaufort Chronicles.* Beaufort, SC: Pluff Mud. 110 pp., $9.95. A new collection of remembrances and essays on small-town life and its simple pleasures.

Towne, Laura. *Letters and Diary Written from the Sea Islands of South Carolina, 1862–1884.* New York: American Biography Series, 1991. 310 pp., $79. Another wonderful journal of a teacher; she established Penn School, the first school for freed slaves in the United States.

Verner, Elizabeth O. *Mellowed by Time.* Charleston, SC: Tradd St. Press, 1978. $15. Sketches and memories of old Charleston by a distinguished artist who favored etchings, pastel, and pencil drawing.

Cultural Studies

Bluffton Historical Preservation Society. *No. II: A Longer Short History of Bluffton, South Carolina and its Environs.* Bluffton, SC: Bluffton Historical Preservation Society, 1988. 49 pp., photos, $9.95. An excellent local history with photographs of classic Lowcountry cottages.

Carawan, Guy and Candy Carawan, eds. *Ain't You Got a Right to the Tree of Life? The People of John's Island, South Carolina—Their Faces, Their Words and Their Songs.* Athens, GA: University of Georgia Press, 1989. 256 pp., photos, $29.95.

Garrity, Janet. *Goin' Down the River: Fish Camps of the Sea Islands.* Hilton Head Island, SC: Lydia Inglett Publishing, 2012. 128 pp., photos, $39.95. A beautiful presentation of the fish camps that dot the hummocks and creeks, with stories of multigenerational families who built and use them still, and their history as special places from the time of Native American settlements. Original and archival photos.

Johnson, Guion G. *A Social History of the Sea Islands.* Westport, CT: Greenwood Press, 1969. 185 pp., index, bibliog., $38.50. A reprint of the 1930 edition of a series in which scholars from the University of North Carolina examined the lives, speech, culture, and folkways of Sea Island natives. Others in the series include *Folk Culture on St. Helena Island* by Guy B. Johnson and *Black Yeomanry* by T. J. Woofter, which, if you can find it, has stirring documentary photographs.

Jones-Jackson, Patricia. *When Roots Die: Endangered Traditions on the Sea Islands.* Athens, GA: University of Georgia Press, 1987. 189 pp., photos, bibliog., $19.95.

Lee, Matt and Ted Lee. *The Lee Bros. Southern Cookbook.* New York: W. W. Norton, 2006. 589 pp., $35. The brothers relocated with their family to Charleston as preteens, and by messing around in the creeks and the kitchen, found, as they put it, that in the Lowcountry food is life. They became entrepreneurs of boiled peanuts in Manhattan because they missed their favorite snacks, and it wasn't long before their amusing prose, goofy self-deprecation, and honest devotion to Lowcountry foodways garnered praise and fans. Their most recent book is *The Lee Bros. Charleston Kitchen.* New York: Clarkson, Potter, 2013. 240 pp., $35. It's an homage to Charleston foodways of the past and present, with old recipes they've researched and updated, archival photographs, stories of local farmers and fishermen, and even walking and driving tours to orient you to the homes where cooking has been essential to the city's culture for more than two centuries.

Parrish, Lydia. *Slave Songs of the Georgia Sea Islands.* Athens, GA: University of Georgia Press, 1992. 252 pp., photos, musical notation, $19.95. A reprint of the 1942 original by the wife of artist Maxfield Parrish, documenting the islanders' songs from the praise house to the play yard.

Taylor, John Martin. *Hoppin' John's Lowcountry Cooking.* New York: Bantam, 1990. 345 pp., illus., $24.

———. *The New Southern Cook: 200 Recipes.* New York: Bantam, 1995. 287 pp., illus., $27.95. A superb follow-up to Taylor's first book, this one ranges a bit further but maintains the author's discriminating judgments and lack of pretension.

Vernon, Amelia Wallace. *African-Americans at Mars Bluff, South Carolina.* Columbia, SC: University of South Carolina Press, 1995. 200 pp., illus., photos, index, bibliog., $16.95. A wonderful documentary account of an African American community north of Charleston.

Welty, Eudora. *The Eye of the Story: Selected Essays and Reviews.* New York: Vintage International, 1990. 355 pp., $14.

Westmacott, Richard. *African-American Gardens and Yards in the Rural South.* Knoxville, TN: University of Tennessee Press, 1992. 175 pp., illus., photos, index, bibliog., $24.95. One of the most thoughtful and inspired books ever written on African American rural life (some in the Lowcountry), it focuses on several families and the way they create color, style, whimsy, and usefulness in their immediate landscape. It is part scholarship, part oral history, and the tone is just right.

Wolfe, Michael C. *The Abundant Life Prevails: Religious Traditions of St. Helena Island.* Waco, TX: Baylor University Press, 2000. 181 pp., bibliog., and extensive chapter notes, $39.95. A tremendously thoughtful book that examines the religious traditions of St. Helena Islanders, in particular the role of Penn School and the missionary tradition.

Fiction

Berendt, John. *Midnight in the Garden of Good and Evil.* New York: Random House, 1994. 388 pp., $22. A wild romp in Savannah—and it's all true.

Conroy, Pat. *The Water Is Wide.* New York: Bantam, 1972. 320 pp., $4.95. This was the book based on Conroy's experiences as a Beaufort County schoolteacher on isolated Daufuskie Island. His other books include *The Great Santini, The Prince of Tides,* and *Beach Music,* and have Beaufort as their setting (even in the movie versions).

Griswold, Francis. *Sea Island Lady.* Beaufort, SC: Beaufort Book Co., 1984. 964 pp., $19.95. A reprint of the 1939 original—a big, fat Southern novel set in Beaufort.

Heyward, Du Bose. *Porgy.* Charleston, SC: Tradd St. Press, 1985. 130 pp., illus., $20. A reprinting of the great tale, set in and around Charleston.

Humphreys, Josephine. *Rich in Love.* New York: Viking Penguin, 1987. 262 pp., $8.95. Set in Mount Pleasant, near Charleston, this novel (basis of the 1993 movie) captures the world view of a precocious 17-year-old girl. The author's other novels, *Dreams of Sleep* (1984) and *The Fireman's Fair* (1991), are also set in the Charleston area.

Naylor, Gloria R. *Mama Day.* New York: Random House, 1989. 312 pp., $9.95. A magical story set in a mythical place that nearly mirrors the Georgia/South Carolina Sea Islands.

Peterkin, Julia. *Scarlet Sister Mary.* Marietta, GA: Cherokee Press, 1991. 352 pp., $18.95. A reprint of the 1928 edition.

Powell, Padgett. *Edisto.* New York: Farrar, Strauss & Giroux, 1984. 192 pp., $11.95. A boy's coming-of-age on a Sea Island.

———. *Edisto Revisited.* New York: Henry Holt, 1996. 145 pp., $20.

A southern magnolia. SC Lowcountry Tourism Commission

Sayers, Valerie. *Due East.* New York: Doubleday, 1987. 264 pp., $15.95. The first novel in a group that chronicles life in a town like Beaufort, where the author grew up. Others include *How I Got Him Back* (1989) and *Who Do You Love* (1991).

Worthington, Curtis, ed. *Literary Charleston: A Lowcountry Reader.* Charleston, SC: Wyrick & Co., 1996. 360 pp., $24.95.

History

Bridenbaugh, Carl. *Myths and Realities: Societies of the Colonial South.* New York: Atheneum, 1963. 208 pp., index, bibliog., from $4 used.

Dollard, John. *Caste and Class in a Southern Town.* Madison, WI: University of Wisconsin Press, 1989. 466 pp., index, $14.50. A reissue of the 1937 work which, while not specifically about the Lowcountry, has everything to say about race relations in small towns throughout the region.

Jacoway, Elizabeth. *Yankee Missionaries in the South: The Penn School Experiment.* Baton Rouge, LA: LSU Press, 1980. 301 pp., index, bibliog., from $5 used.

Jones, Katharine M. *Port Royal under Six Flags.* Indianapolis, IN: Bobbs-Merrill, 1960. 368 pp., illus., bibliog., from $15 used. A good general introduction to the area, with long passages quoting original documents.

Rogers, George. *Charleston in the Age of the Pinckneys.* Columbia, SC: University of South Carolina Press, 1984. 198 pp., index, $9.95. If there is one book you should read about Charleston's heyday, this is it.

Rose, Willie Lee. *Rehearsal for Reconstruction: The Port Royal Experiment.* New York: Oxford University Press, 1976. 450 pp., index, bibliog., $13.95. A beautifully written and meticulously researched account of the Northern abolitionists who went to the Sea Islands of Beaufort at the time of the Civil War. If you have a serious interest in the subject, the bibliography of this book is where you should start.

Rosen, Robert. *A Short History of Charleston.* San Francisco: Lexikos, 1982. 160 pp., illus., photos, bibliog., $8.95. A popular introduction to Charleston by a native son.

Rosengarten, Theodore. *Tombee: Portrait of a Cotton Planter.* New York: McGraw, 1988. 752 pp., index, $15. This prize-winning book reproduces the diaries of an antebellum St. Helena Islander, Thomas B. Chaplin, and creates a context of explanation for them. This is the story—not the myth—of life on a cotton plantation, handled in vivid prose by the region's best historian.

Rowland, Lawrence, Alexander Moore, and George Rogers. *The History of Beaufort County, South Carolina: 1514–1861.* Columbia, SC: University of South Carolina Press, 1996. 480 pp., index, bibliog., maps, $39.95. The first volume of the authoritative yet readable history of the area, which brings the Native American story into new focus and weeds out the antebellum myths about Beaufort and plantation culture.

Stampp, Kenneth. *The Peculiar Institution: Slavery in the Ante-Bellum South.* New York: Vintage, 1989. Index, $10. A classic study, first published in 1956.

Wise, Stephen R. *Lifeline of the Confederacy: Blockade Running during the Civil War.* Columbia, SC: University of South Carolina Press, 1988. 403 pp., illus., index, $16.95.

————. *Gate of Hell: Campaign for Charleston Harbor, 1863.* Columbia, SC: University of South Carolina Press, 1994. 218 pp., illus., index, $29.95.

Wood, Peter. *Black Majority: Negroes in Colonial South Carolina from 1670 through the Stono Rebellion.* New York: W. W. Norton, 1975. 384 pp., index, $9.95.

Photographic Studies

Blagden, Tom. *The Lowcountry.* Greensboro, NC: Legacy Publications, 1988. 104 pp., photos, $49.95. Views of the coastal world by an immensely talented photographer. His words of introduction and praise for the region's natural beauty resonate with visitors and locals alike.

————. *South Carolina's Wetland Wilderness: The ACE Basin.* Englewood, CO: Westcliffe Publishers, Inc., 1992. 110 pp., $29.95. A sumptuous study of the land and estuarine ecosystem in and around the Ashepoo, Combahee, and Edisto Rivers; much of the area is protected by federal, state, local, and private organizations.

Dabbs, Edith, ed. *Face of an Island.* New York: Wyrick & Co., 1971. New edition. Used editions start at $35; first editions start at $170. An album of early 20th-century photographs taken on St. Helena Island by Leigh Richmond Miner and reproduced from the glass plates. A treasure.

Ellis, Ray. *South by Southeast.* Birmingham, AL: Oxmoor House, 1983. 122 pp., $50. Watercolors of the coastal region by a noted painter and Hilton Head resident.

Isley, Jane, Agnes Baldwin, and William P. Baldwin. *Plantations of the Lowcountry.* Greensboro, NC: Legacy Publishing, 1987. 151 pp., $19.95. Color photographs and histories of historic homes.

McLaren, Lynn, and Gerhard Spieler. *Ebb Tide, Flood Tide.* Columbia, SC: University of South Carolina Press, 1991. 105 pp., $40. Color photographs of favorite Beaufort sites.

Schultz, Constance, ed. *A South Carolina Album, 1936–1948.* Columbia, SC: University of South Carolina Press, 1992. 143 pp., from $10 used. A collection of photographs taken under the auspices of the Farm Security Administration and later under the direction of its chief, Roy Stryker.

Recreation/Travel

Baldwin, William P. III. *Lowcountry Daytrips: Plantations, Gardens, and a Natural History of the Charleston Region.* Greensboro, NC: Legacy Publications, 1993. 283 pp., illus., photos, index, bibliog., maps, $18.95. Written by a Lowcountry native, it is a model of organization (with maps and mileages clearly spelled out), good design, practicality, and a writing style that lends itself to reading aloud.

Ballantine, Todd. *Tideland Treasures.* Columbia, SC: University of South Carolina Press, 1991. 218 pp., $15.95.

Federal Writers' Project Staff. *South Carolina: The WPA Guide to the Palmetto State.* Walter B. Edgar, ed. Columbia, SC: University of South Carolina Press, 1988. 514 pp., photos, index, $16.95. A reprint of the superb guide.

Georgia Conservancy. *A Guide to the Georgia Coast.* Savannah, GA: The Georgia Conservancy, 1989. 199 pp., illus., index, $6.

Index